ATOMIC ROBO

VOLUME FIVE

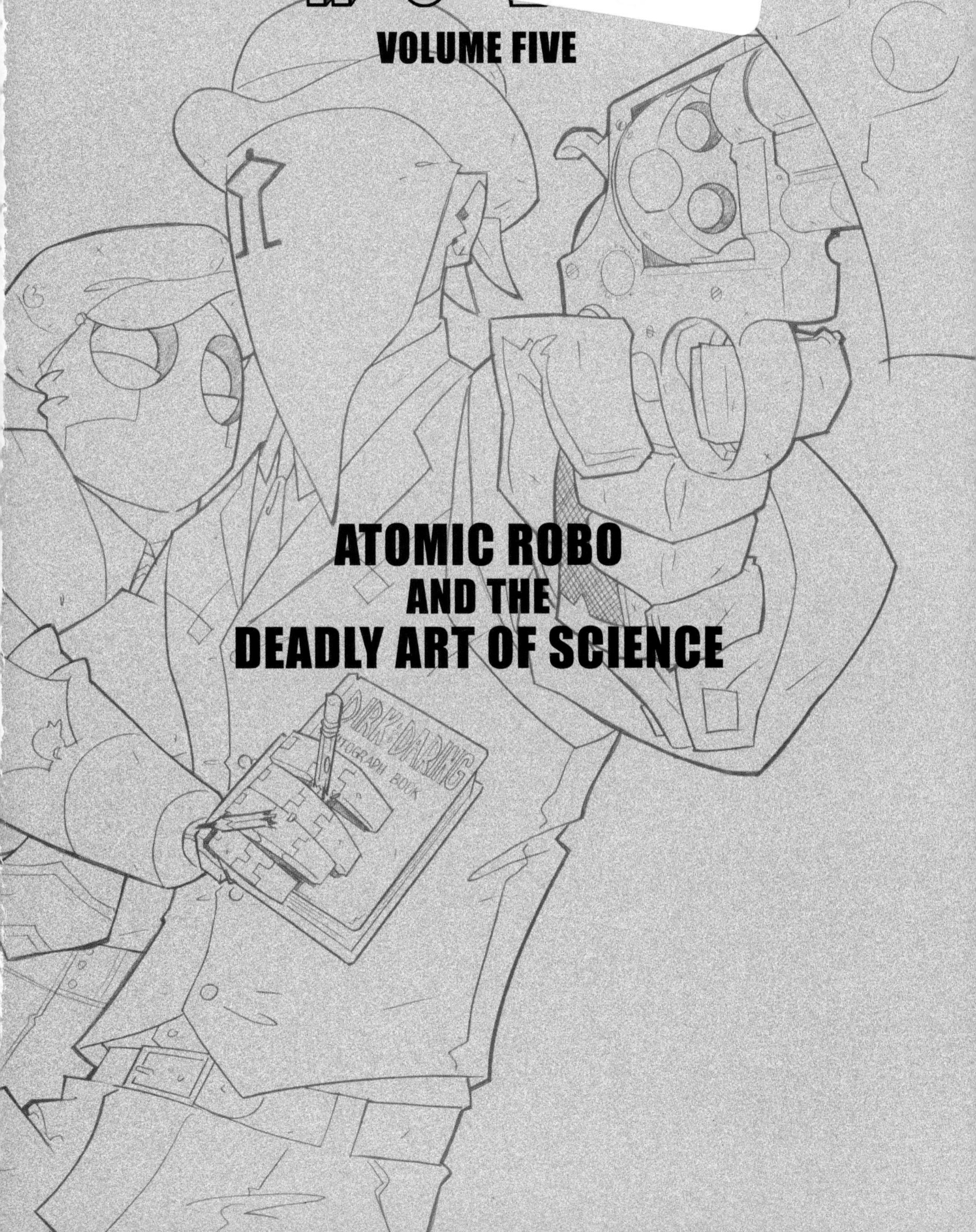

ATOMIC ROBO AND THE DEADLY ART OF SCIENCE

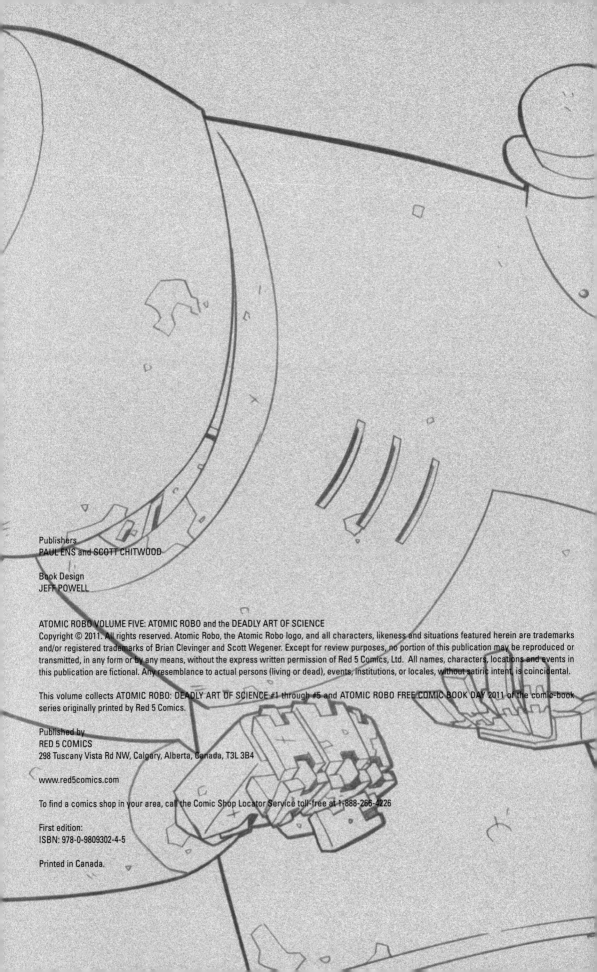

Publishers
PAUL ENS and SCOTT CHITWOOD

Book Design
JEFF POWELL

ATOMIC ROBO VOLUME FIVE: ATOMIC ROBO and the DEADLY ART OF SCIENCE

This volume collects ATOMIC ROBO: DEADLY ART OF SCIENCE #1 through #5 and ATOMIC ROBO FREE COMIC BOOK DAY 2011 of the comic-book series originally printed by Red 5 Comics.

Published by
RED 5 COMICS
298 Tuscany Vista Rd NW, Calgary, Alberta, Canada, T3L 3B4

www.red5comics.com

To find a comics shop in your area, call the Comic Shop Locator Service toll-free at 1-888-266-4226

First edition:
ISBN: 978-0-9809302-4-5

Printed in Canada.

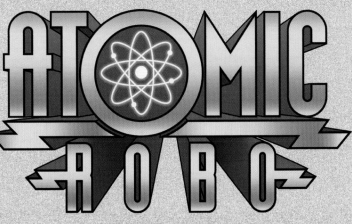

ATOMIC ROBO

VOLUME FIVE

ATOMIC ROBO AND THE DEADLY ART OF SCIENCE

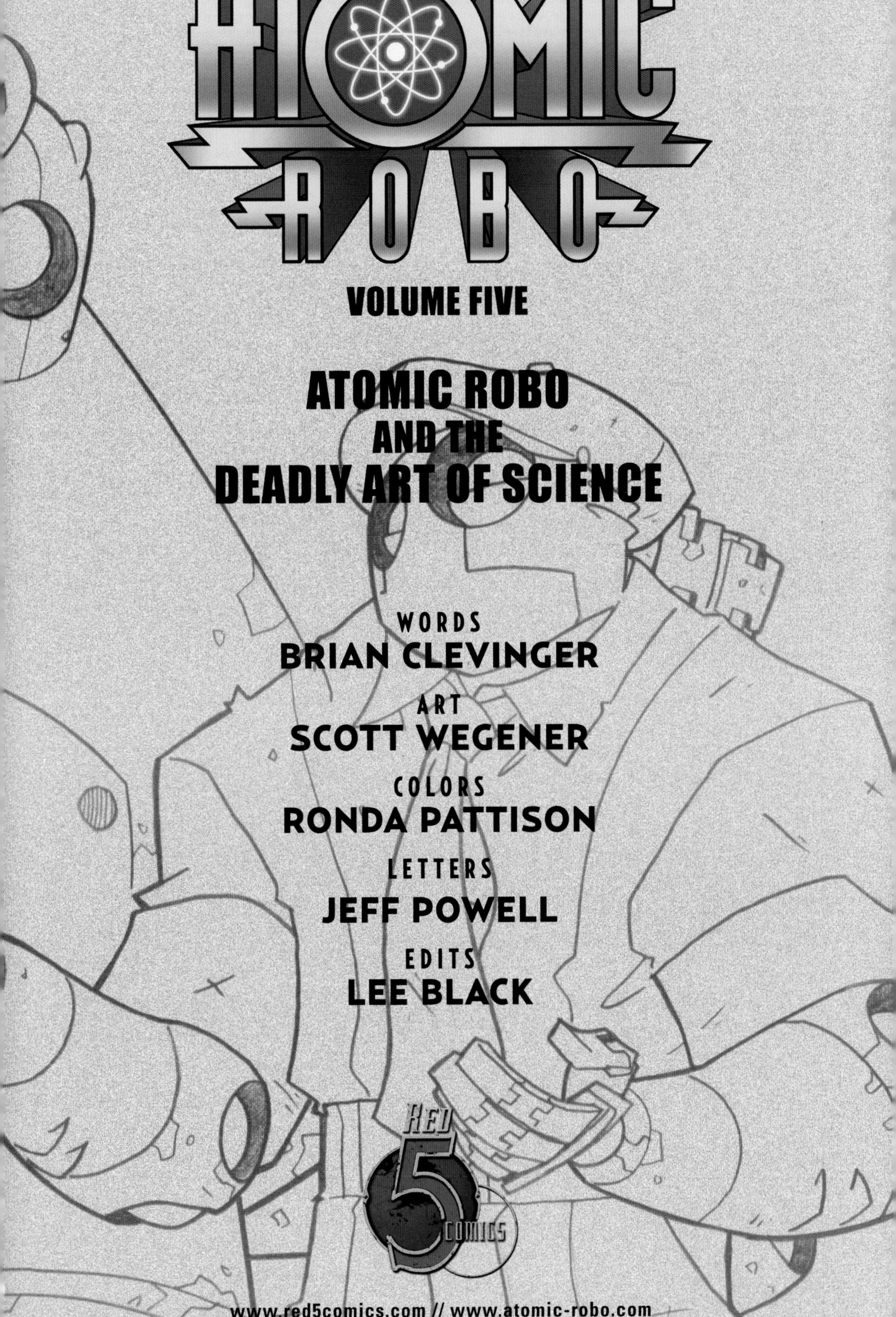

WORDS
BRIAN CLEVINGER

ART
SCOTT WEGENER

COLORS
RONDA PATTISON

LETTERS
JEFF POWELL

EDITS
LEE BLACK

RED 5 COMICS

www.red5comics.com // www.atomic-robo.com

INTRODUCTION

A few years ago I picked up a copy of "Atomic Robo" on impulse. I like comics. I like robots. I'd like this, right?

Wrong. I **loved** it.

"Atomic Robo" #2 was the issue that sealed the deal, with utterly self-assured pacing in a story that featured a wisecracking, art-deco robot soldier, gorgeously colored, clean-lined art, giant ants, World War II flashbacks, and mile-a-minute quipping (including "I used my violence on them," which may be my favorite comic book line of all time). All this mayhem was framed by melancholy bookends as surprising as they were moving, with a final line that almost played like a non sequitur but instead put the button on the story's theme in a beautifully understated and gently ridiculous way.

In short, writer Brian Clevinger, artist Scott Wegener, colorist Ronda Pattison and letterer Jeff Powell hit the pop culture sweet spot for me, combining glorious genre excess with genuine emotional resonance. And I've been reading the adventures of their marvelous creation ever since.

The hijinks continue apace with the volume you hold in your hands today, a "Year One" story that shows how a young, pulp-reading, newsboy-cap-wearing robo-lad with light-up eyes became the gun-toting Atomic Robo of today.

Adventure! Romance! Action Science! Secret History! You'll even learn why Tesla ate crackers – and it might just make you mist up a bit.

Life is good. And "Atomic Robo" makes it better.

Greg Pak
May 2011, New York City

Greg Pak is a filmmaker and comic book writer best known for his feature film "Robot Stories" and Marvel Comics series such as "Planet Hulk" and "Magneto Testament."

Wait, when did we make five of these things? Good lord, it seems like just the other day I was accosting a stranger named Scott Wegener with some ideas about a robot who's also a scientist.

Oddly enough, this volume is a synthesis of those early days. Back then Scott was bouncing around an old school gun-toting pulp action hero. We turned him into Jack Tarot and made him Robo's reluctant mentor.

Sorry about that, Jack.

Brian Clevinger
May 2011, Richmond VA

Brian Clevinger will one day learn how to write.

This one is for the ladies. First, its for my mom, who opened her home to us at a time when we desperately needed a change of scenery. I never realized how much I missed New York City until we moved back. Thank you.

Second, this is for my Emma -our little Widget, who's not so little anymore. It was so much fun putting you into an Atomic Robo story. You're a rad little girl.

And finally, this is for Dorinda. I agonized pretty hard over that page where Robo kisses Helen. I had no idea how to approach it without being cheesey, creepy, or both. And then I thought about our first date, sitting in the car, outside your apartment. We were both fairly certain that you'd never agree to a second date.

And then we kissed.

Scott Wegener
May 2011, Staten Island NY

Scott Wegener complained about every single page you're about to read.

THE MAN WITH TWO SKULLS

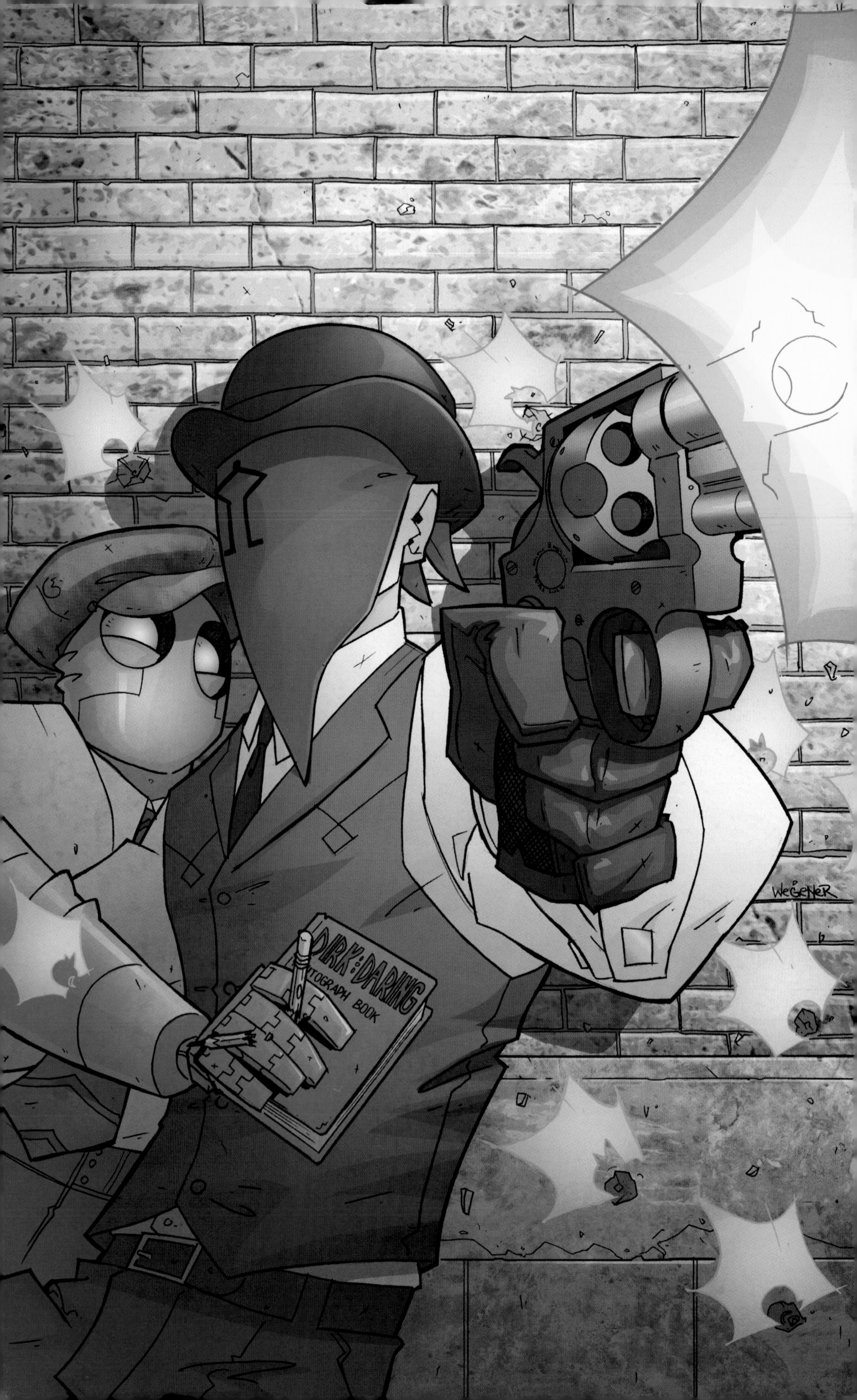
DIRK DARING
TOGRAPH BOOK
WEGENER

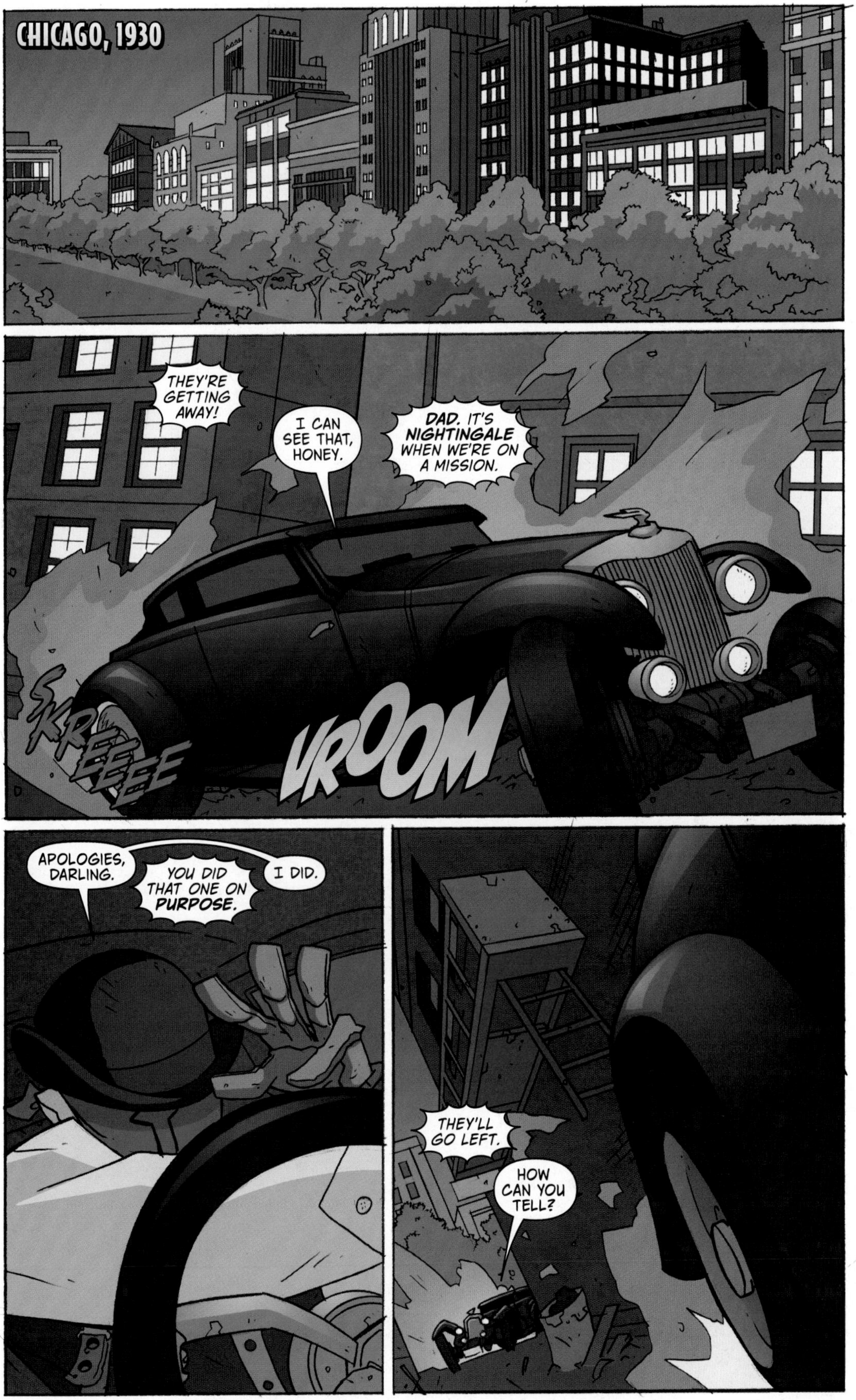
CHICAGO, 1930
THEY'RE GETTING AWAY!
I CAN SEE THAT, HONEY.
DAD. IT'S NIGHTINGALE WHEN WE'RE ON A MISSION.
SKREEEEEE
VROOM
APOLOGIES, DARLING.
YOU DID THAT ONE ON PURPOSE.
I DID.
THEY'LL GO LEFT.
HOW CAN YOU TELL?

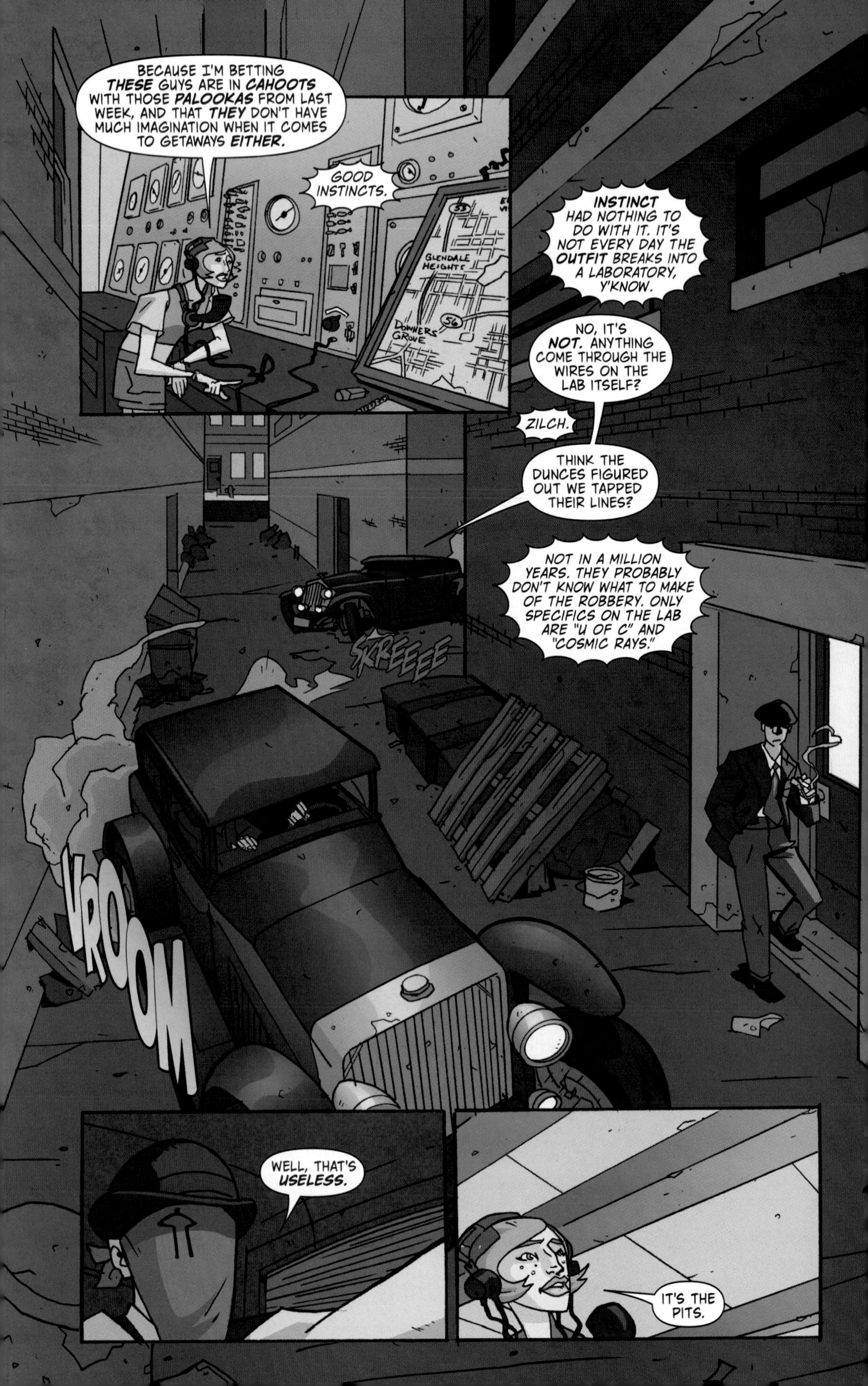

BECAUSE I'M BETTING THESE GUYS ARE IN CAHOOTS WITH THOSE PALOOKAS FROM LAST WEEK, AND THAT THEY DON'T HAVE MUCH IMAGINATION WHEN IT COMES TO GETAWAYS EITHER.
GOOD INSTINCTS.
53
GLENDALE HEIGHTS
DOWNERS GROVE
56
INSTINCT HAD NOTHING TO DO WITH IT. IT'S NOT EVERY DAY THE OUTFIT BREAKS INTO A LABORATORY, Y'KNOW.
NO, IT'S NOT. ANYTHING COME THROUGH THE WIRES ON THE LAB ITSELF?
ZILCH.
THINK THE DUNCES FIGURED OUT WE TAPPED THEIR LINES?
NOT IN A MILLION YEARS. THEY PROBABLY DON'T KNOW WHAT TO MAKE OF THE ROBBERY. ONLY SPECIFICS ON THE LAB ARE "U OF C" AND "COSMIC RAYS."
SKREEEEE
VROOM
WELL, THAT'S USELESS.
IT'S THE PITS.

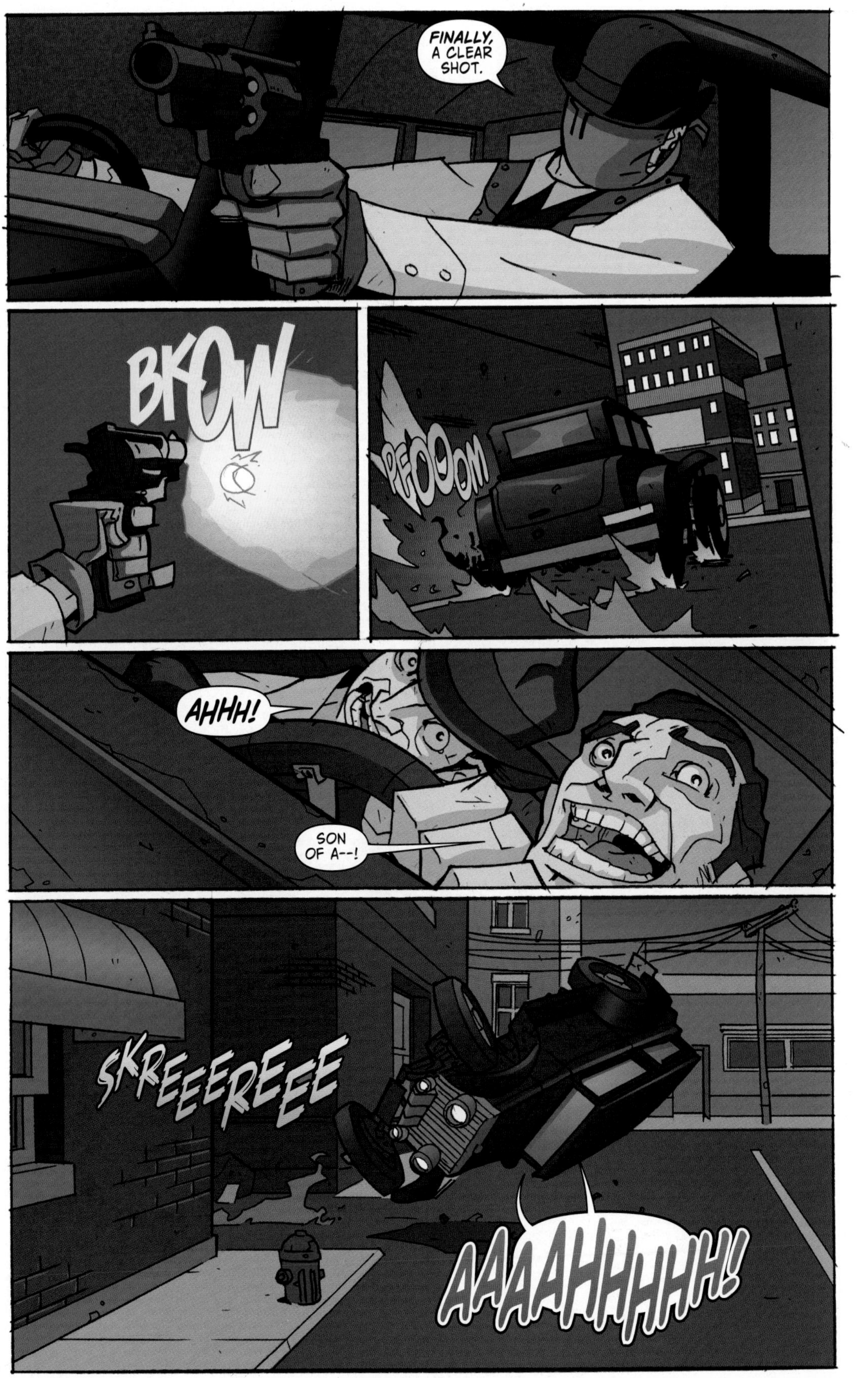
FINALLY, A CLEAR SHOT.
BKOW
PFOOOM
AHHH!
SON OF A--!
SKREEEREEE
AAAAHHHHH!

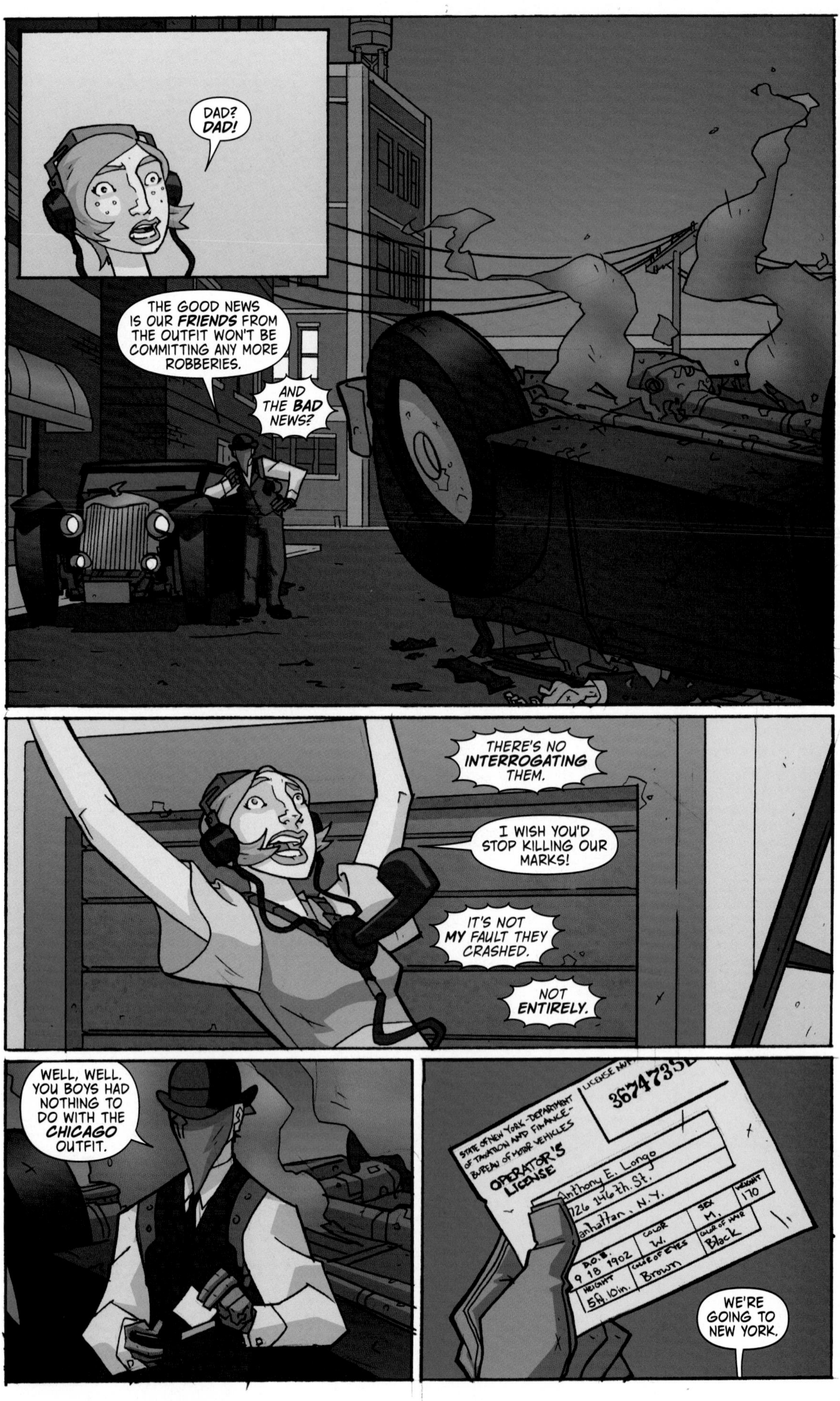
DAD? DAD!
THE GOOD NEWS IS OUR FRIENDS FROM THE OUTFIT WON'T BE COMMITTING ANY MORE ROBBERIES.
AND THE BAD NEWS?
THERE'S NO INTERROGATING THEM.
I WISH YOU'D STOP KILLING OUR MARKS!
IT'S NOT MY FAULT THEY CRASHED.
NOT ENTIRELY.
WELL, WELL. YOU BOYS HAD NOTHING TO DO WITH THE CHICAGO OUTFIT.
STATE OF NEW YORK - DEPARTMENT OF TAXATION AND FINANCE - BUREAU OF MOTOR VEHICLES
OPERATOR'S LICENSE
Anthony E. Longo
M.
170
W.
Black
9 18 1902
Brown
5ft. 10in.
WE'RE GOING TO NEW YORK.

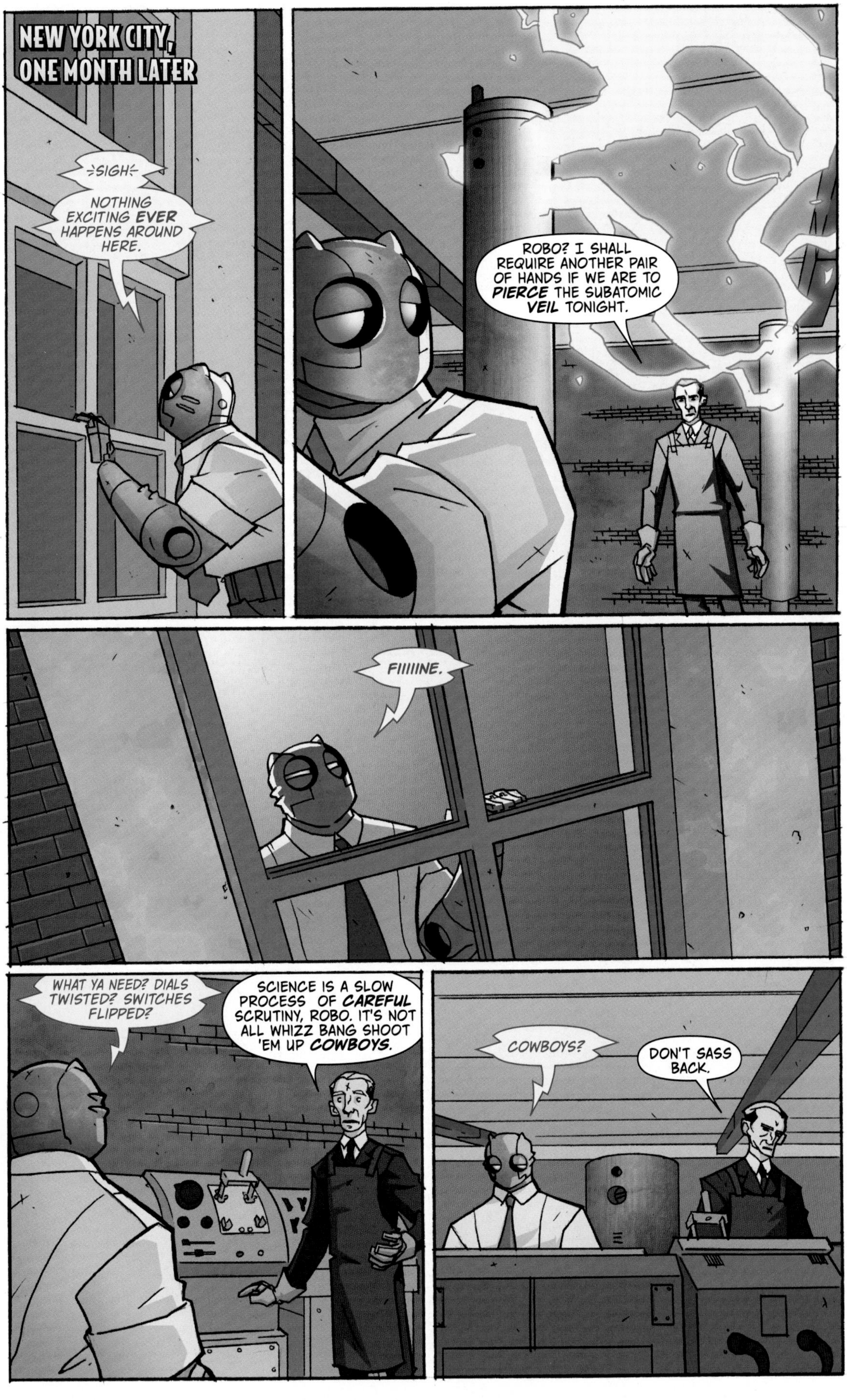
NEW YORK CITY, ONE MONTH LATER
SIGH
NOTHING EXCITING EVER HAPPENS AROUND HERE.
ROBO? I SHALL REQUIRE ANOTHER PAIR OF HANDS IF WE ARE TO PIERCE THE SUBATOMIC VEIL TONIGHT.
FIIIIINE.
WHAT YA NEED? DIALS TWISTED? SWITCHES FLIPPED?
SCIENCE IS A SLOW PROCESS OF CAREFUL SCRUTINY, ROBO. IT'S NOT ALL WHIZZ BANG SHOOT 'EM UP COWBOYS.
COWBOYS?
DON'T SASS BACK.

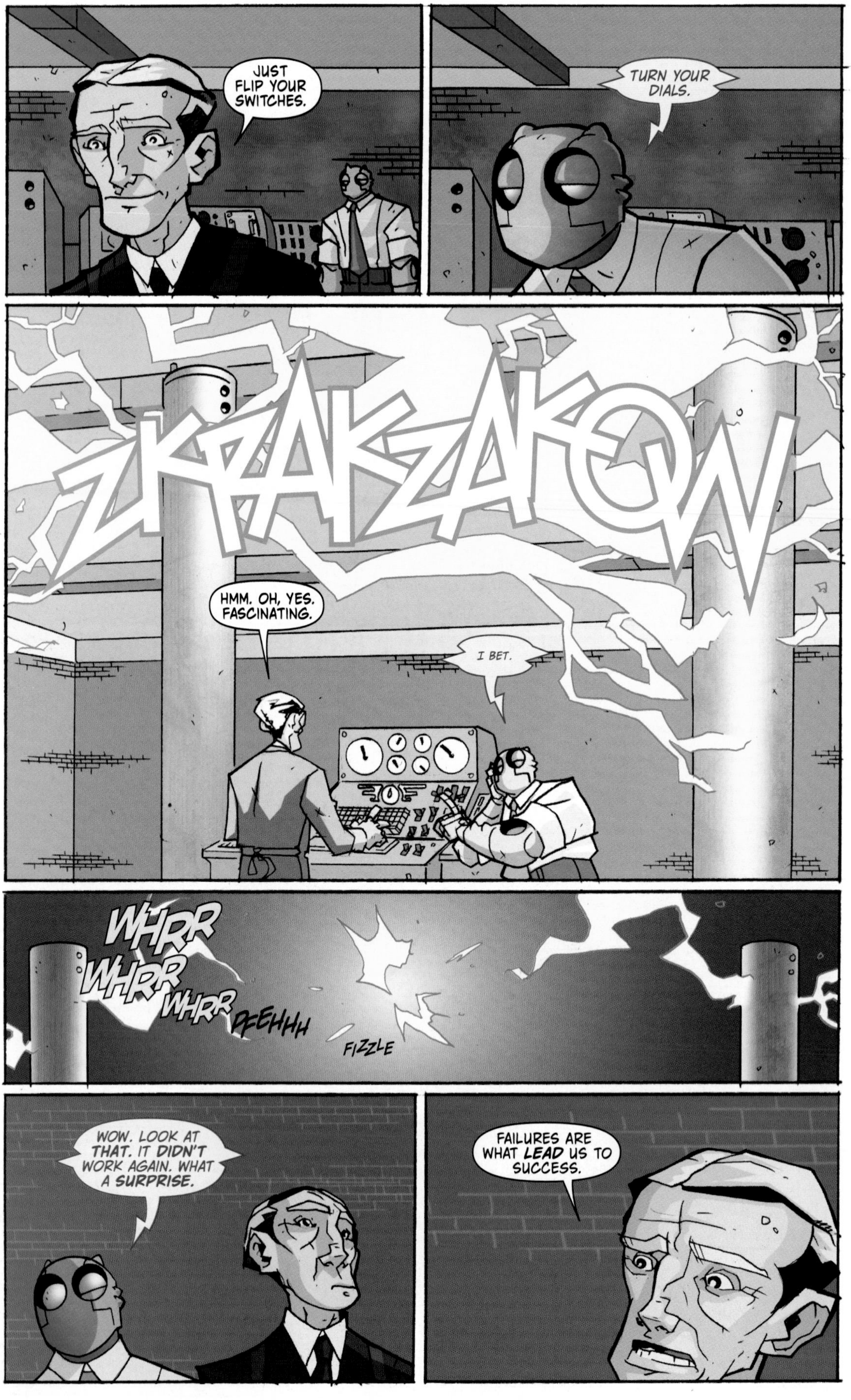
JUST FLIP YOUR SWITCHES.
TURN YOUR DIALS.
ZKRAKZAKOW
HMM. OH, YES. FASCINATING.
I BET.
WHRR
WHRR
WHRR
PFEHHH
FIZZLE
WOW. LOOK AT **THAT**. IT **DIDN'T** WORK AGAIN. WHAT A **SURPRISE**.
FAILURES ARE WHAT **LEAD** US TO SUCCESS.

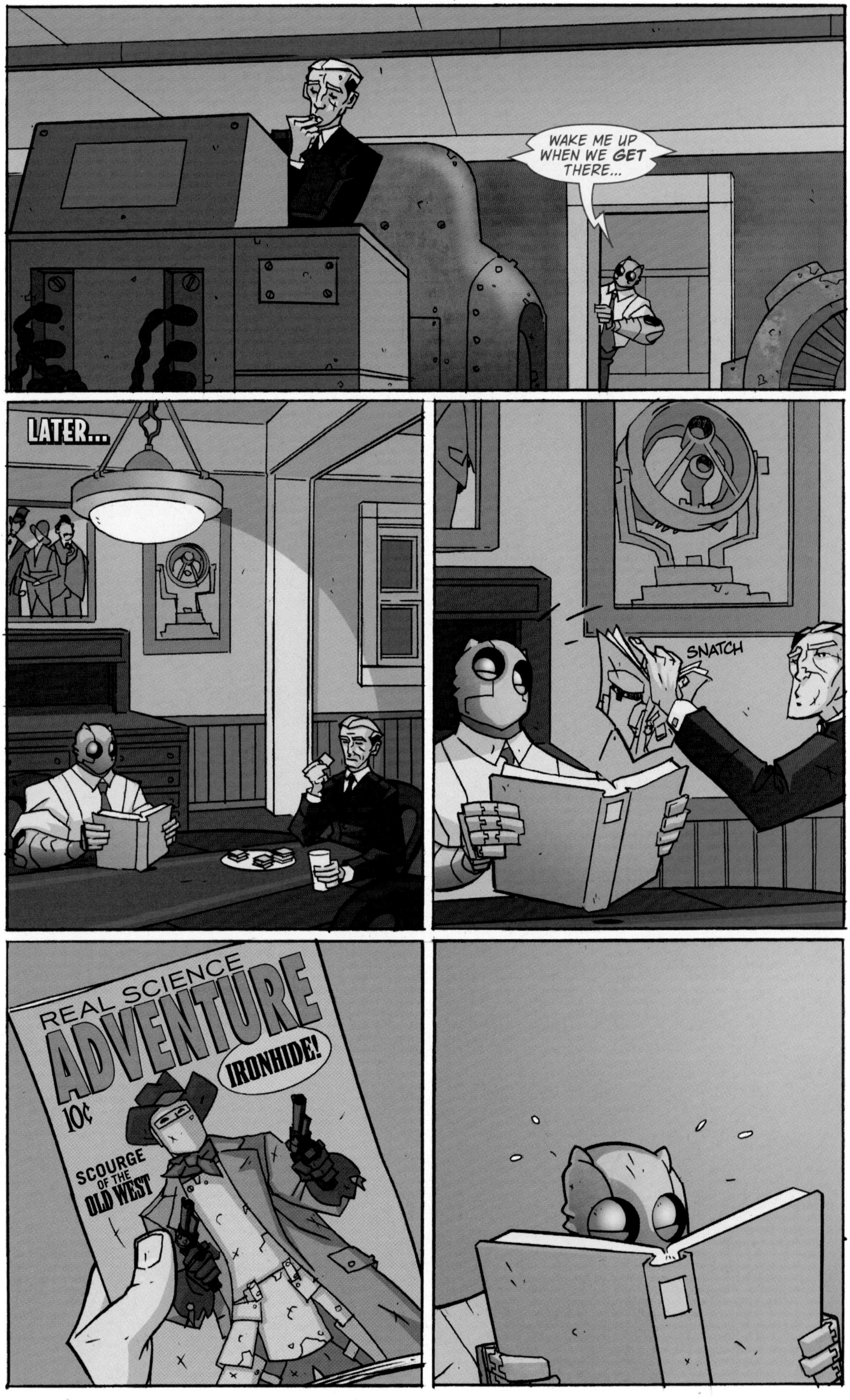
WAKE ME UP WHEN WE GET THERE...
LATER...
SNATCH
REAL SCIENCE ADVENTURE
IRONHIDE!
10¢
SCOURGE OF THE OLD WEST

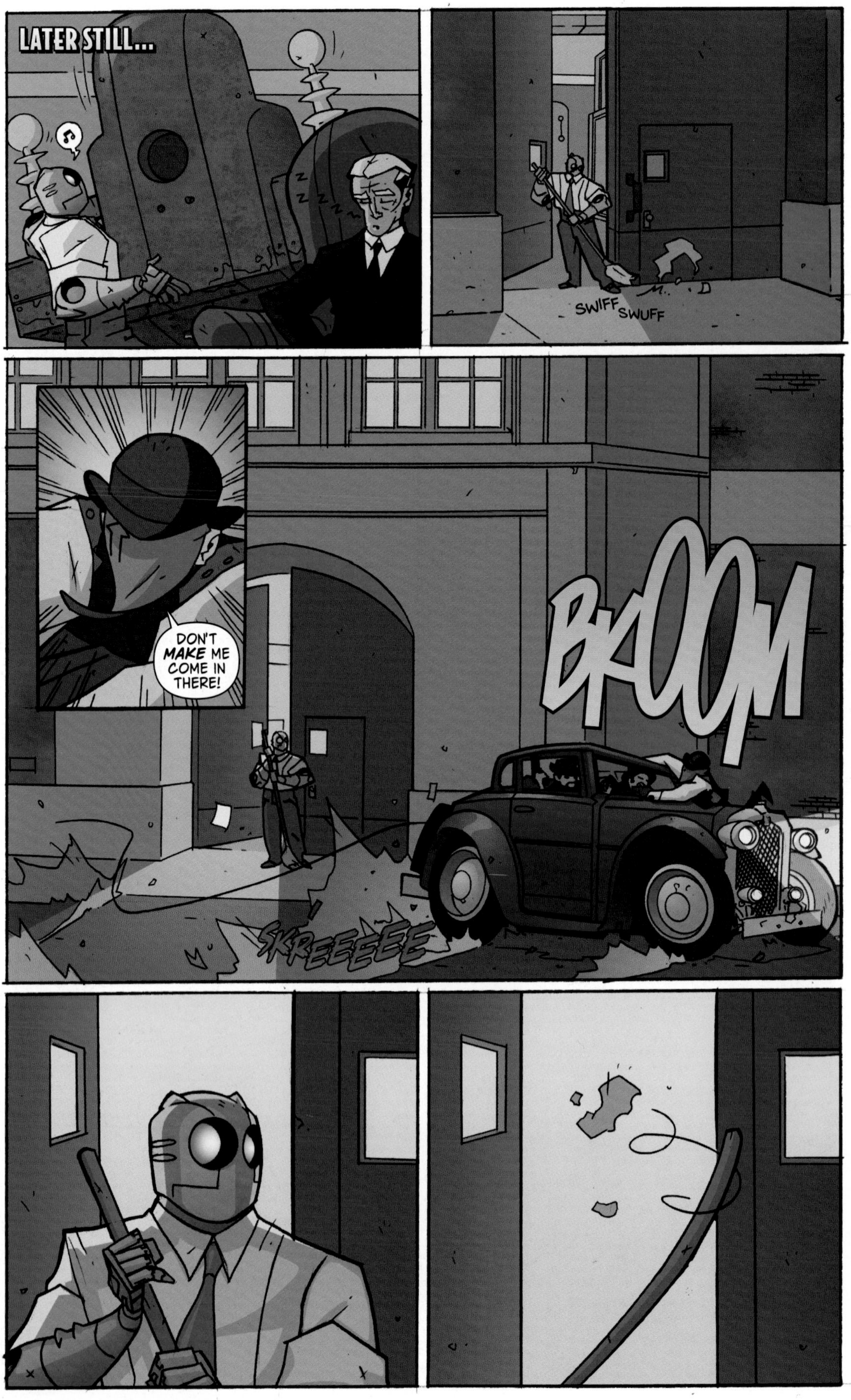
LATER STILL...
SWIFF SWUFF
DON'T MAKE ME COME IN THERE!
BKOOM
SKREEEEEE

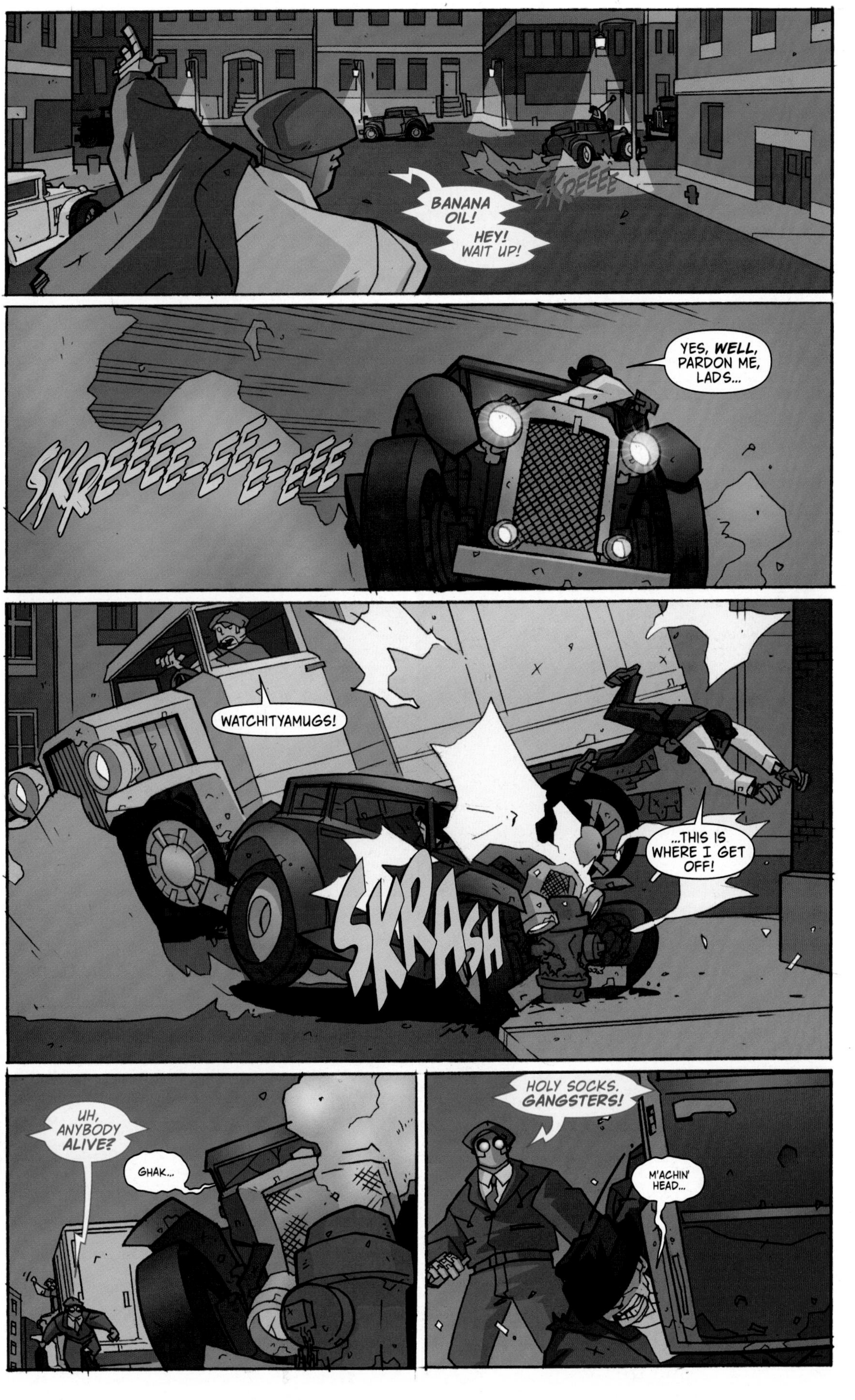

BANANA OIL!
HEY! WAIT UP!
SKREEEE
YES, **WELL**, PARDON ME, LADS...
SKREEEEE-EEE-E-EEE
WATCHITYAMUGS!
...THIS IS WHERE I GET OFF!
SKRASH
UH, ANYBODY **ALIVE?**
GHAK...
HOLY SOCKS. **GANGSTERS!**
M'ACHIN' HEAD...

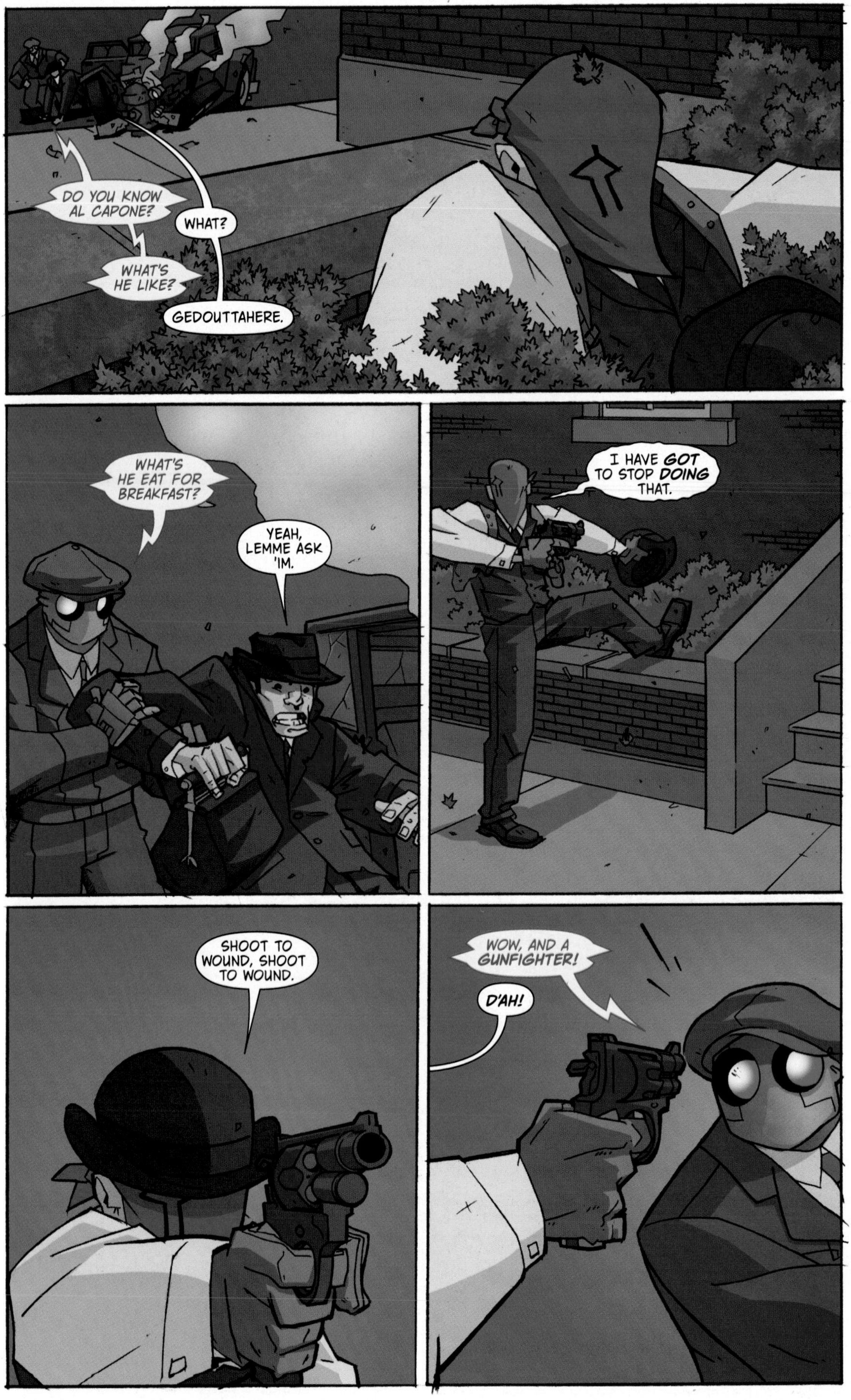
DO YOU KNOW AL CAPONE?
WHAT?
WHAT'S HE LIKE?
GEDOUTTAHERE.
WHAT'S HE EAT FOR BREAKFAST?
YEAH, LEMME ASK 'IM.
I HAVE **GOT** TO STOP **DOING** THAT.
SHOOT TO WOUND, SHOOT TO WOUND.
WOW, AND A **GUNFIGHTER!**
D'AH!

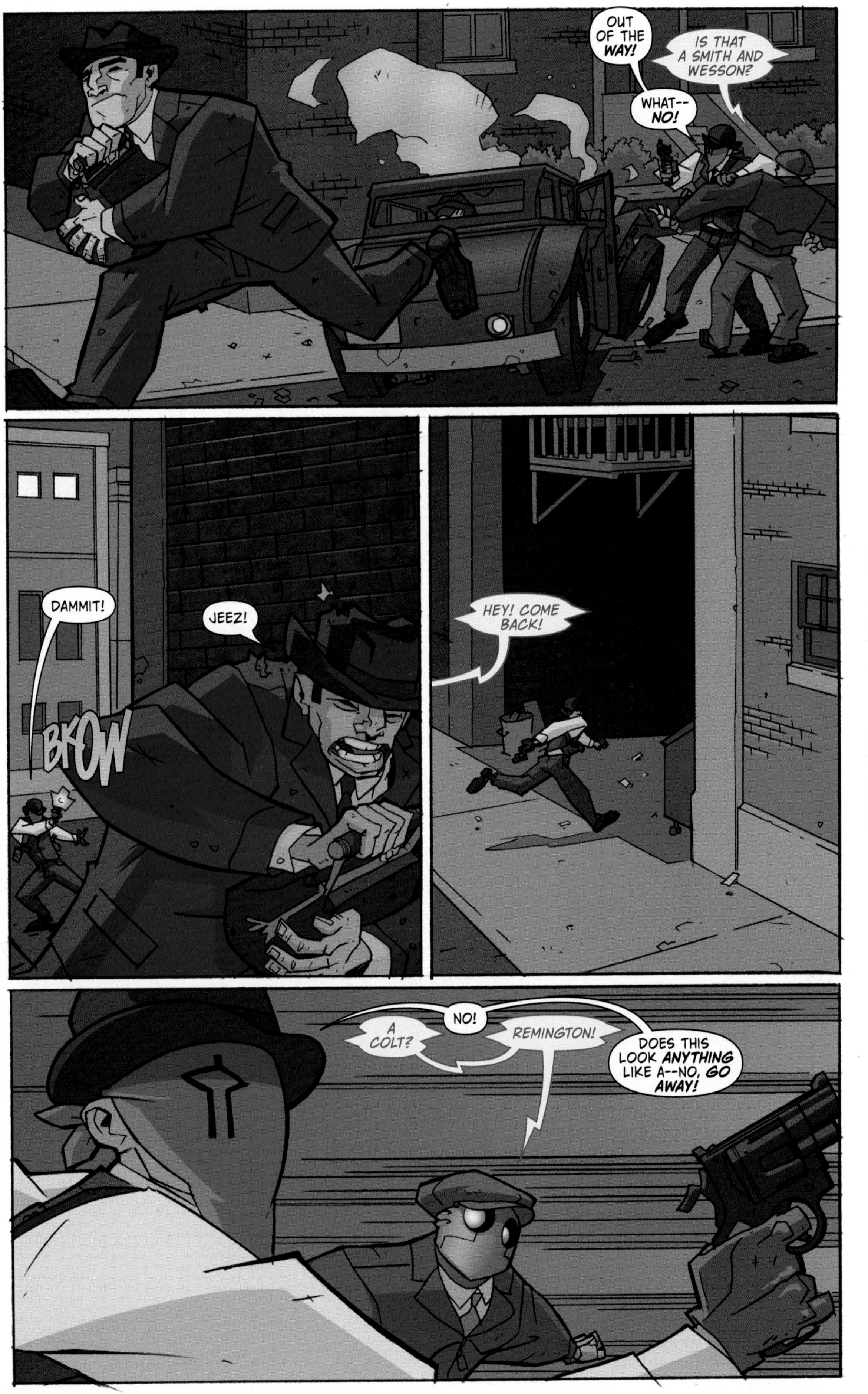
OUT OF THE WAY!
IS THAT A SMITH AND WESSON?
WHAT-- NO!
DAMMIT!
JEEZ!
BKOW
HEY! COME BACK!
A COLT?
NO!
REMINGTON!
DOES THIS LOOK ANYTHING LIKE A--NO, GO AWAY!

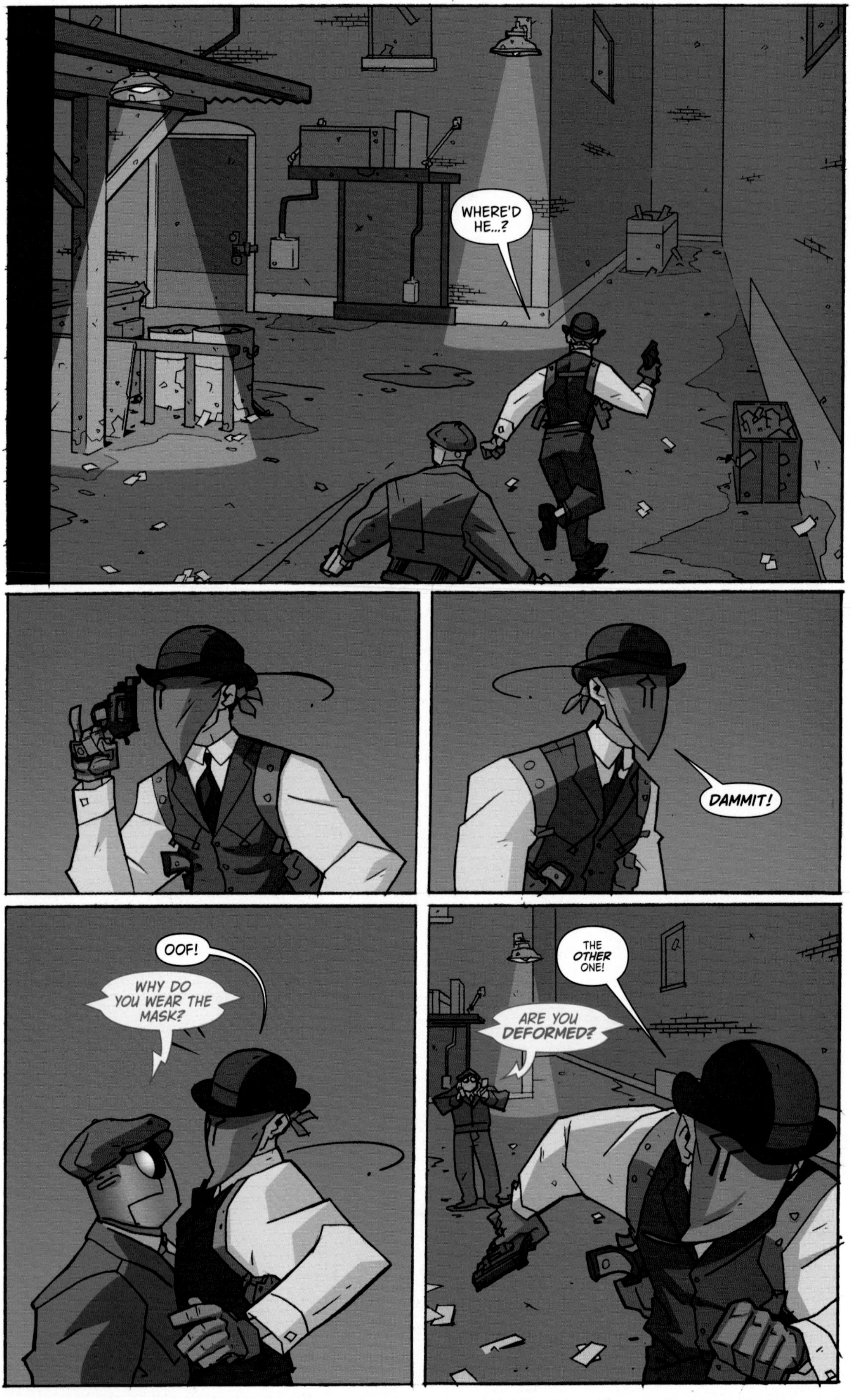
WHERE'D HE...?
DAMMIT!
OOF!
WHY DO YOU WEAR THE MASK?
ARE YOU DEFORMED?
THE OTHER ONE!

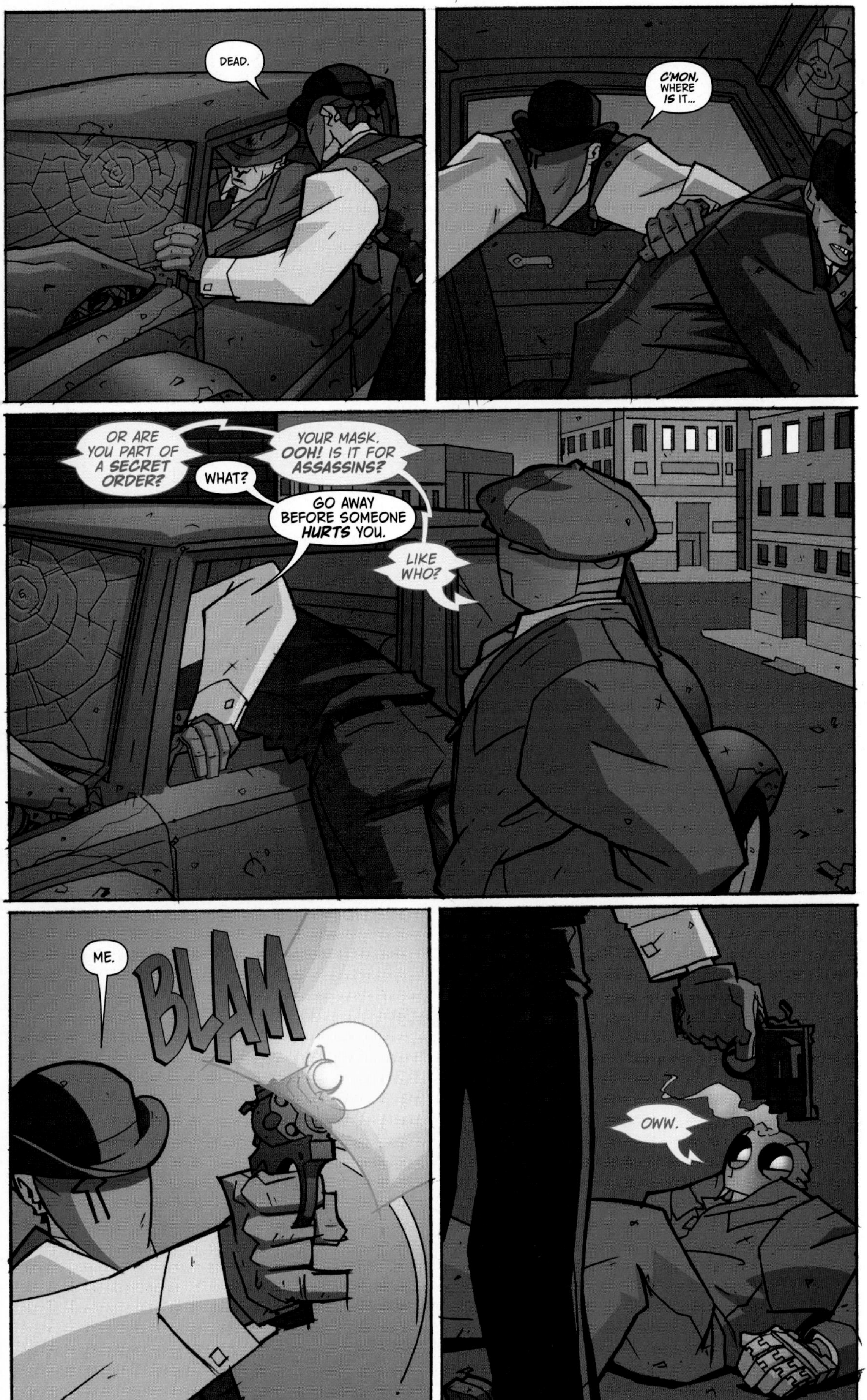
DEAD.
C'MON, WHERE IS IT...
YOUR MASK. OOH! IS IT FOR ASSASSINS?
OR ARE YOU PART OF A SECRET ORDER?
WHAT?
GO AWAY BEFORE SOMEONE HURTS YOU.
LIKE WHO?
ME.
BLAM
OWW.

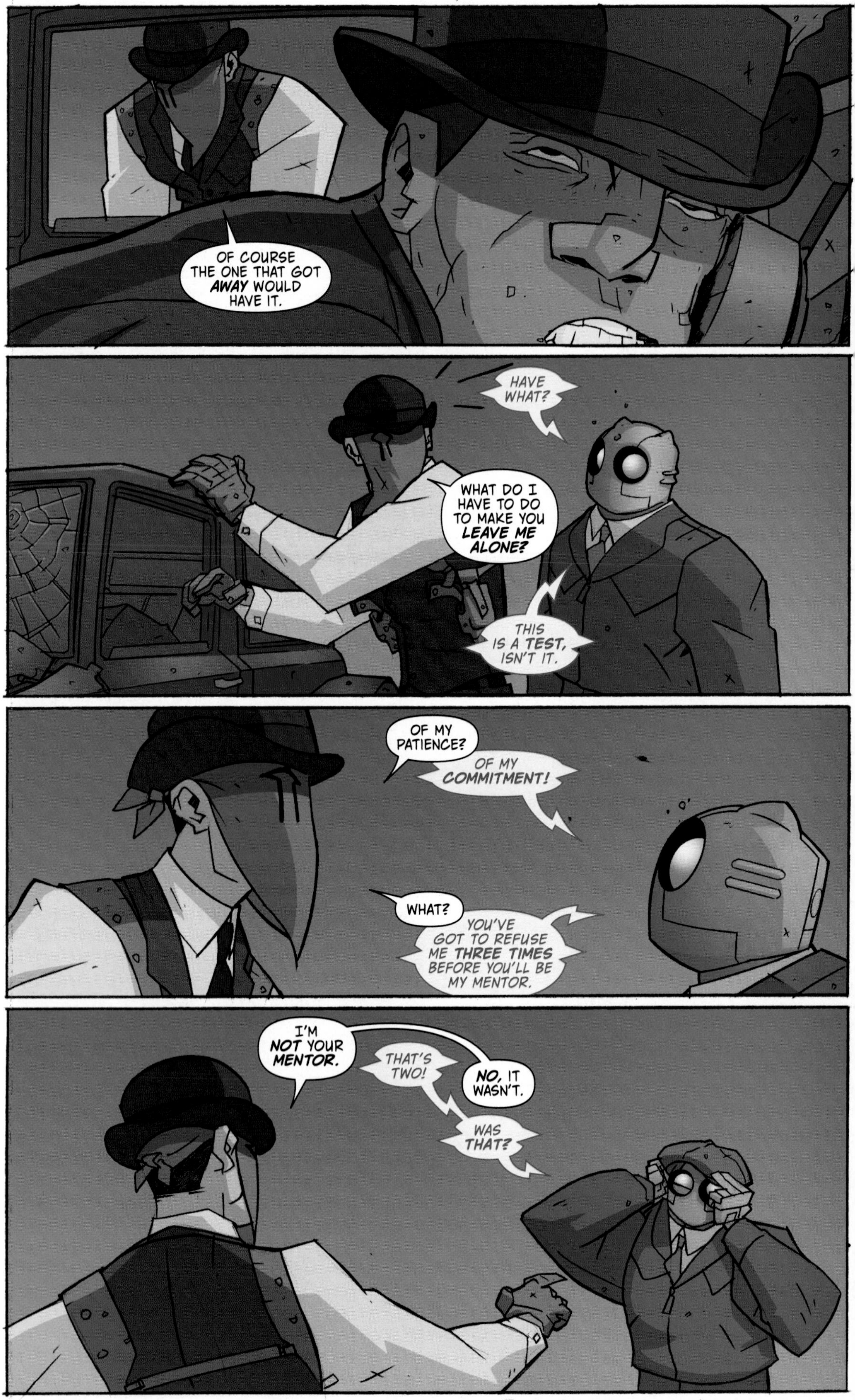

OF COURSE THE ONE THAT GOT **AWAY** WOULD HAVE IT.
HAVE WHAT?
WHAT DO I HAVE TO DO TO MAKE YOU **LEAVE ME ALONE?**
THIS IS A **TEST,** ISN'T IT.
OF MY PATIENCE?
OF MY **COMMITMENT!**
WHAT?
YOU'VE GOT TO REFUSE ME **THREE TIMES** BEFORE YOU'LL BE MY MENTOR.
I'M **NOT** YOUR **MENTOR.**
THAT'S TWO!
NO, IT WASN'T.
WAS **THAT?**

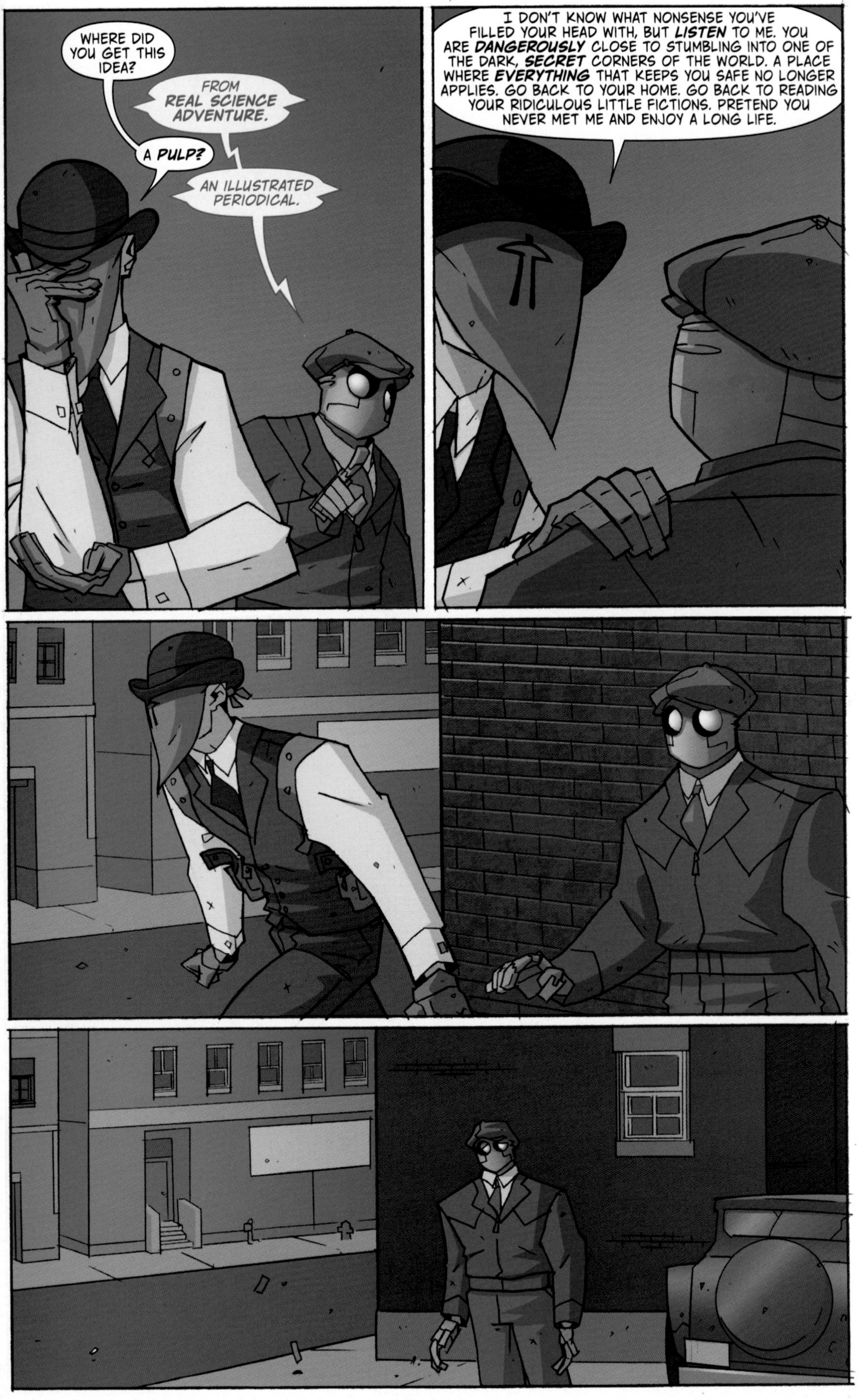
WHERE DID YOU GET THIS IDEA?
FROM REAL SCIENCE ADVENTURE.
A PULP?
AN ILLUSTRATED PERIODICAL.
I DON'T KNOW WHAT NONSENSE YOU'VE FILLED YOUR HEAD WITH, BUT LISTEN TO ME. YOU ARE DANGEROUSLY CLOSE TO STUMBLING INTO ONE OF THE DARK, SECRET CORNERS OF THE WORLD. A PLACE WHERE EVERYTHING THAT KEEPS YOU SAFE NO LONGER APPLIES. GO BACK TO YOUR HOME. GO BACK TO READING YOUR RIDICULOUS LITTLE FICTIONS. PRETEND YOU NEVER MET ME AND ENJOY A LONG LIFE.

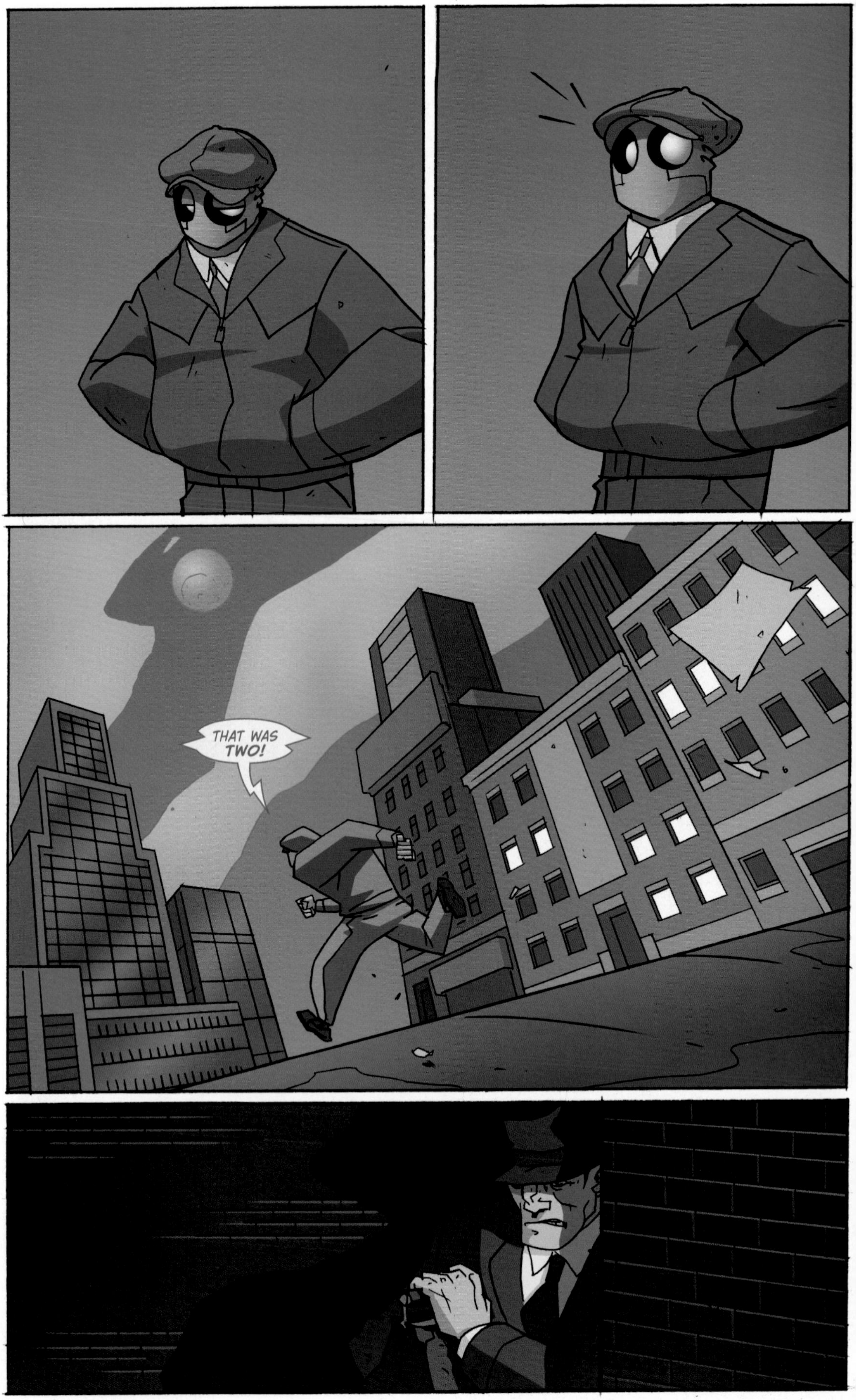
THAT WAS TWO!

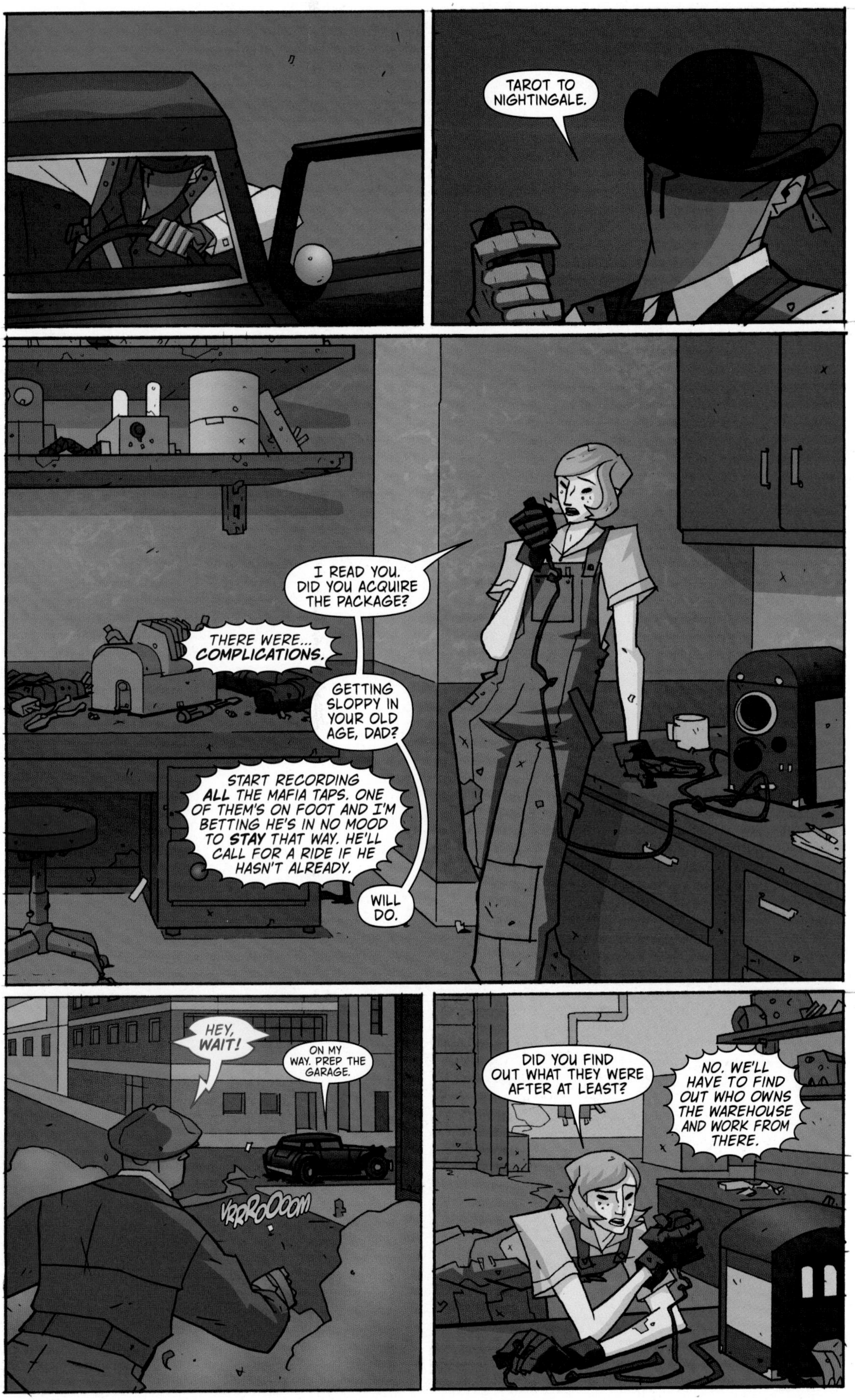
TAROT TO NIGHTINGALE.
I READ YOU. DID YOU ACQUIRE THE PACKAGE?
THERE WERE... **COMPLICATIONS.**
GETTING SLOPPY IN YOUR OLD AGE, DAD?
START RECORDING **ALL** THE MAFIA TAPS. ONE OF THEM'S ON FOOT AND I'M BETTING HE'S IN NO MOOD TO **STAY** THAT WAY. HE'LL CALL FOR A RIDE IF HE HASN'T ALREADY.
WILL DO.
HEY, **WAIT!**
ON MY WAY. PREP THE GARAGE.
VRRROOOOM
DID YOU FIND OUT WHAT THEY WERE AFTER AT LEAST?
NO. WE'LL HAVE TO FIND OUT WHO OWNS THE WAREHOUSE AND WORK FROM THERE.

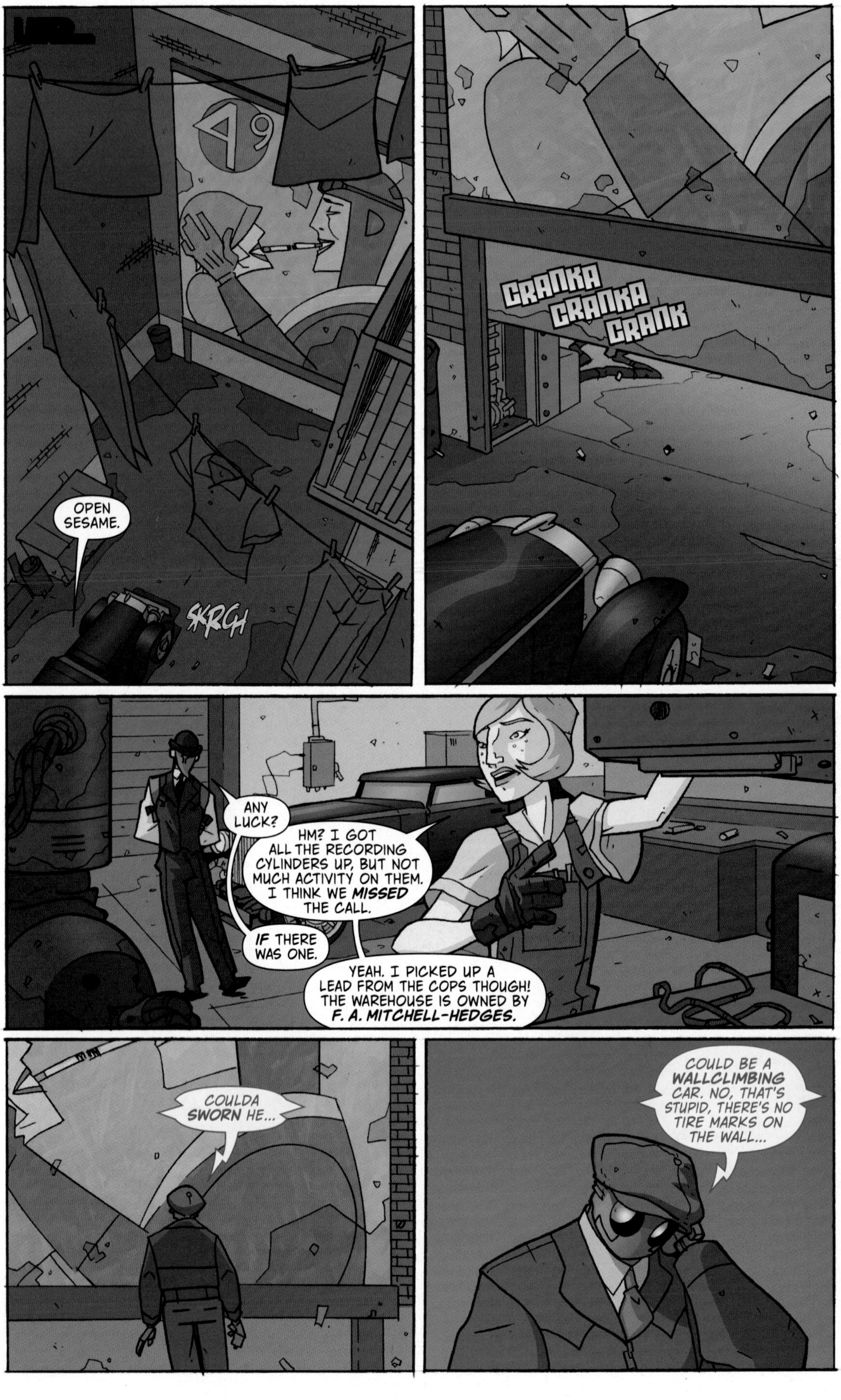
OPEN SESAME.
SKRCH
CRANKA CRANKA CRANK
ANY LUCK?
HM? I GOT ALL THE RECORDING CYLINDERS UP, BUT NOT MUCH ACTIVITY ON THEM. I THINK WE **MISSED** THE CALL.
IF THERE WAS ONE.
YEAH. I PICKED UP A LEAD FROM THE COPS THOUGH! THE WAREHOUSE IS OWNED BY ***F. A. MITCHELL-HEDGES.***
*COULDA **SWORN** HE...*
*COULD BE A **WALLCLIMBING** CAR. NO, THAT'S STUPID, THERE'S NO TIRE MARKS ON THE WALL...*

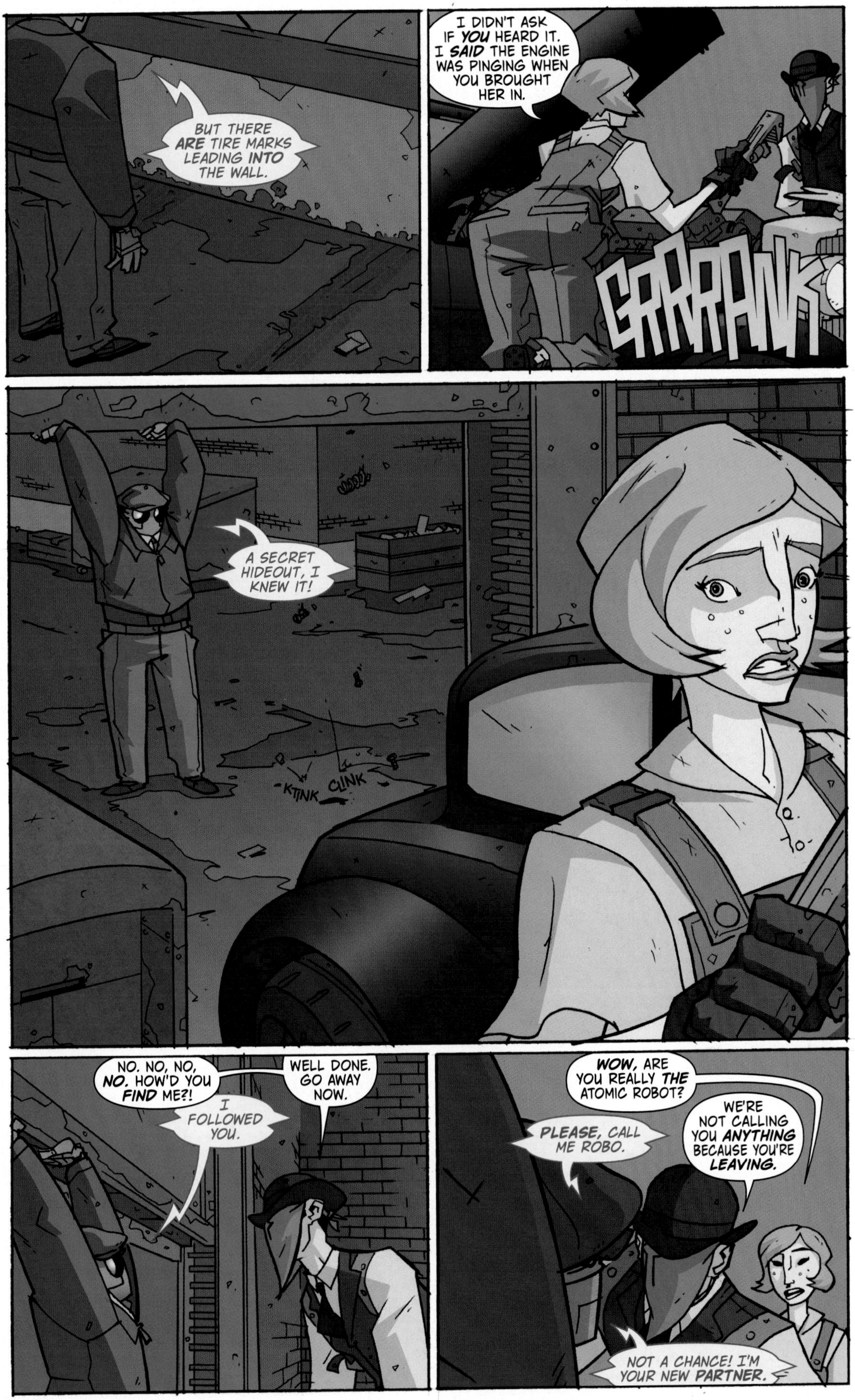
BUT THERE ARE TIRE MARKS LEADING INTO THE WALL.
I DIDN'T ASK IF YOU HEARD IT. I SAID THE ENGINE WAS PINGING WHEN YOU BROUGHT HER IN.
GRRRANK
A SECRET HIDEOUT, I KNEW IT!
KTINK
CLINK
NO. NO, NO, NO. HOW'D YOU FIND ME?!
I FOLLOWED YOU.
WELL DONE. GO AWAY NOW.
WOW, ARE YOU REALLY THE ATOMIC ROBOT?
PLEASE, CALL ME ROBO.
WE'RE NOT CALLING YOU ANYTHING BECAUSE YOU'RE LEAVING.
NOT A CHANCE! I'M YOUR NEW PARTNER.

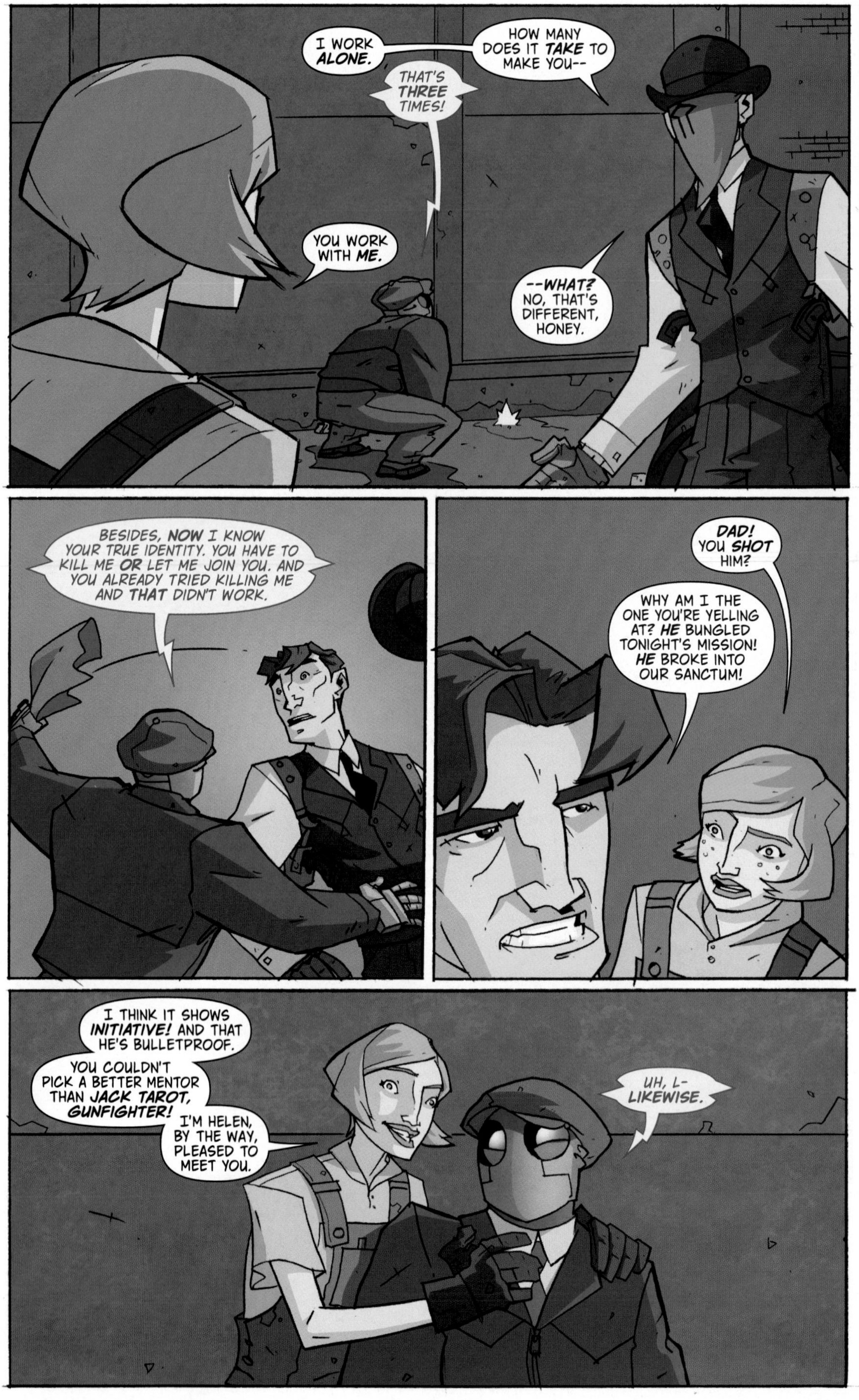
I WORK ALONE.
HOW MANY DOES IT TAKE TO MAKE YOU--
THAT'S THREE TIMES!
YOU WORK WITH ME.
--WHAT? NO, THAT'S DIFFERENT, HONEY.
BESIDES, NOW I KNOW YOUR TRUE IDENTITY. YOU HAVE TO KILL ME OR LET ME JOIN YOU. AND YOU ALREADY TRIED KILLING ME AND THAT DIDN'T WORK.
DAD! YOU SHOT HIM?
WHY AM I THE ONE YOU'RE YELLING AT? HE BUNGLED TONIGHT'S MISSION! HE BROKE INTO OUR SANCTUM!
I THINK IT SHOWS INITIATIVE! AND THAT HE'S BULLETPROOF.
YOU COULDN'T PICK A BETTER MENTOR THAN JACK TAROT, GUNFIGHTER!
I'M HELEN, BY THE WAY, PLEASED TO MEET YOU.
UH, L-LIKEWISE.

MEANWHILE, AT THE DOCKS...

WHAT TOOK SO LONG?

YEAH, GOOD TO SEE YOU *TOO*, DOC.

I HAVEN'T TIME FOR *PLEASANTRIES.* IS THAT THE *ITEM?*

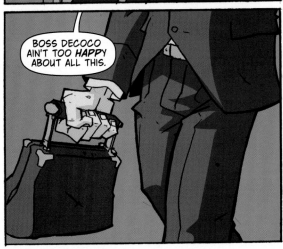

BOSS DECOCO AIN'T TOO *HAPPY* ABOUT ALL THIS.

HE ISN'T *PAID* TO HAVE AN OPINION ON THE MATTER.

IT'S CAUSIN' *TROUBLE.* THE POLICE *KNOW* THEIR PLACE. BUT WE GOT THIS MASKED *WACKADOO* DOGGIN' US NOW. HELL, HE *KILLED* KNUCKLES.

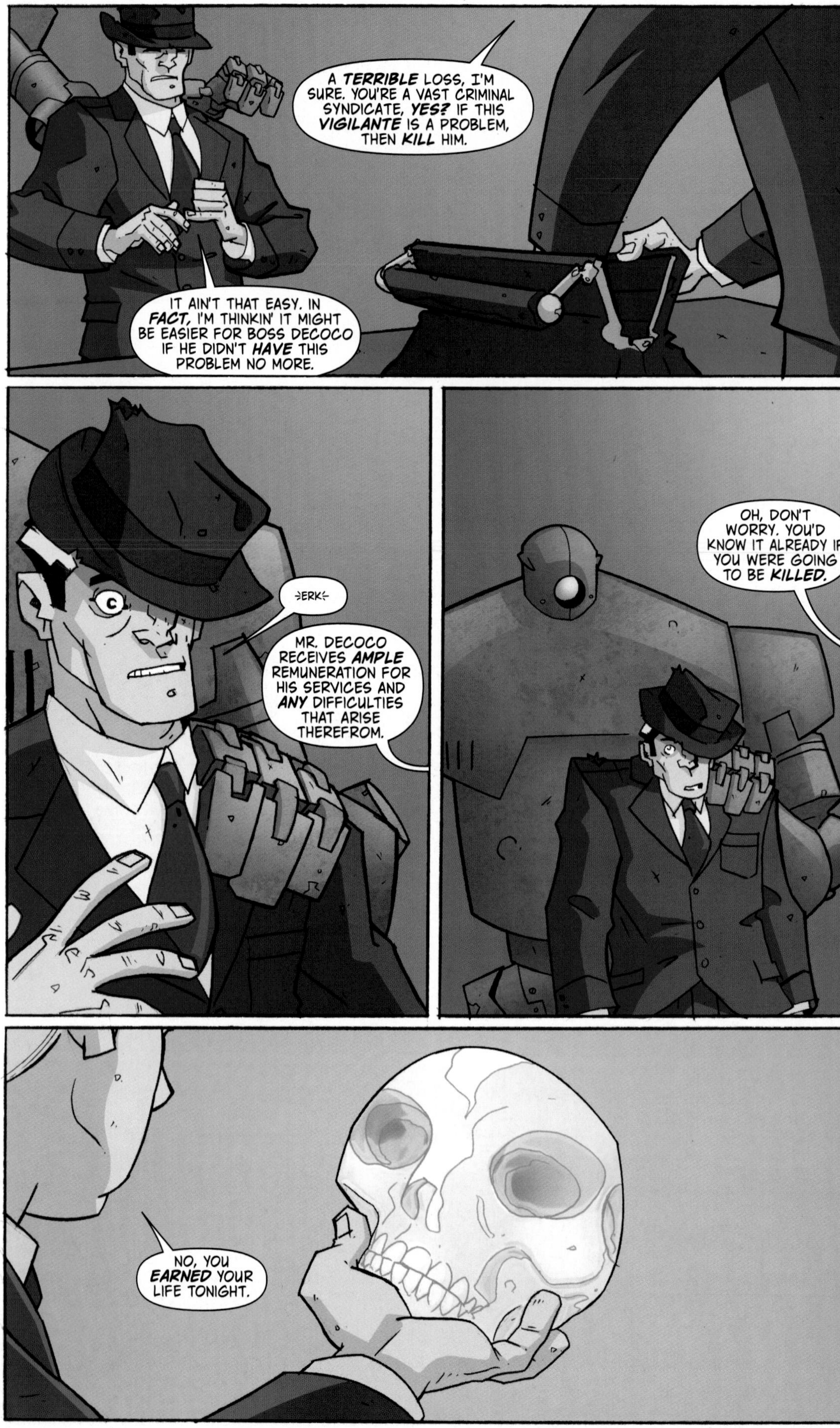
A TERRIBLE LOSS, I'M SURE. YOU'RE A VAST CRIMINAL SYNDICATE, YES? IF THIS VIGILANTE IS A PROBLEM, THEN KILL HIM.
IT AIN'T THAT EASY. IN FACT, I'M THINKIN' IT MIGHT BE EASIER FOR BOSS DECOCO IF HE DIDN'T HAVE THIS PROBLEM NO MORE.
ERK
MR. DECOCO RECEIVES AMPLE REMUNERATION FOR HIS SERVICES AND ANY DIFFICULTIES THAT ARISE THEREFROM.
OH, DON'T WORRY. YOU'D KNOW IT ALREADY IF YOU WERE GOING TO BE KILLED.
NO, YOU EARNED YOUR LIFE TONIGHT.

THE ROBOT WHO WOULDN'T GO AWAY

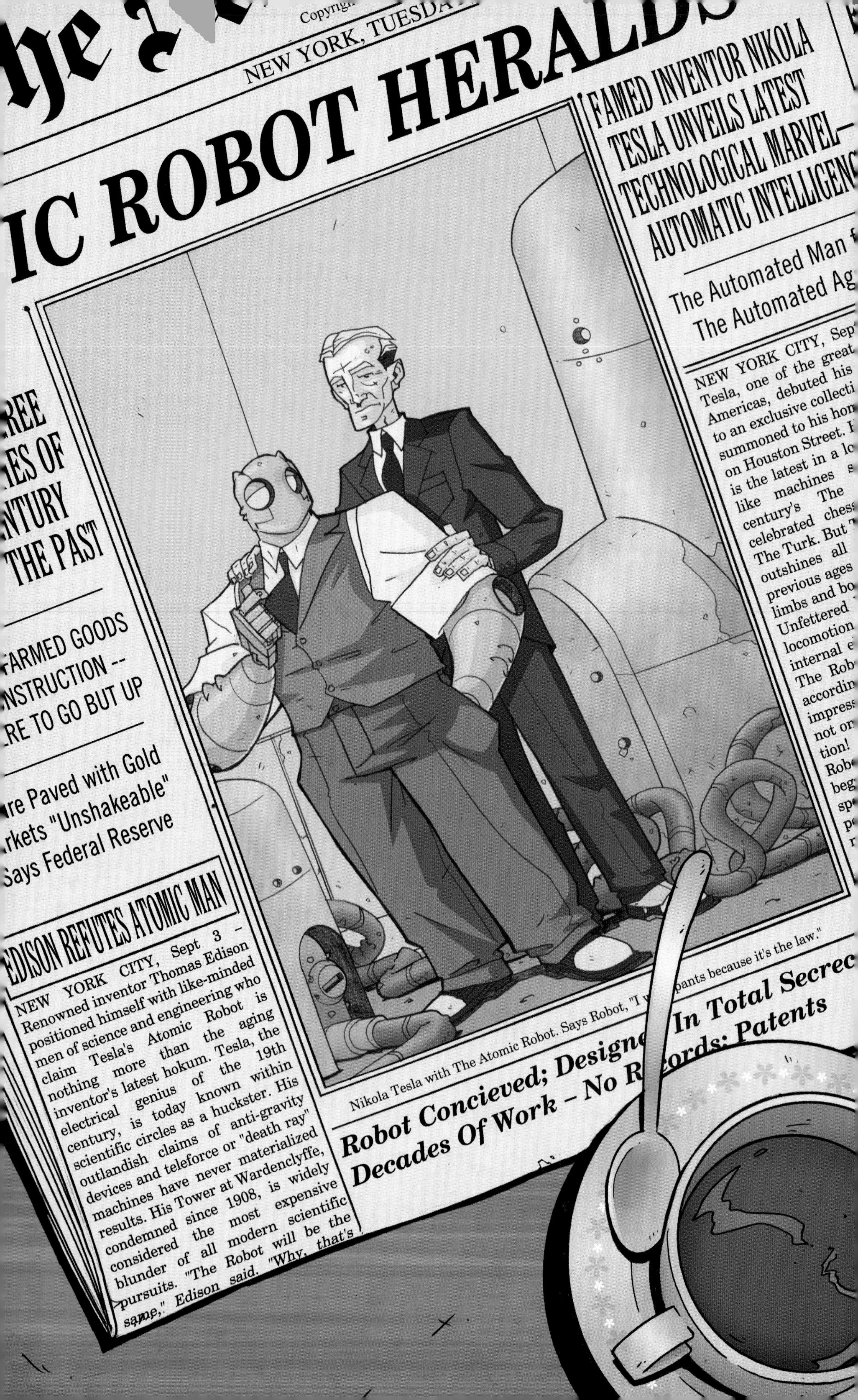
NEW YORK, TUESDA
IC ROBOT HERALDS
FAMED INVENTOR NIKOLA TESLA UNVEILS LATEST TECHNOLOGICAL MARVEL— AUTOMATIC INTELLIGENC
The Automated Man f
The Automated Ag
NEW YORK CITY, Sept Tesla, one of the great Americas, debuted his to an exclusive collecti summoned to his hon on Houston Street. is the latest in a lo like machines s century's The celebrated chess The Turk. But T outshines all previous ages limbs and bo Unfettered locomotion internal e The Rob accordin impress not on tion! Robo beg sp p
REE
IES OF
NTURY
THE PAST
FARMED GOODS
NSTRUCTION --
RE TO GO BUT UP
re Paved with Gold
rkets "Unshakeable"
Says Federal Reserve
EDISON REFUTES ATOMIC MAN
NEW YORK CITY, Sept 3 – Renowned inventor Thomas Edison positioned himself with like-minded men of science and engineering who claim Tesla's Atomic Robot is nothing more than the aging inventor's latest hokum. Tesla, the electrical genius of the 19th century, is today known within scientific circles as a huckster. His outlandish claims of anti-gravity devices and teleforce or "death ray" machines have never materialized results. His Tower at Wardenclyffe, condemned since 1908, is widely considered the most expensive blunder of all modern scientific pursuits. "The Robot will be the same," Edison said. "Why, that's
Nikola Tesla with The Atomic Robot. Says Robot, "I w pants because it's the law."
Robot Concieved; Designe In Total Secrec
Decades Of Work – No R ords: Patents

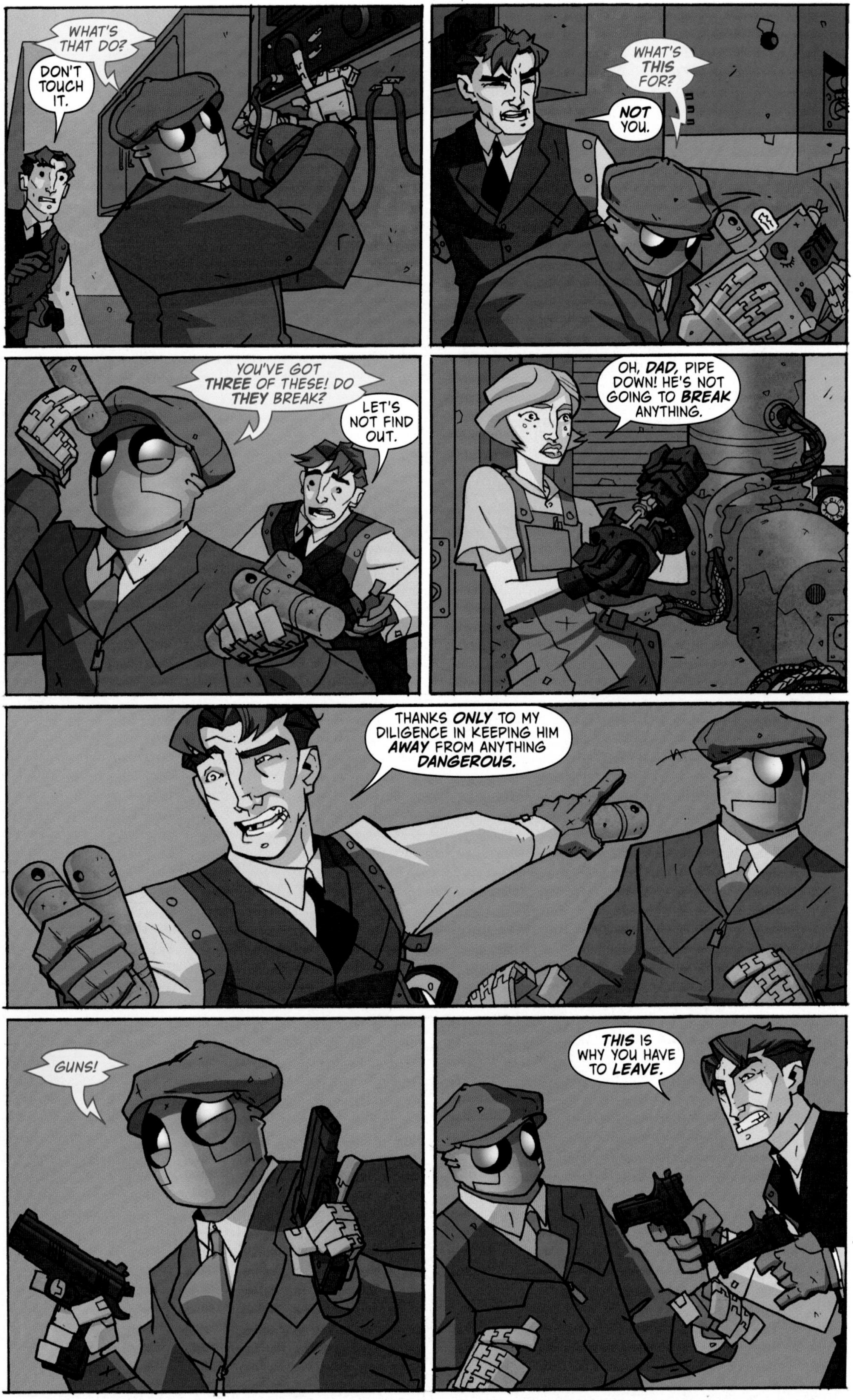
WHAT'S THAT DO?
DON'T TOUCH IT.
WHAT'S THIS FOR?
NOT YOU.
YOU'VE GOT THREE OF THESE! DO THEY BREAK?
LET'S NOT FIND OUT.
OH, DAD, PIPE DOWN! HE'S NOT GOING TO BREAK ANYTHING.
THANKS ONLY TO MY DILIGENCE IN KEEPING HIM AWAY FROM ANYTHING DANGEROUS.
GUNS!
THIS IS WHY YOU HAVE TO LEAVE.

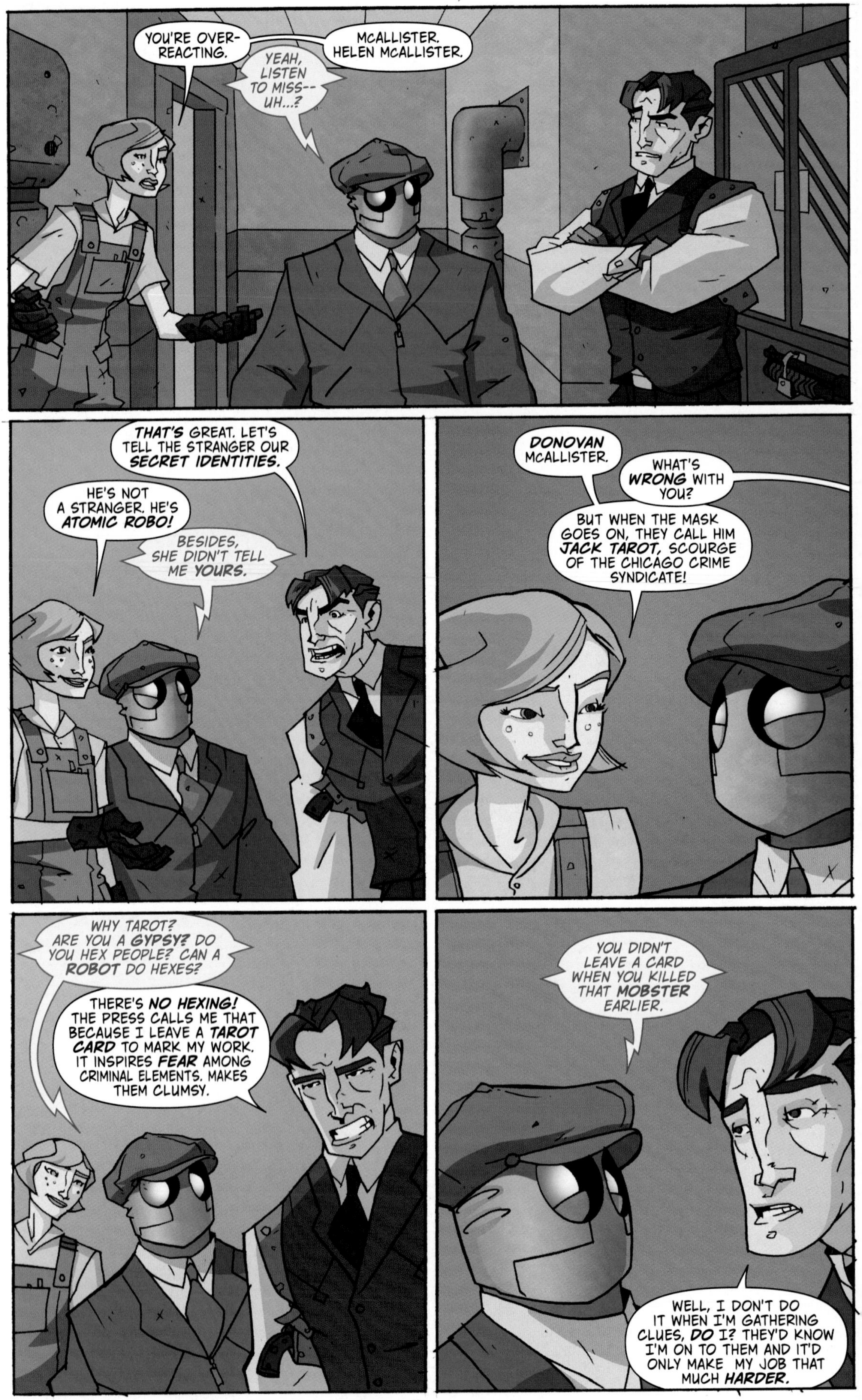
YOU'RE OVER-REACTING.
YEAH, LISTEN TO MISS-- UH...?
McALLISTER. HELEN McALLISTER.
THAT'S GREAT. LET'S TELL THE STRANGER OUR SECRET IDENTITIES.
HE'S NOT A STRANGER. HE'S ATOMIC ROBO!
BESIDES, SHE DIDN'T TELL ME YOURS.
DONOVAN McALLISTER.
WHAT'S WRONG WITH YOU?
BUT WHEN THE MASK GOES ON, THEY CALL HIM JACK TAROT, SCOURGE OF THE CHICAGO CRIME SYNDICATE!
WHY TAROT? ARE YOU A GYPSY? DO YOU HEX PEOPLE? CAN A ROBOT DO HEXES?
THERE'S NO HEXING! THE PRESS CALLS ME THAT BECAUSE I LEAVE A TAROT CARD TO MARK MY WORK. IT INSPIRES FEAR AMONG CRIMINAL ELEMENTS. MAKES THEM CLUMSY.
YOU DIDN'T LEAVE A CARD WHEN YOU KILLED THAT MOBSTER EARLIER.
WELL, I DON'T DO IT WHEN I'M GATHERING CLUES, DO I? THEY'D KNOW I'M ON TO THEM AND IT'D ONLY MAKE MY JOB THAT MUCH HARDER.

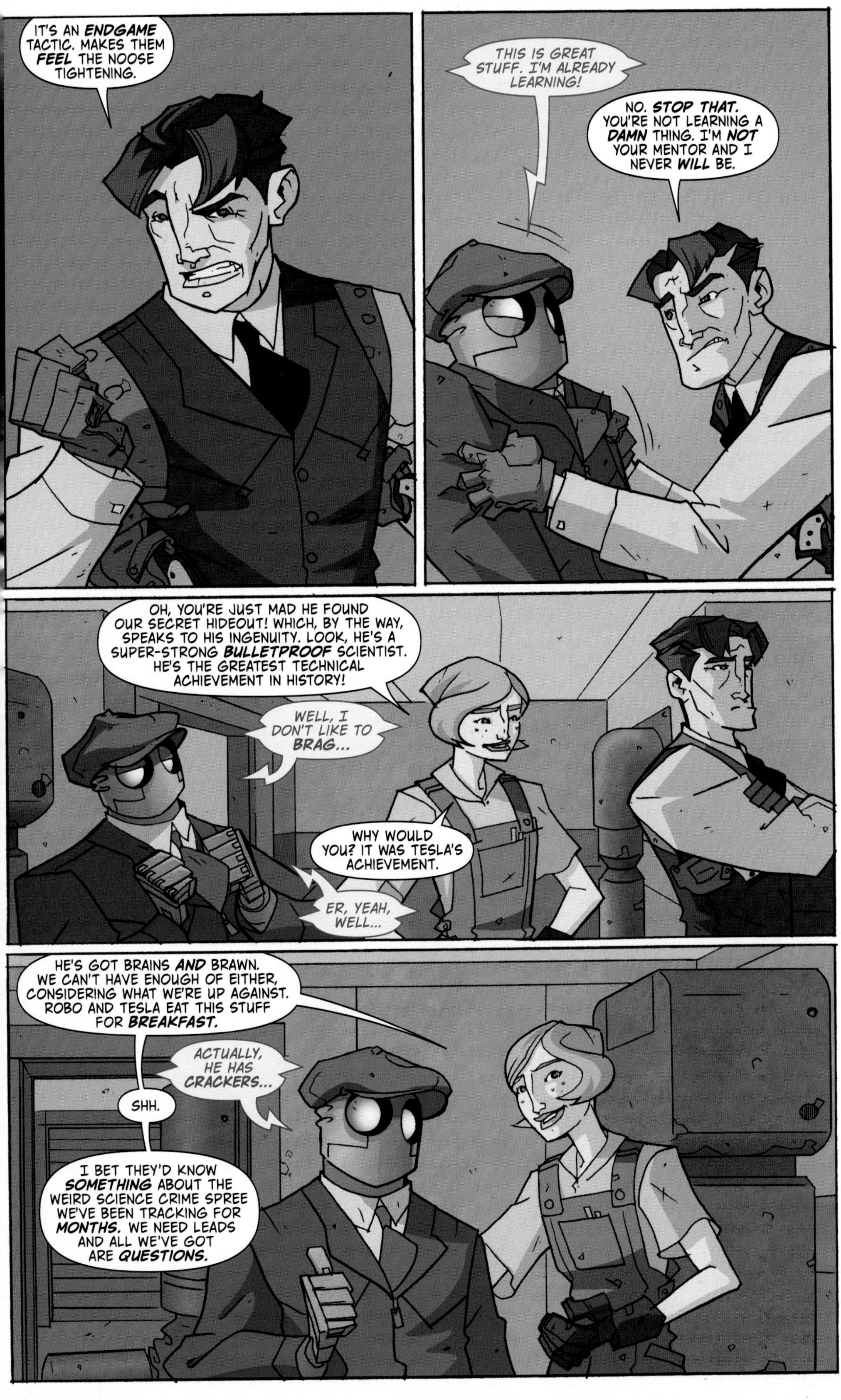
IT'S AN ENDGAME TACTIC. MAKES THEM FEEL THE NOOSE TIGHTENING.
THIS IS GREAT STUFF. I'M ALREADY LEARNING!
NO. STOP THAT. YOU'RE NOT LEARNING A DAMN THING. I'M NOT YOUR MENTOR AND I NEVER WILL BE.
OH, YOU'RE JUST MAD HE FOUND OUR SECRET HIDEOUT! WHICH, BY THE WAY, SPEAKS TO HIS INGENUITY. LOOK, HE'S A SUPER-STRONG BULLETPROOF SCIENTIST. HE'S THE GREATEST TECHNICAL ACHIEVEMENT IN HISTORY!
WELL, I DON'T LIKE TO BRAG...
WHY WOULD YOU? IT WAS TESLA'S ACHIEVEMENT.
ER, YEAH, WELL...
HE'S GOT BRAINS AND BRAWN. WE CAN'T HAVE ENOUGH OF EITHER, CONSIDERING WHAT WE'RE UP AGAINST. ROBO AND TESLA EAT THIS STUFF FOR BREAKFAST.
ACTUALLY, HE HAS CRACKERS...
SHH.
I BET THEY'D KNOW SOMETHING ABOUT THE WEIRD SCIENCE CRIME SPREE WE'VE BEEN TRACKING FOR MONTHS. WE NEED LEADS AND ALL WE'VE GOT ARE QUESTIONS.

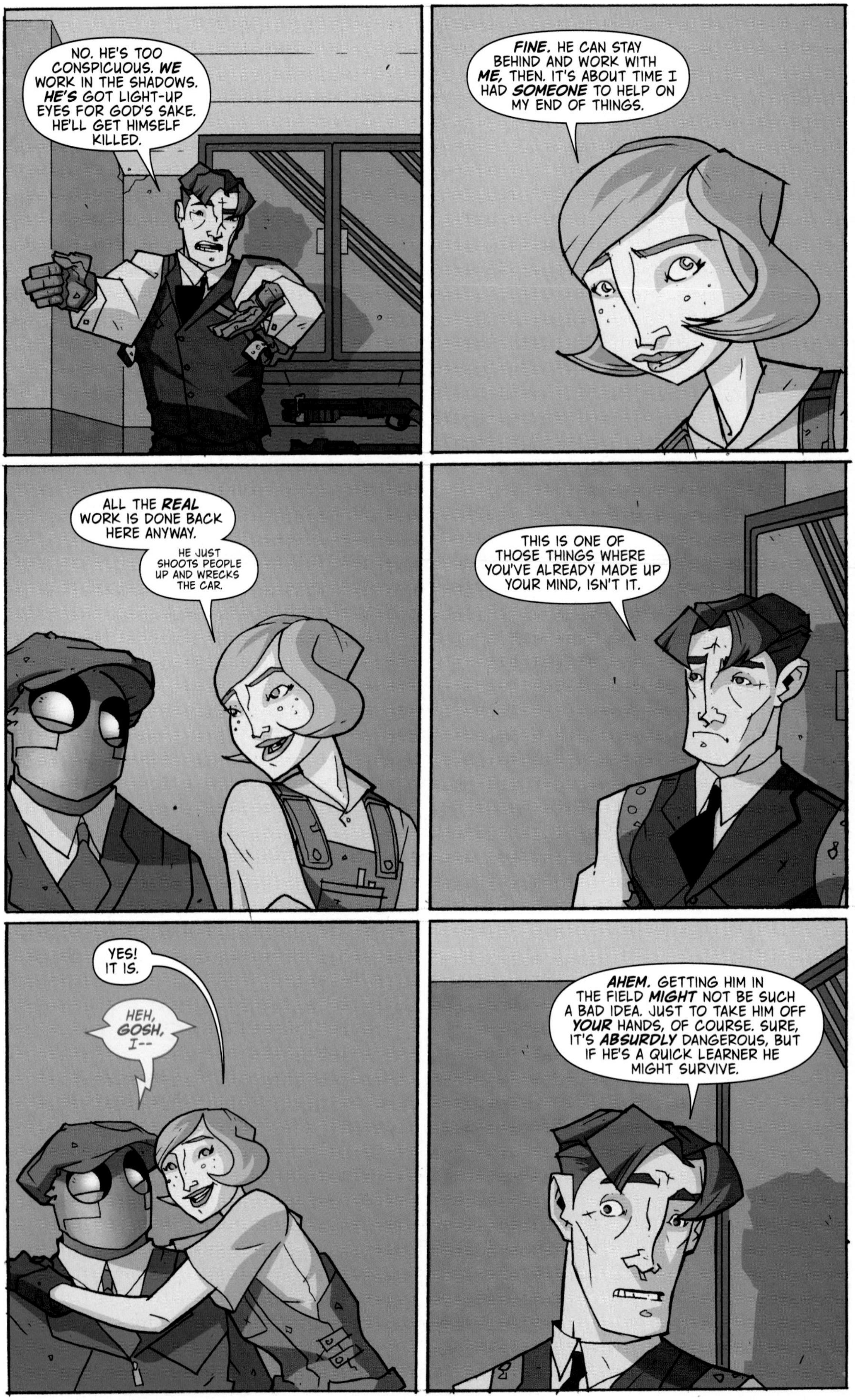
NO. HE'S TOO CONSPICUOUS. WE WORK IN THE SHADOWS. HE'S GOT LIGHT-UP EYES FOR GOD'S SAKE. HE'LL GET HIMSELF KILLED.
FINE. HE CAN STAY BEHIND AND WORK WITH ME, THEN. IT'S ABOUT TIME I HAD SOMEONE TO HELP ON MY END OF THINGS.
ALL THE REAL WORK IS DONE BACK HERE ANYWAY.
HE JUST SHOOTS PEOPLE UP AND WRECKS THE CAR.
THIS IS ONE OF THOSE THINGS WHERE YOU'VE ALREADY MADE UP YOUR MIND, ISN'T IT.
YES! IT IS.
HEH, GOSH, I--
AHEM. GETTING HIM IN THE FIELD MIGHT NOT BE SUCH A BAD IDEA. JUST TO TAKE HIM OFF YOUR HANDS, OF COURSE. SURE, IT'S ABSURDLY DANGEROUS, BUT IF HE'S A QUICK LEARNER HE MIGHT SURVIVE.

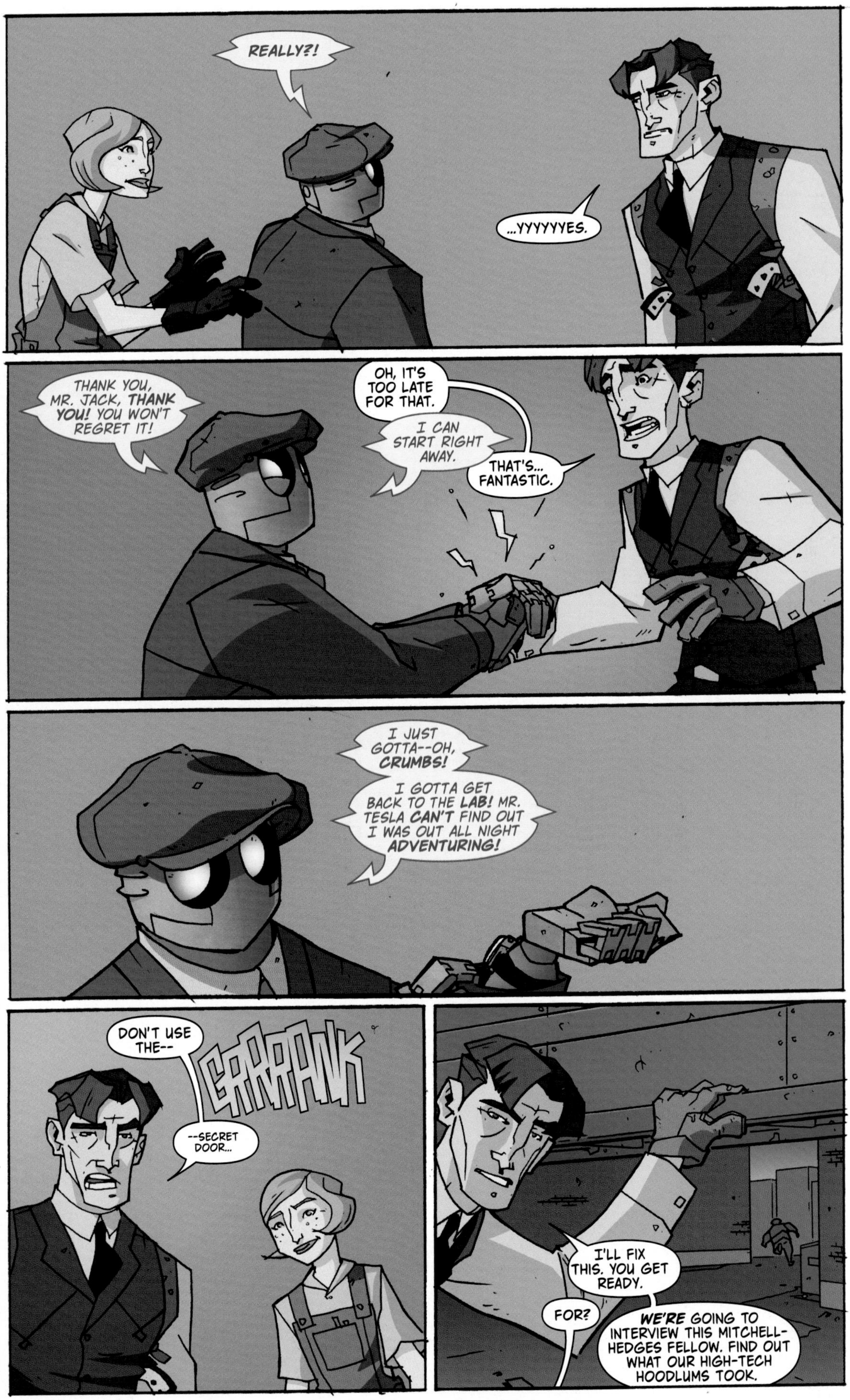
REALLY?!
...YYYYYYES.
THANK YOU, MR. JACK, THANK YOU! YOU WON'T REGRET IT!
OH, IT'S TOO LATE FOR THAT.
I CAN START RIGHT AWAY.
THAT'S... FANTASTIC.
I JUST GOTTA--OH, CRUMBS!
I GOTTA GET BACK TO THE LAB! MR. TESLA CAN'T FIND OUT I WAS OUT ALL NIGHT ADVENTURING!
DON'T USE THE--
GRRRANK
--SECRET DOOR...
I'LL FIX THIS. YOU GET READY.
FOR?
WE'RE GOING TO INTERVIEW THIS MITCHELL-HEDGES FELLOW. FIND OUT WHAT OUR HIGH-TECH HOODLUMS TOOK.

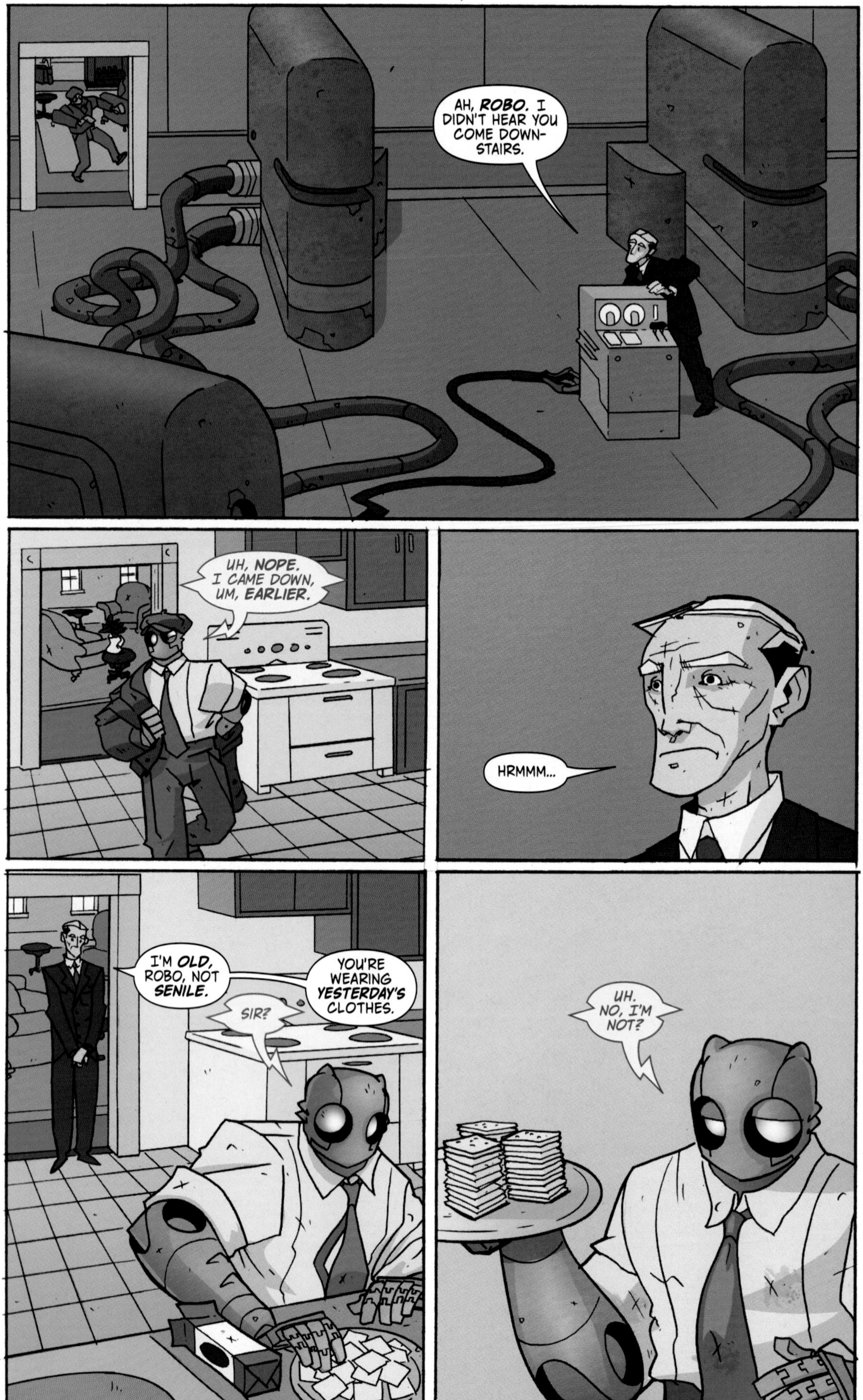
AH, ROBO. I DIDN'T HEAR YOU COME DOWN-STAIRS.
UH, NOPE. I CAME DOWN, UM, EARLIER.
HRMMM...
I'M OLD, ROBO, NOT SENILE.
YOU'RE WEARING YESTERDAY'S CLOTHES.
SIR?
UH. NO, I'M NOT?

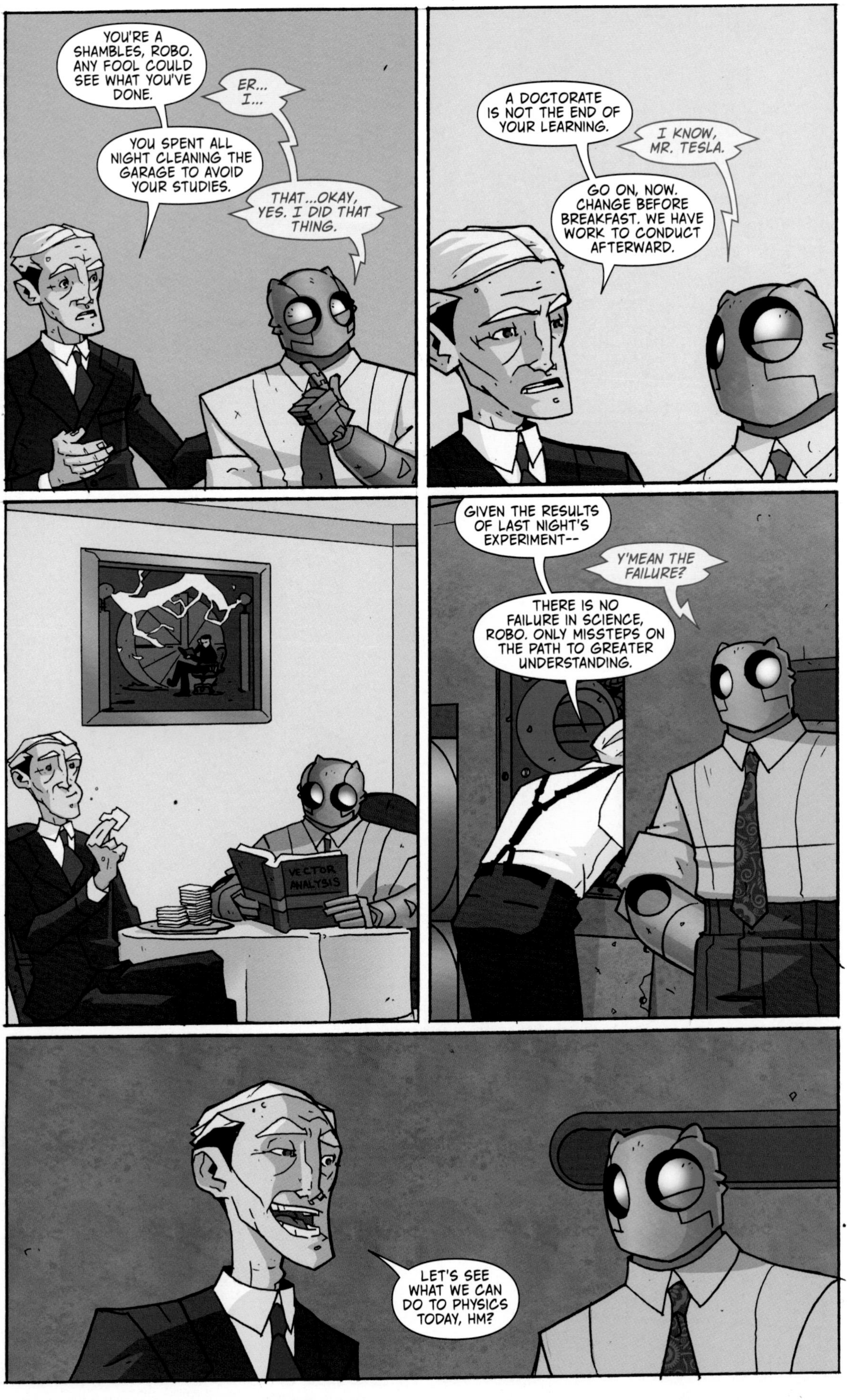
YOU'RE A SHAMBLES, ROBO. ANY FOOL COULD SEE WHAT YOU'VE DONE.
ER... I...
YOU SPENT ALL NIGHT CLEANING THE GARAGE TO AVOID YOUR STUDIES.
THAT...OKAY, YES. I DID THAT THING.
A DOCTORATE IS NOT THE END OF YOUR LEARNING.
I KNOW, MR. TESLA.
GO ON, NOW. CHANGE BEFORE BREAKFAST. WE HAVE WORK TO CONDUCT AFTERWARD.
VECTOR ANALYSIS
GIVEN THE RESULTS OF LAST NIGHT'S EXPERIMENT--
Y'MEAN THE FAILURE?
THERE IS NO FAILURE IN SCIENCE, ROBO. ONLY MISSTEPS ON THE PATH TO GREATER UNDERSTANDING.
LET'S SEE WHAT WE CAN DO TO PHYSICS TODAY, HM?

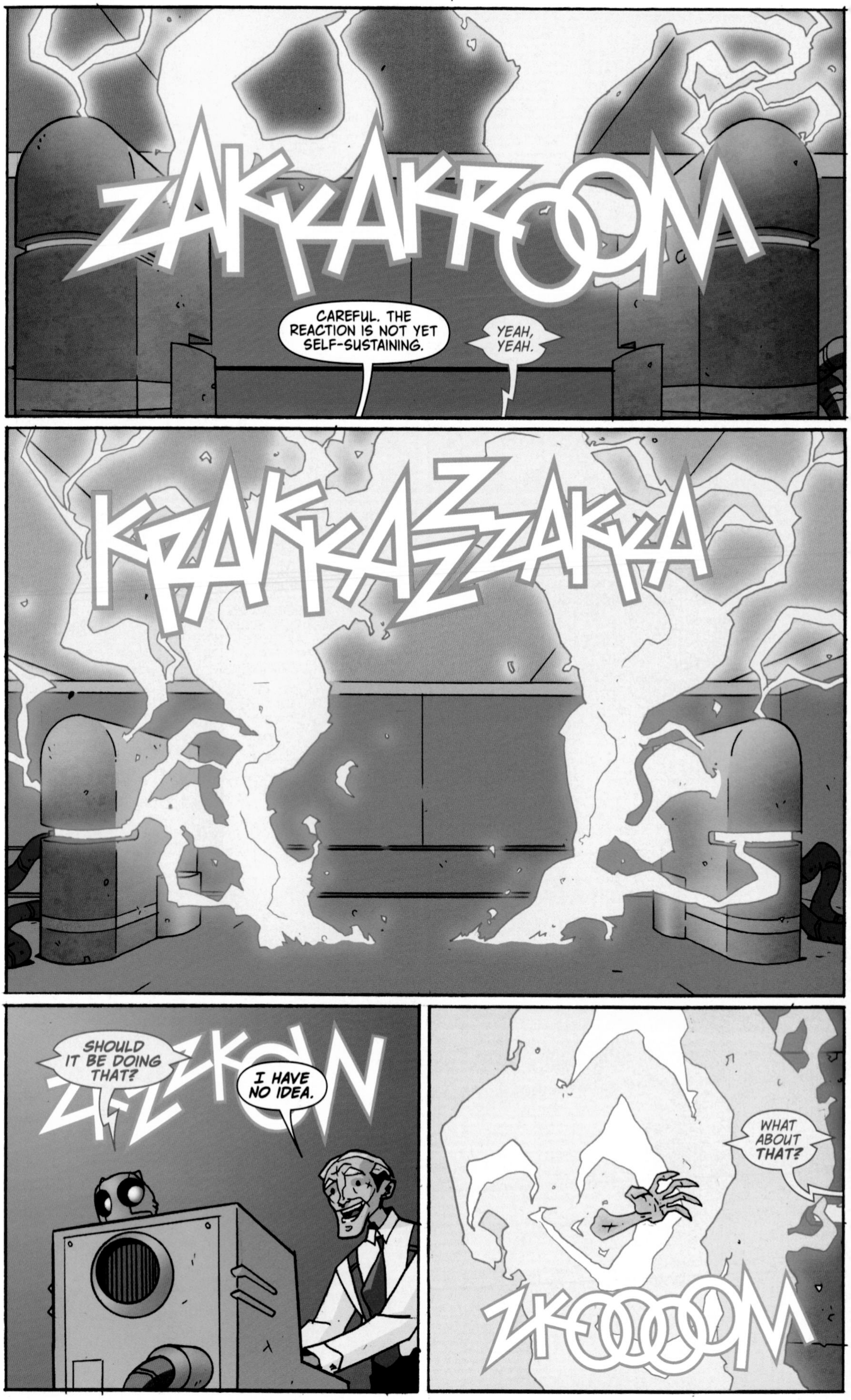
ZAKKAKROOM
CAREFUL. THE REACTION IS NOT YET SELF-SUSTAINING.
YEAH, YEAH.
KRAKKAZZZAKKA
SHOULD IT BE DOING THAT?
ZZZZKOW
I HAVE NO IDEA.
WHAT ABOUT THAT?
ZKOOOOM

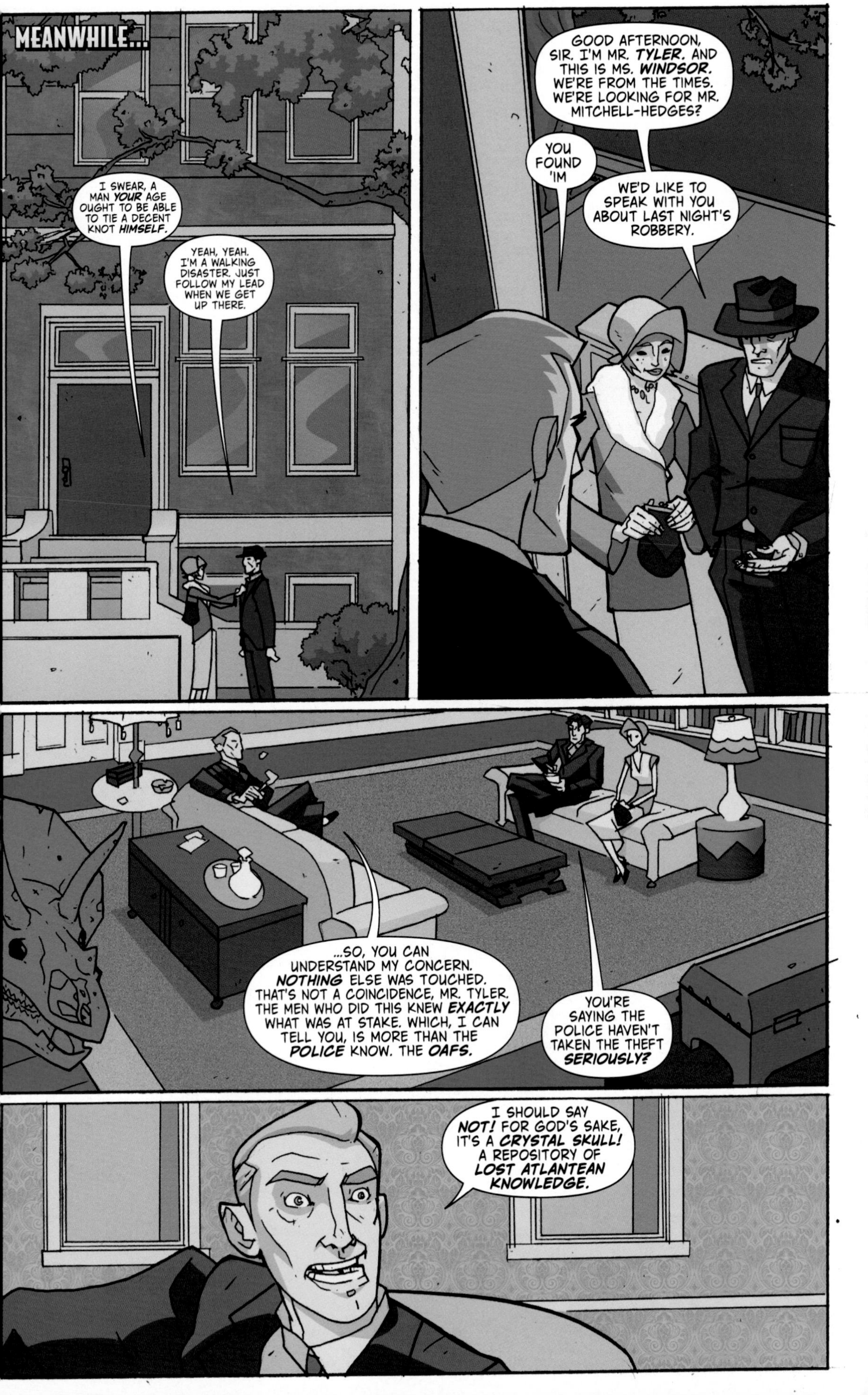
MEANWHILE...
I SWEAR, A MAN YOUR AGE OUGHT TO BE ABLE TO TIE A DECENT KNOT HIMSELF.
YEAH, YEAH. I'M A WALKING DISASTER. JUST FOLLOW MY LEAD WHEN WE GET UP THERE.
GOOD AFTERNOON, SIR. I'M MR. TYLER. AND THIS IS MS. WINDSOR. WE'RE FROM THE TIMES. WE'RE LOOKING FOR MR. MITCHELL-HEDGES?
YOU FOUND 'IM
WE'D LIKE TO SPEAK WITH YOU ABOUT LAST NIGHT'S ROBBERY.
...SO, YOU CAN UNDERSTAND MY CONCERN. NOTHING ELSE WAS TOUCHED. THAT'S NOT A COINCIDENCE, MR. TYLER. THE MEN WHO DID THIS KNEW EXACTLY WHAT WAS AT STAKE. WHICH, I CAN TELL YOU, IS MORE THAN THE POLICE KNOW. THE OAFS.
YOU'RE SAYING THE POLICE HAVEN'T TAKEN THE THEFT SERIOUSLY?
I SHOULD SAY NOT! FOR GOD'S SAKE, IT'S A CRYSTAL SKULL! A REPOSITORY OF LOST ATLANTEAN KNOWLEDGE.

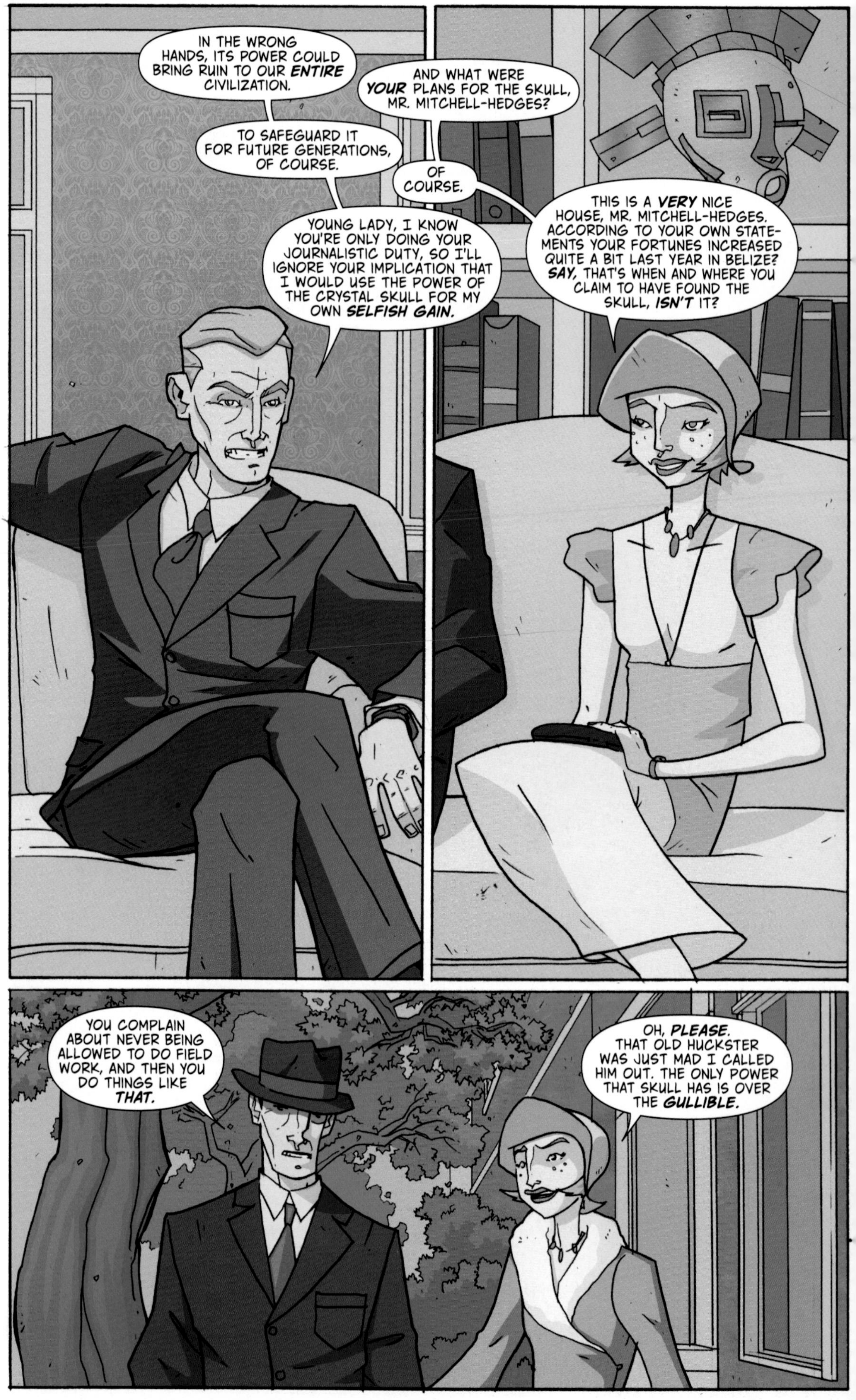

IN THE WRONG HANDS, ITS POWER COULD BRING RUIN TO OUR ENTIRE CIVILIZATION.
AND WHAT WERE YOUR PLANS FOR THE SKULL, MR. MITCHELL-HEDGES?
TO SAFEGUARD IT FOR FUTURE GENERATIONS, OF COURSE.
OF COURSE.
YOUNG LADY, I KNOW YOU'RE ONLY DOING YOUR JOURNALISTIC DUTY, SO I'LL IGNORE YOUR IMPLICATION THAT I WOULD USE THE POWER OF THE CRYSTAL SKULL FOR MY OWN SELFISH GAIN.
THIS IS A VERY NICE HOUSE, MR. MITCHELL-HEDGES. ACCORDING TO YOUR OWN STATEMENTS YOUR FORTUNES INCREASED QUITE A BIT LAST YEAR IN BELIZE? SAY, THAT'S WHEN AND WHERE YOU CLAIM TO HAVE FOUND THE SKULL, ISN'T IT?
YOU COMPLAIN ABOUT NEVER BEING ALLOWED TO DO FIELD WORK, AND THEN YOU DO THINGS LIKE THAT.
OH, PLEASE. THAT OLD HUCKSTER WAS JUST MAD I CALLED HIM OUT. THE ONLY POWER THAT SKULL HAS IS OVER THE GULLIBLE.

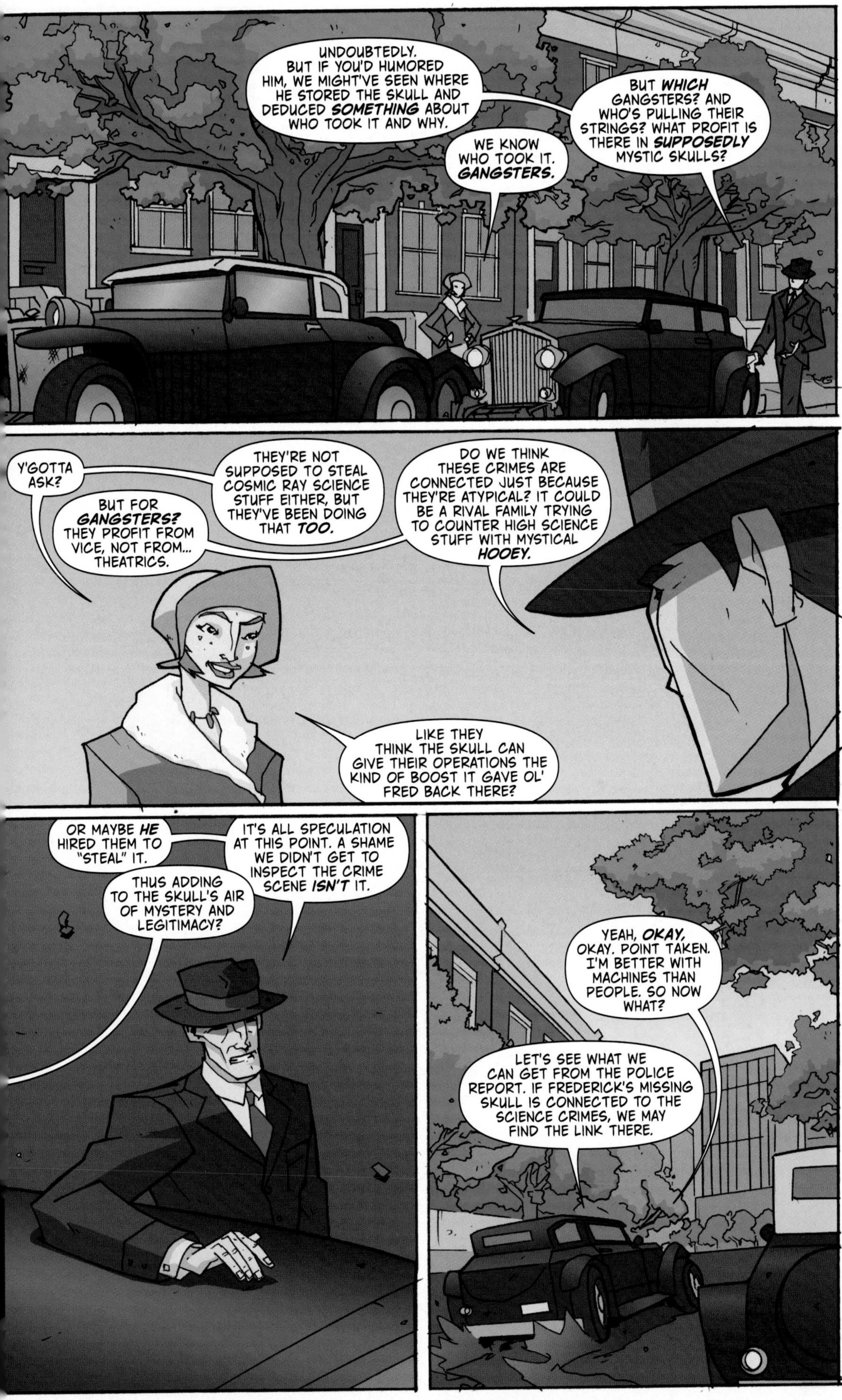
UNDOUBTEDLY. BUT IF YOU'D HUMORED HIM, WE MIGHT'VE SEEN WHERE HE STORED THE SKULL AND DEDUCED SOMETHING ABOUT WHO TOOK IT AND WHY.
WE KNOW WHO TOOK IT. GANGSTERS.
BUT WHICH GANGSTERS? AND WHO'S PULLING THEIR STRINGS? WHAT PROFIT IS THERE IN SUPPOSEDLY MYSTIC SKULLS?
Y'GOTTA ASK?
BUT FOR GANGSTERS? THEY PROFIT FROM VICE, NOT FROM... THEATRICS.
THEY'RE NOT SUPPOSED TO STEAL COSMIC RAY SCIENCE STUFF EITHER, BUT THEY'VE BEEN DOING THAT TOO.
DO WE THINK THESE CRIMES ARE CONNECTED JUST BECAUSE THEY'RE ATYPICAL? IT COULD BE A RIVAL FAMILY TRYING TO COUNTER HIGH SCIENCE STUFF WITH MYSTICAL HOOEY.
LIKE THEY THINK THE SKULL CAN GIVE THEIR OPERATIONS THE KIND OF BOOST IT GAVE OL' FRED BACK THERE?
OR MAYBE HE HIRED THEM TO "STEAL" IT.
THUS ADDING TO THE SKULL'S AIR OF MYSTERY AND LEGITIMACY?
IT'S ALL SPECULATION AT THIS POINT. A SHAME WE DIDN'T GET TO INSPECT THE CRIME SCENE ISN'T IT.
YEAH, OKAY, OKAY. POINT TAKEN. I'M BETTER WITH MACHINES THAN PEOPLE. SO NOW WHAT?
LET'S SEE WHAT WE CAN GET FROM THE POLICE REPORT. IF FREDERICK'S MISSING SKULL IS CONNECTED TO THE SCIENCE CRIMES, WE MAY FIND THE LINK THERE.

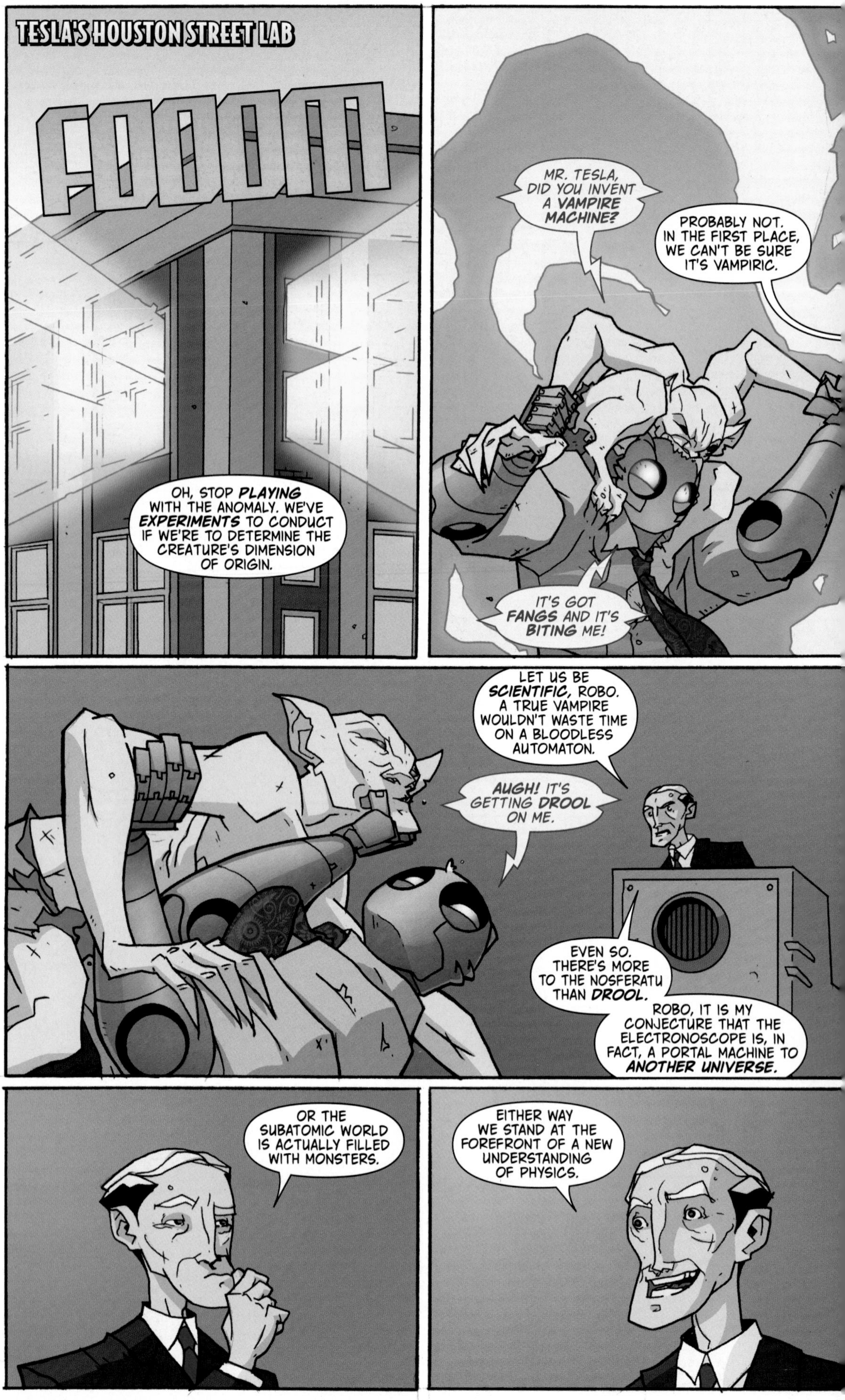
TESLA'S HOUSTON STREET LAB
FOOOM
OH, STOP PLAYING WITH THE ANOMALY. WE'VE EXPERIMENTS TO CONDUCT IF WE'RE TO DETERMINE THE CREATURE'S DIMENSION OF ORIGIN.
MR. TESLA, DID YOU INVENT A VAMPIRE MACHINE?
PROBABLY NOT. IN THE FIRST PLACE, WE CAN'T BE SURE IT'S VAMPIRIC.
IT'S GOT FANGS AND IT'S BITING ME!
LET US BE SCIENTIFIC, ROBO. A TRUE VAMPIRE WOULDN'T WASTE TIME ON A BLOODLESS AUTOMATON.
AUGH! IT'S GETTING DROOL ON ME.
EVEN SO. THERE'S MORE TO THE NOSFERATU THAN DROOL.
ROBO, IT IS MY CONJECTURE THAT THE ELECTRONOSCOPE IS, IN FACT, A PORTAL MACHINE TO ANOTHER UNIVERSE.
OR THE SUBATOMIC WORLD IS ACTUALLY FILLED WITH MONSTERS.
EITHER WAY WE STAND AT THE FOREFRONT OF A NEW UNDERSTANDING OF PHYSICS.

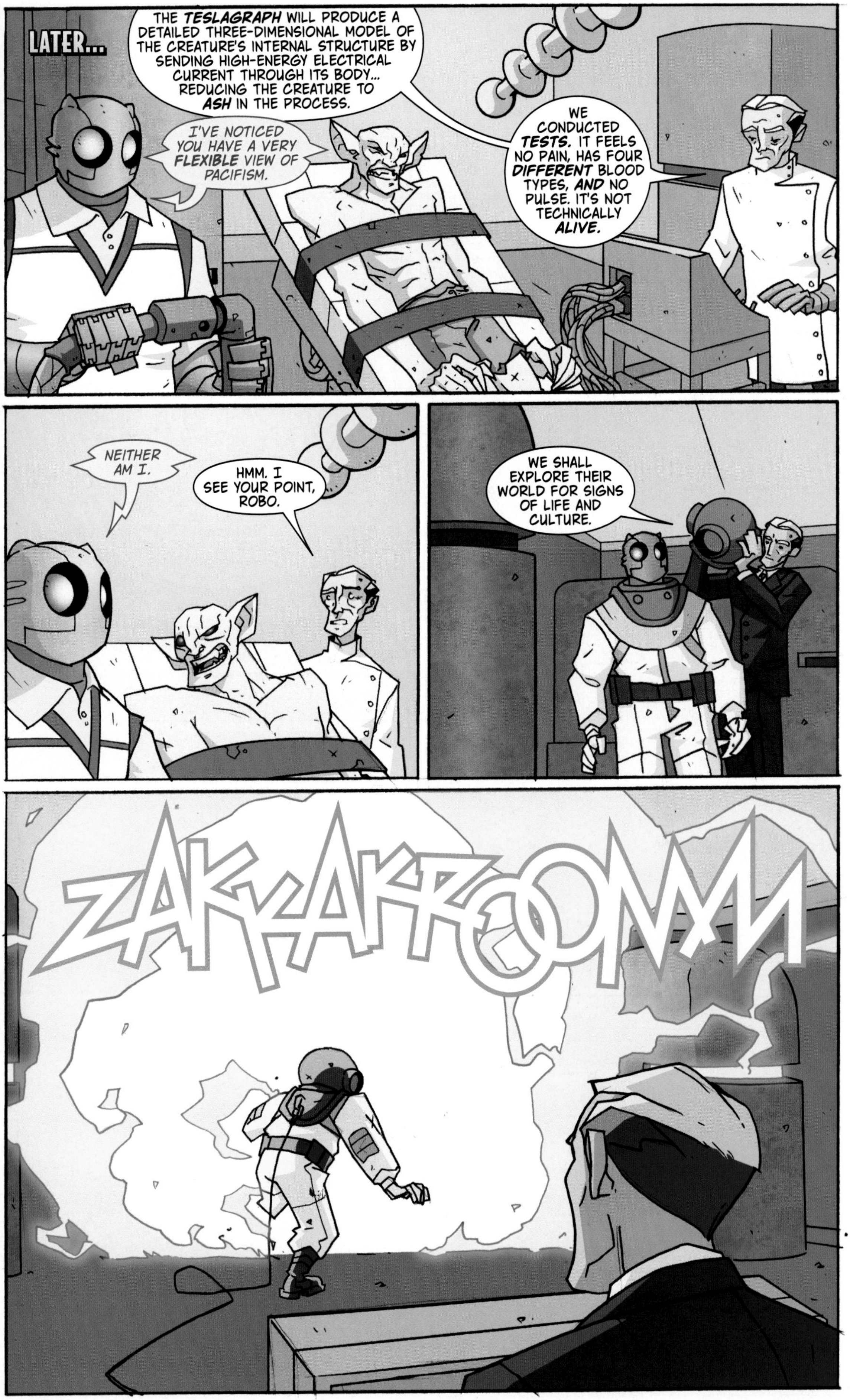
LATER...
THE TESLAGRAPH WILL PRODUCE A DETAILED THREE-DIMENSIONAL MODEL OF THE CREATURE'S INTERNAL STRUCTURE BY SENDING HIGH-ENERGY ELECTRICAL CURRENT THROUGH ITS BODY... REDUCING THE CREATURE TO ASH IN THE PROCESS.
I'VE NOTICED YOU HAVE A VERY FLEXIBLE VIEW OF PACIFISM.
WE CONDUCTED TESTS. IT FEELS NO PAIN, HAS FOUR DIFFERENT BLOOD TYPES, AND NO PULSE. IT'S NOT TECHNICALLY ALIVE.
NEITHER AM I.
HMM. I SEE YOUR POINT, ROBO.
WE SHALL EXPLORE THEIR WORLD FOR SIGNS OF LIFE AND CULTURE.
ZAKKAKROOMM

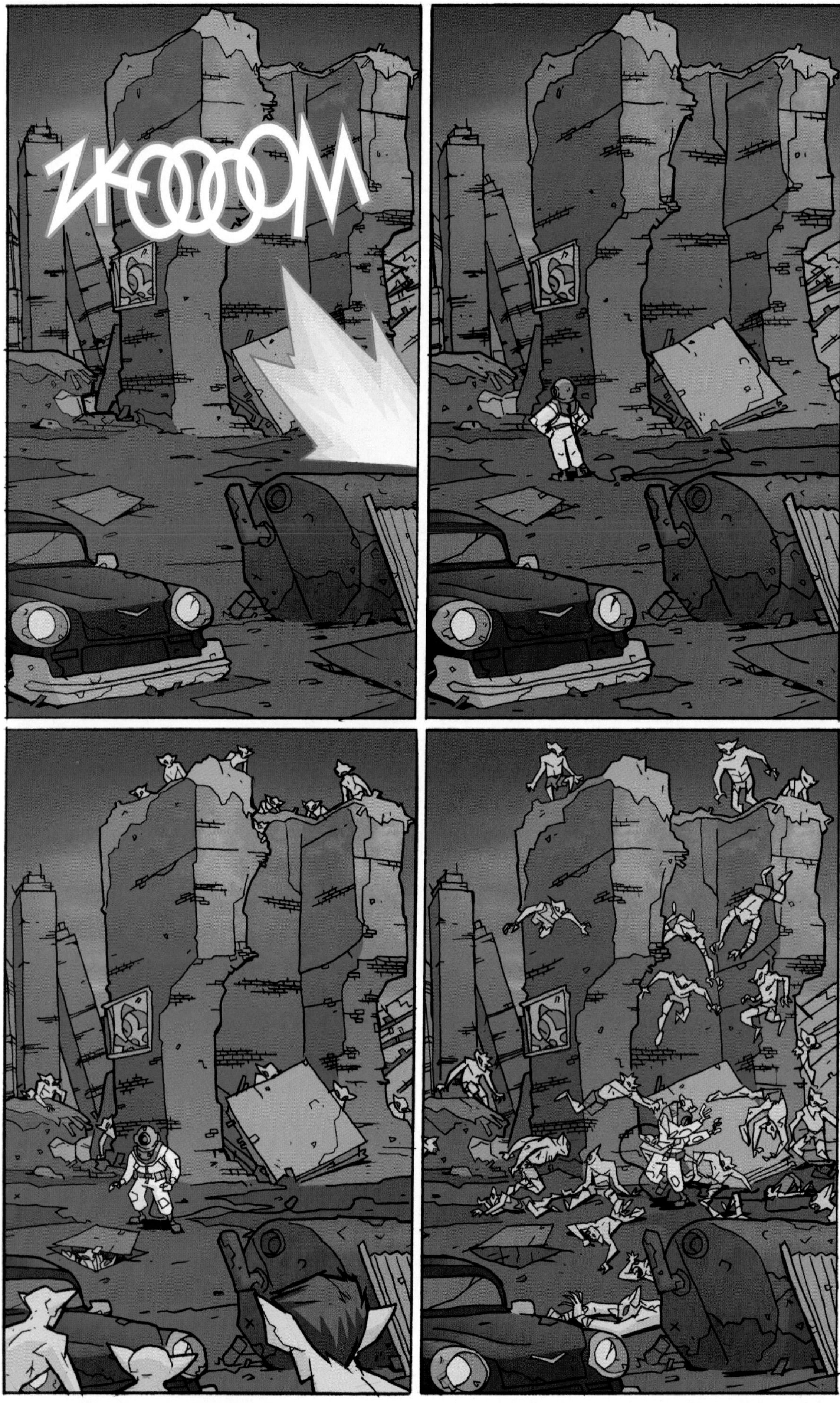
ZKOOOOM

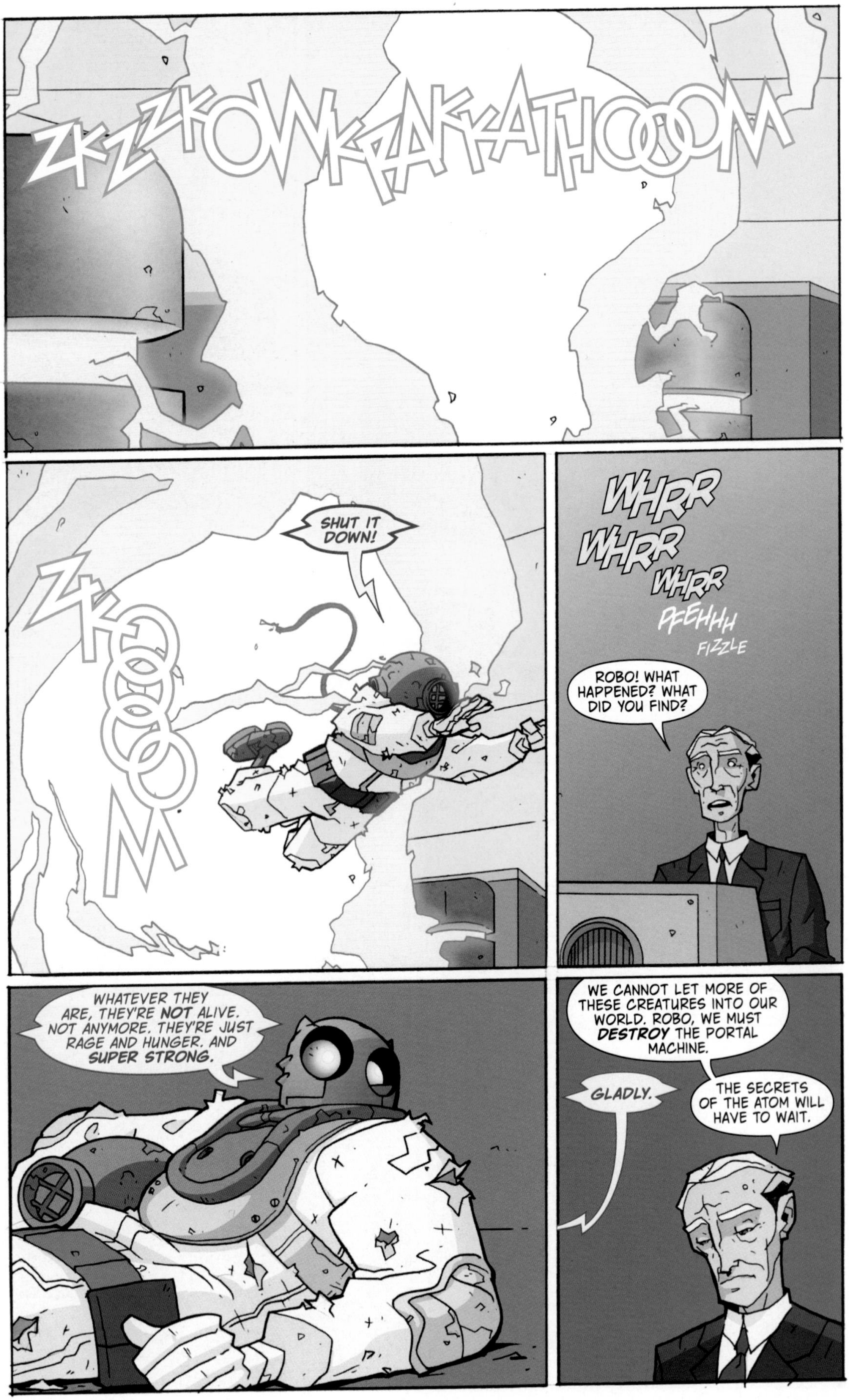
ZKZZKOWKRAKKATHOOOOM
ZKGOOOOOM
SHUT IT DOWN!
WHRR
WHRR
WHRR
PFEHHH
FIZZLE
ROBO! WHAT HAPPENED? WHAT DID YOU FIND?
WHATEVER THEY ARE, THEY'RE **NOT** ALIVE. NOT ANYMORE. THEY'RE JUST RAGE AND HUNGER. AND **SUPER STRONG.**
WE CANNOT LET MORE OF THESE CREATURES INTO OUR WORLD. ROBO, WE MUST **DESTROY** THE PORTAL MACHINE.
THE SECRETS OF THE ATOM WILL HAVE TO WAIT.
GLADLY.

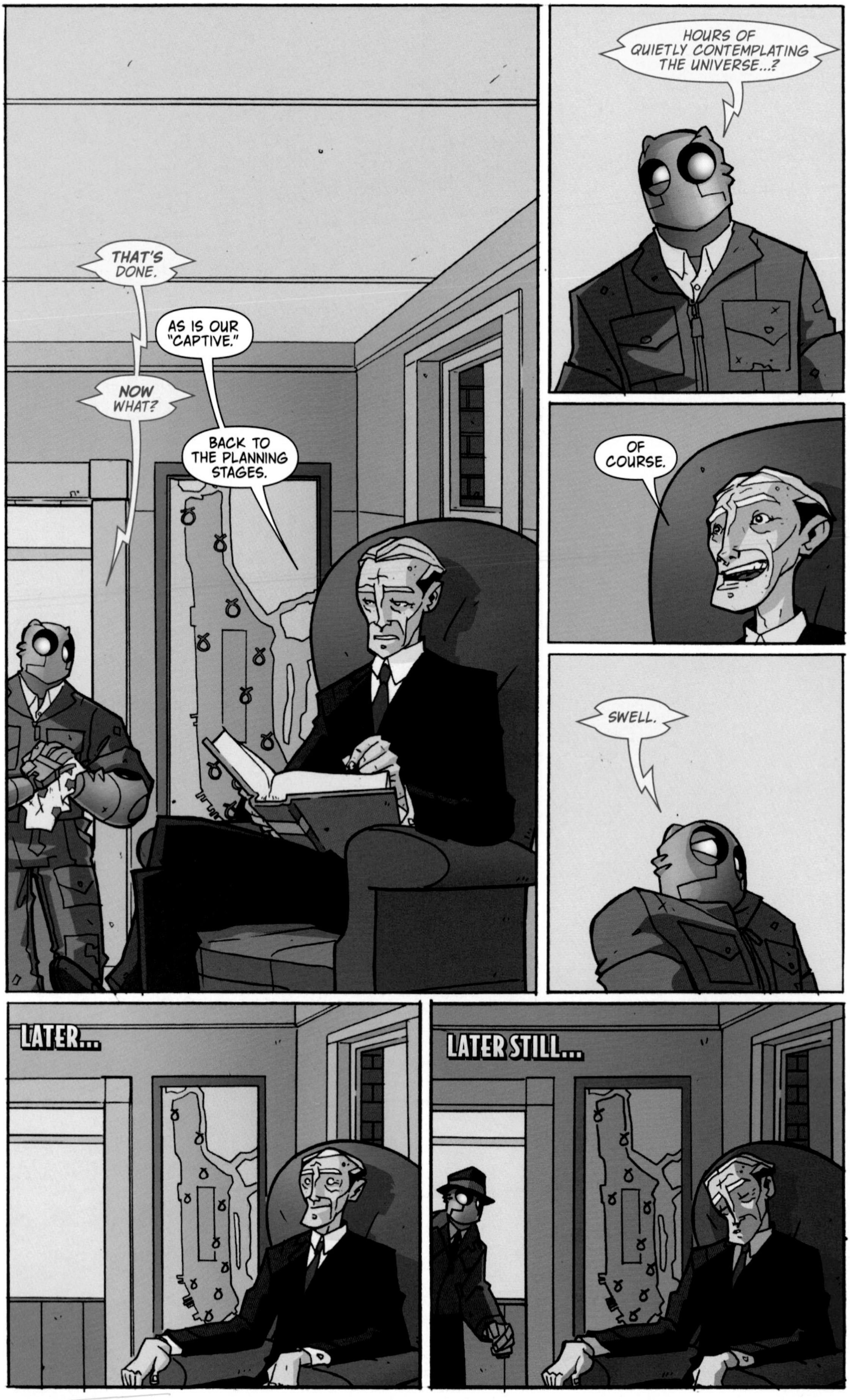
THAT'S DONE.
AS IS OUR "CAPTIVE."
NOW WHAT?
BACK TO THE PLANNING STAGES.
HOURS OF QUIETLY CONTEMPLATING THE UNIVERSE...?
OF COURSE.
SWELL.
LATER...
LATER STILL...

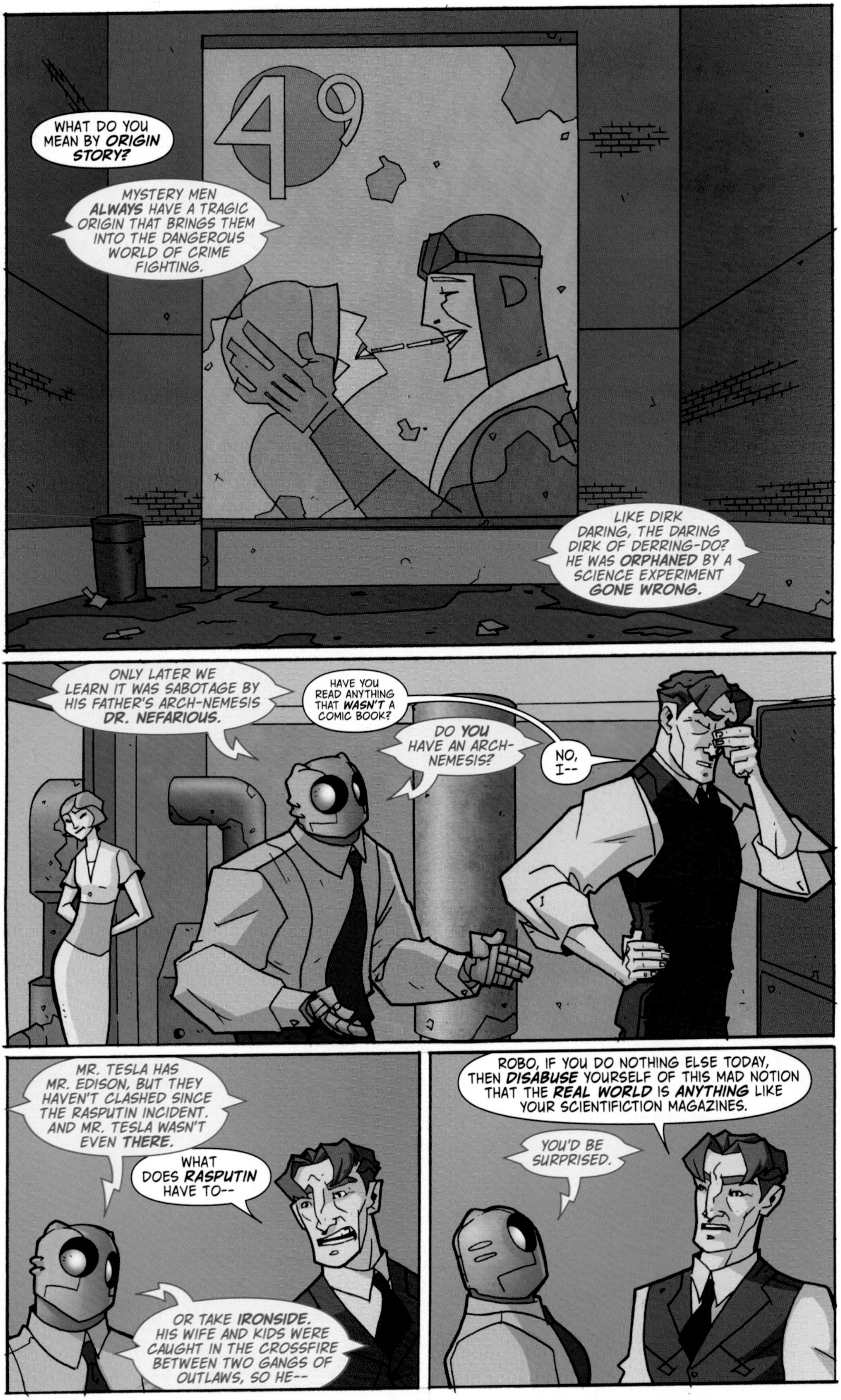
WHAT DO YOU MEAN BY ORIGIN STORY?
MYSTERY MEN ALWAYS HAVE A TRAGIC ORIGIN THAT BRINGS THEM INTO THE DANGEROUS WORLD OF CRIME FIGHTING.
LIKE DIRK DARING, THE DARING DIRK OF DERRING-DO? HE WAS ORPHANED BY A SCIENCE EXPERIMENT GONE WRONG.
ONLY LATER WE LEARN IT WAS SABOTAGE BY HIS FATHER'S ARCH-NEMESIS DR. NEFARIOUS.
HAVE YOU READ ANYTHING THAT WASN'T A COMIC BOOK?
DO YOU HAVE AN ARCH-NEMESIS?
NO, I--
MR. TESLA HAS MR. EDISON, BUT THEY HAVEN'T CLASHED SINCE THE RASPUTIN INCIDENT. AND MR. TESLA WASN'T EVEN THERE.
WHAT DOES RASPUTIN HAVE TO--
OR TAKE IRONSIDE. HIS WIFE AND KIDS WERE CAUGHT IN THE CROSSFIRE BETWEEN TWO GANGS OF OUTLAWS, SO HE--
ROBO, IF YOU DO NOTHING ELSE TODAY, THEN DISABUSE YOURSELF OF THIS MAD NOTION THAT THE REAL WORLD IS ANYTHING LIKE YOUR SCIENTIFICTION MAGAZINES.
YOU'D BE SURPRISED.

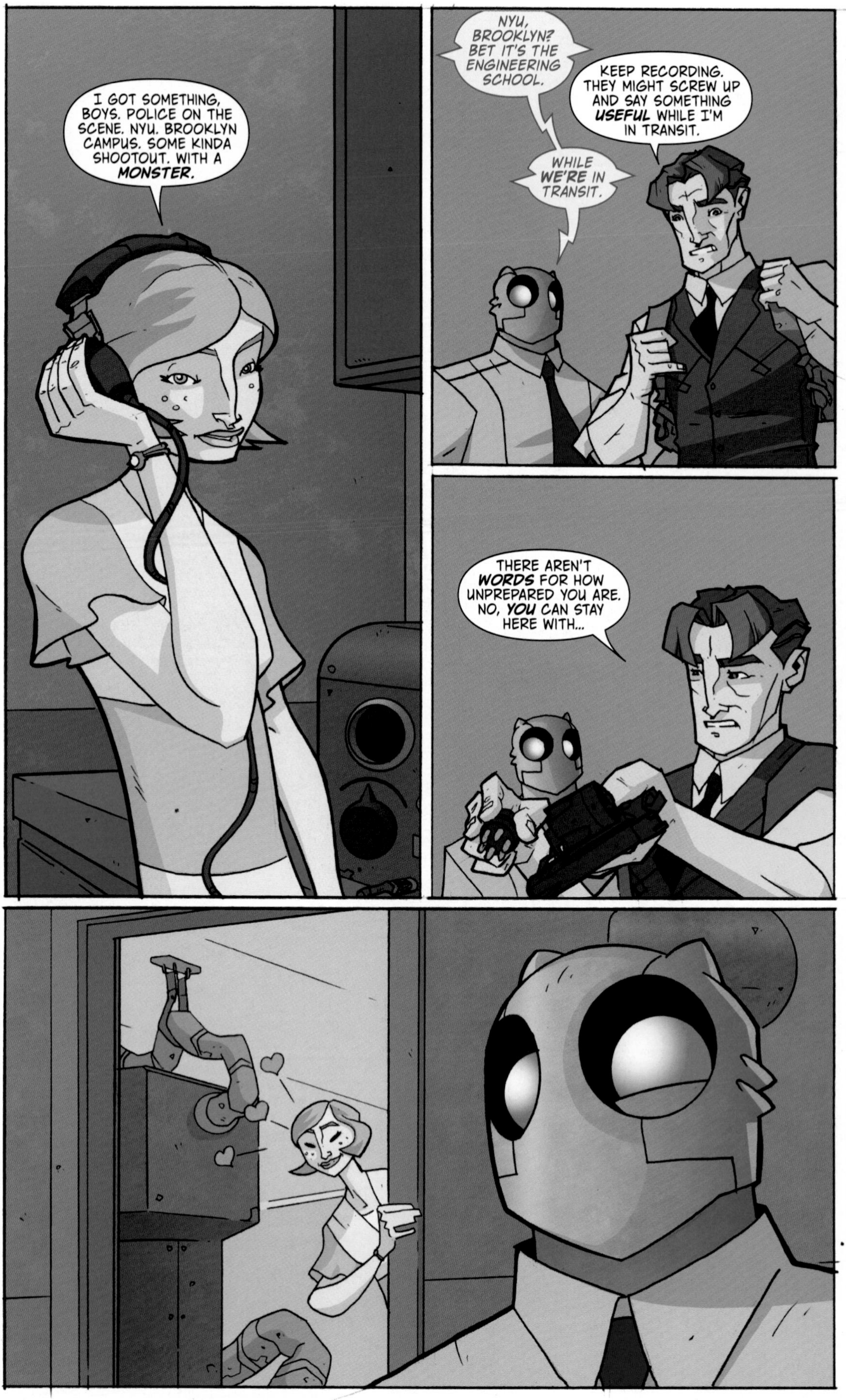
I GOT SOMETHING, BOYS. POLICE ON THE SCENE. NYU. BROOKLYN CAMPUS. SOME KINDA SHOOTOUT. WITH A **MONSTER.**
NYU, BROOKLYN? BET IT'S THE ENGINEERING SCHOOL.
KEEP RECORDING. THEY MIGHT SCREW UP AND SAY SOMETHING **USEFUL** WHILE I'M IN TRANSIT.
WHILE **WE'RE** IN TRANSIT.
THERE AREN'T **WORDS** FOR HOW UNPREPARED YOU ARE. NO, **YOU** CAN STAY HERE WITH...

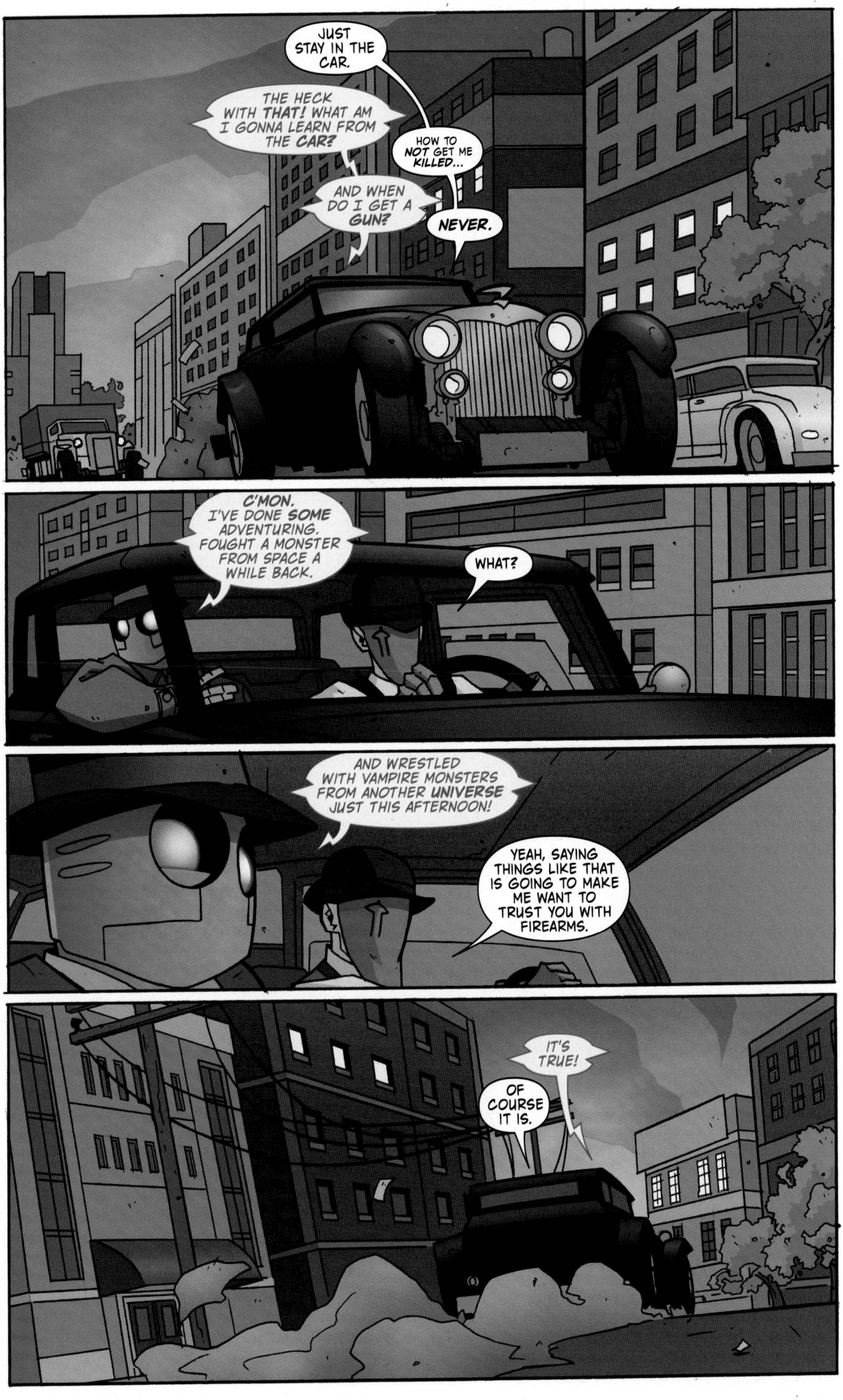
JUST STAY IN THE CAR.
THE HECK WITH THAT! WHAT AM I GONNA LEARN FROM THE CAR?
HOW TO NOT GET ME KILLED...
AND WHEN DO I GET A GUN?
NEVER.
C'MON. I'VE DONE SOME ADVENTURING. FOUGHT A MONSTER FROM SPACE A WHILE BACK.
WHAT?
AND WRESTLED WITH VAMPIRE MONSTERS FROM ANOTHER UNIVERSE JUST THIS AFTERNOON!
YEAH, SAYING THINGS LIKE THAT IS GOING TO MAKE ME WANT TO TRUST YOU WITH FIREARMS.
IT'S TRUE!
OF COURSE IT IS.

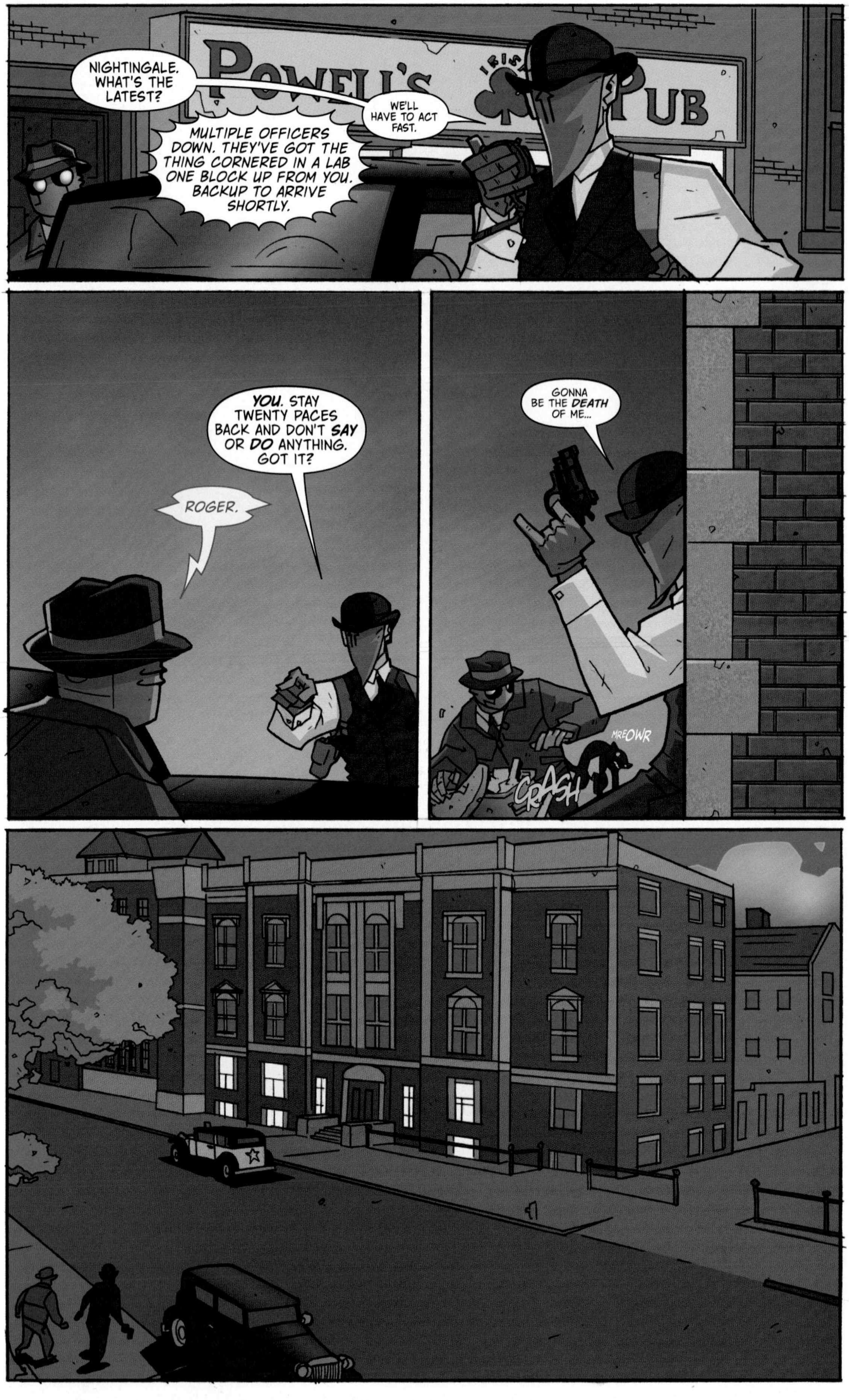
POWELL'S
NIGHTINGALE. WHAT'S THE LATEST?
MULTIPLE OFFICERS DOWN. THEY'VE GOT THE THING CORNERED IN A LAB ONE BLOCK UP FROM YOU. BACKUP TO ARRIVE SHORTLY.
WE'LL HAVE TO ACT FAST.
YOU. STAY TWENTY PACES BACK AND DON'T SAY OR DO ANYTHING. GOT IT?
ROGER.
GONNA BE THE DEATH OF ME...
MREOWR
CRASH

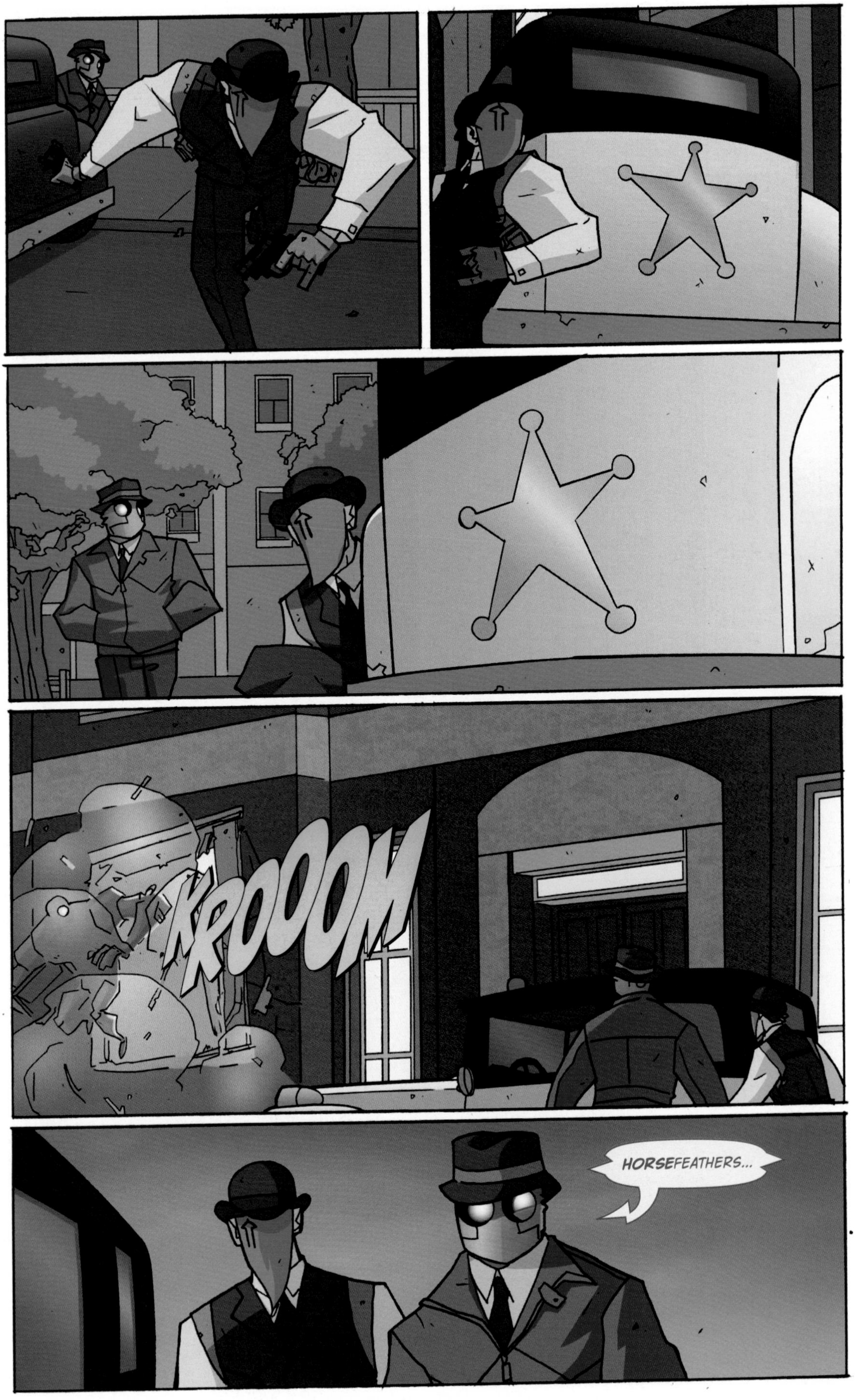
KROOOM
HORSEFEATHERS...

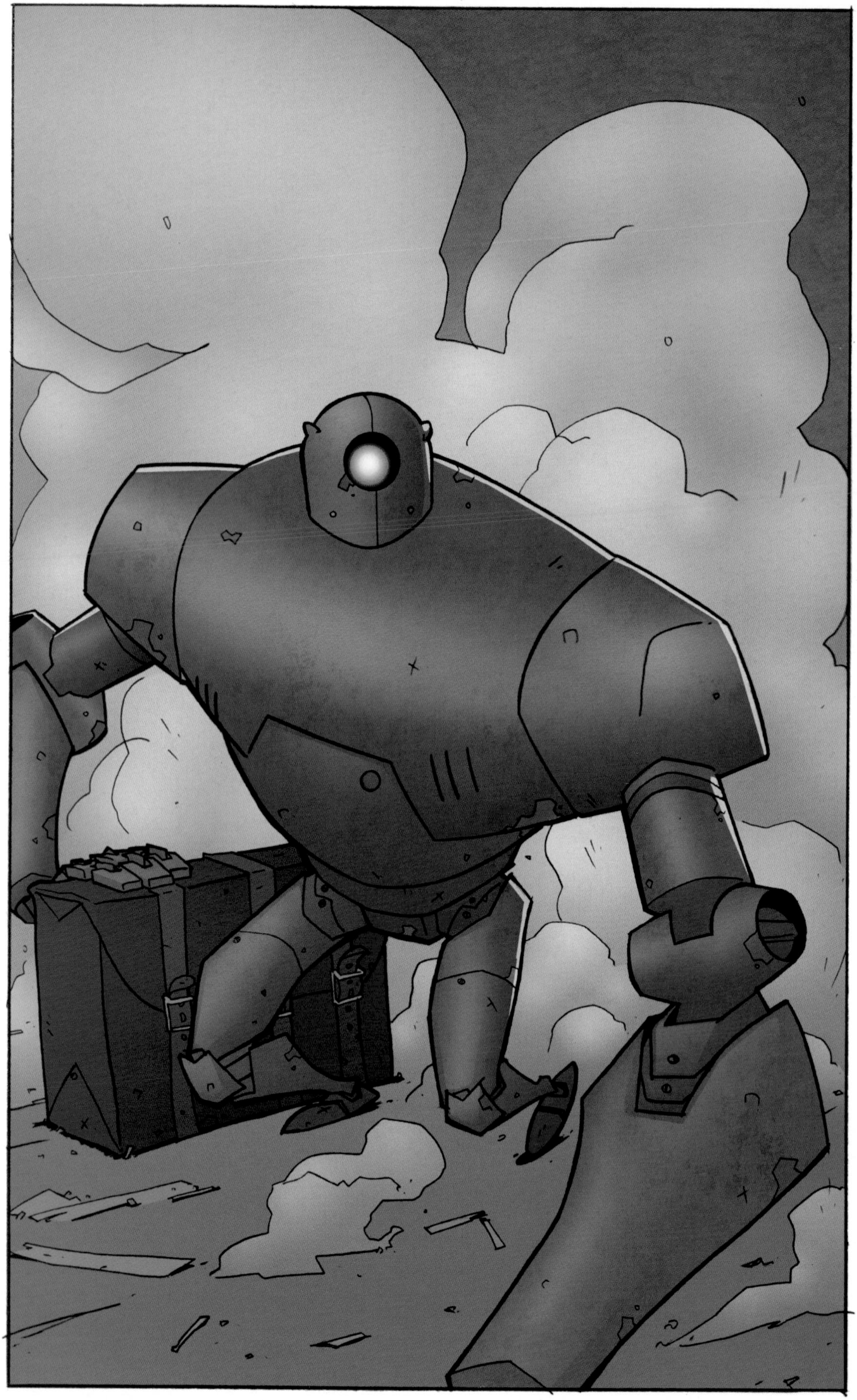

KISS KISS,
BANG BANG

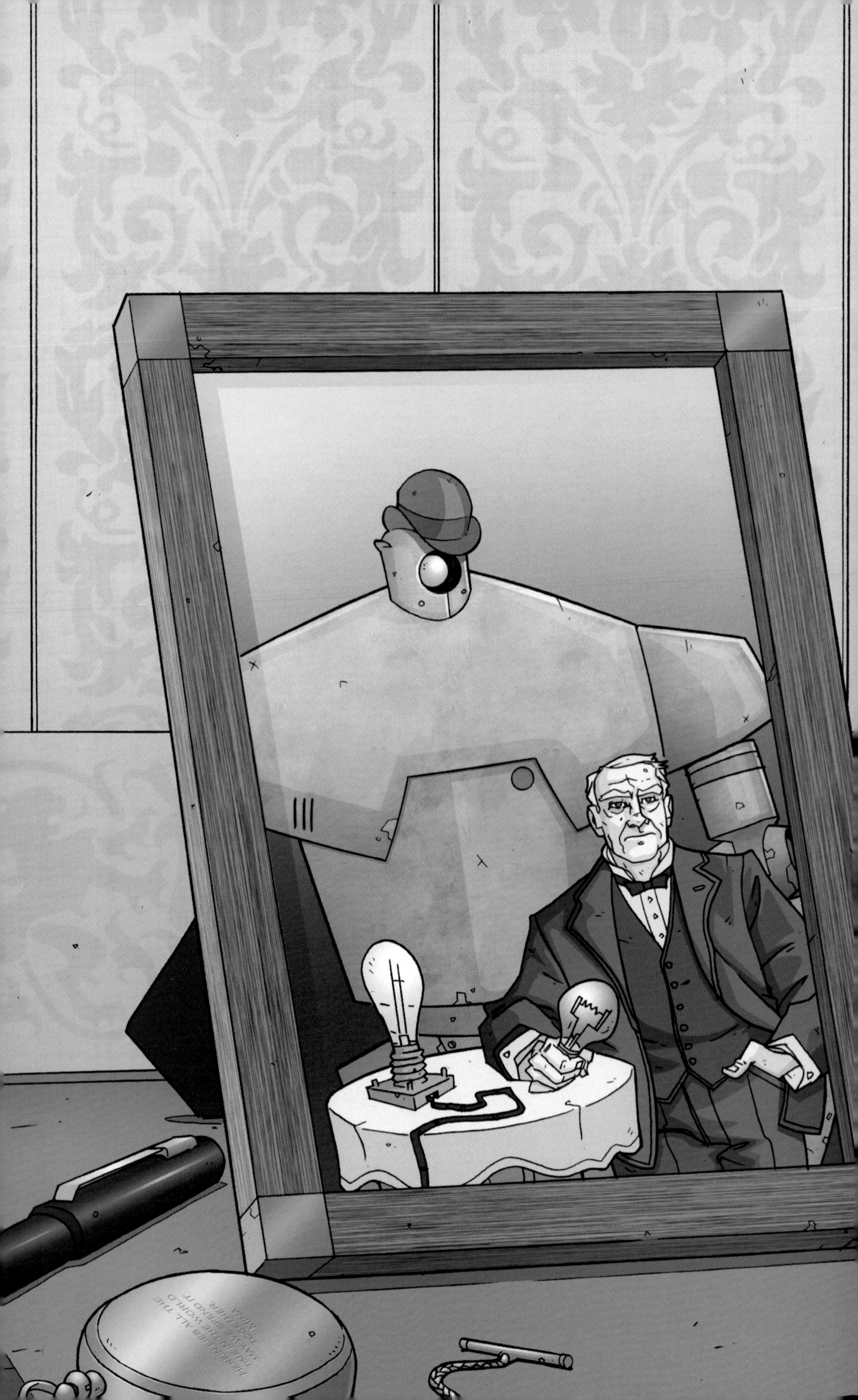
HEREIN LIES ALL THE
TIME IN THE WORLD
MAY WE SPEND IT
TOGETHER.
MINA

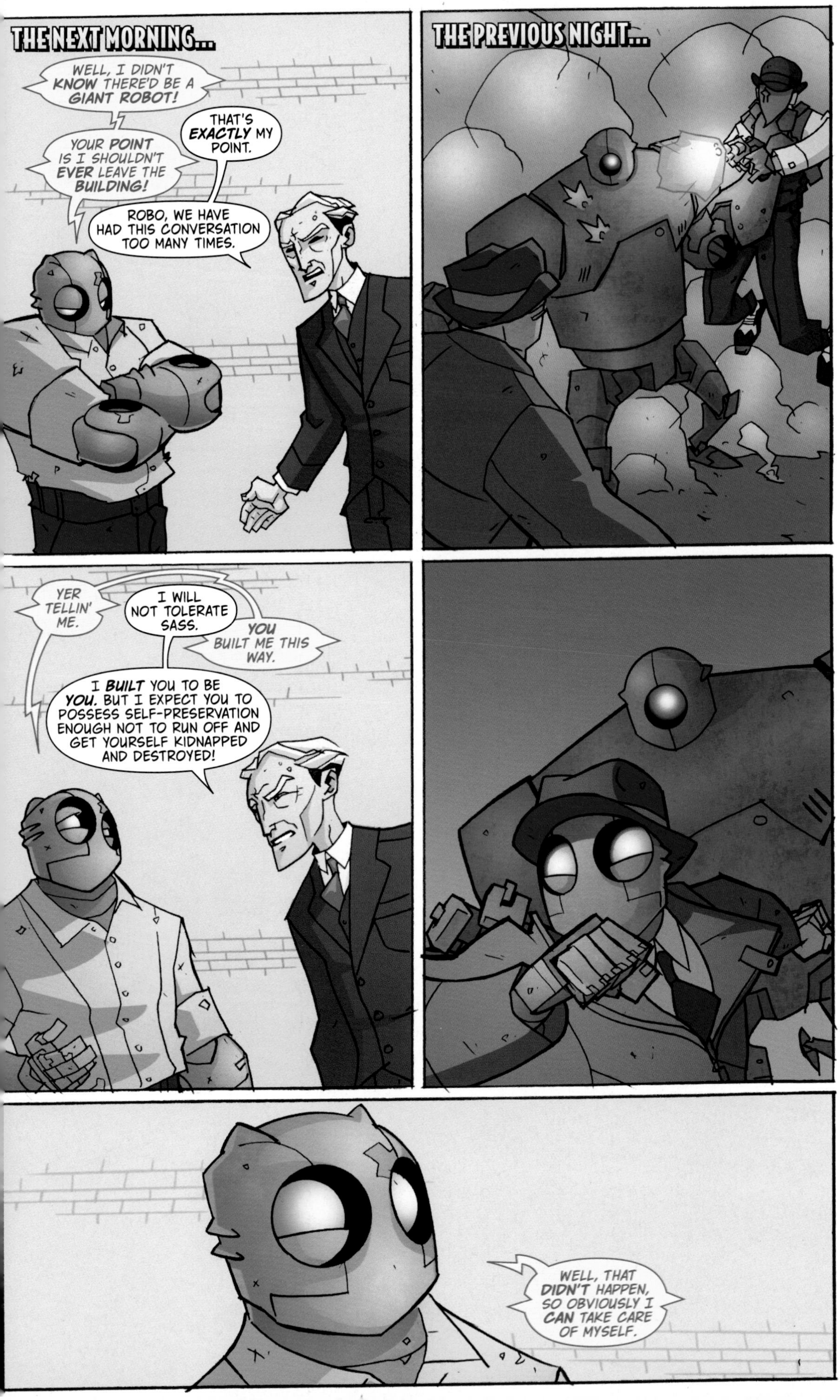
THE NEXT MORNING...
WELL, I DIDN'T KNOW THERE'D BE A GIANT ROBOT!
YOUR POINT IS I SHOULDN'T EVER LEAVE THE BUILDING!
THAT'S EXACTLY MY POINT.
ROBO, WE HAVE HAD THIS CONVERSATION TOO MANY TIMES.
THE PREVIOUS NIGHT...
YER TELLIN' ME.
I WILL NOT TOLERATE SASS.
YOU BUILT ME THIS WAY.
I BUILT YOU TO BE YOU. BUT I EXPECT YOU TO POSSESS SELF-PRESERVATION ENOUGH NOT TO RUN OFF AND GET YOURSELF KIDNAPPED AND DESTROYED!
WELL, THAT DIDN'T HAPPEN, SO OBVIOUSLY I CAN TAKE CARE OF MYSELF.

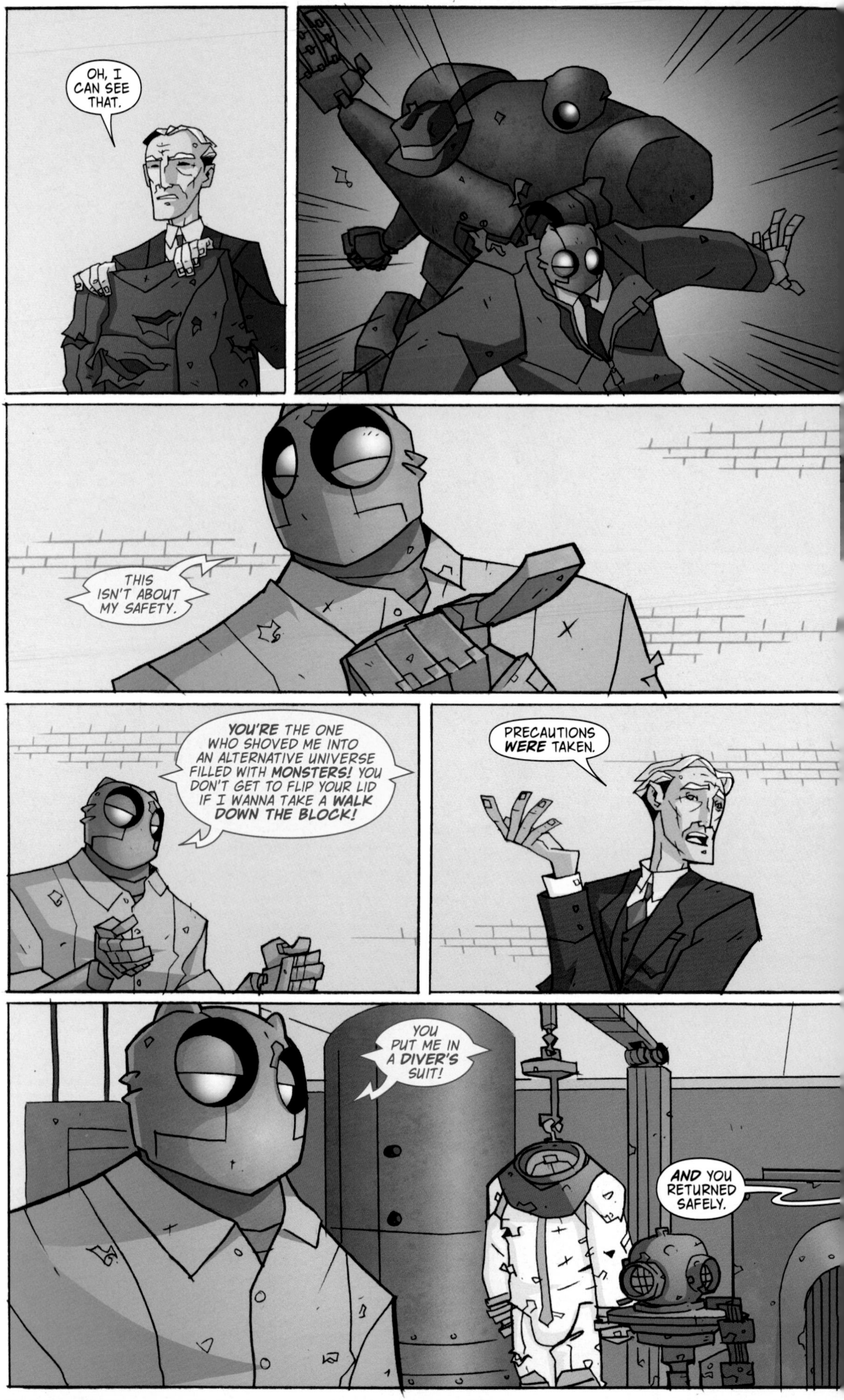
OH, I CAN SEE THAT.
THIS ISN'T ABOUT MY SAFETY.
YOU'RE THE ONE WHO SHOVED ME INTO AN ALTERNATIVE UNIVERSE FILLED WITH **MONSTERS!** YOU DON'T GET TO FLIP YOUR LID IF I WANNA TAKE A **WALK DOWN THE BLOCK!**
PRECAUTIONS **WERE** TAKEN.
YOU PUT ME IN A **DIVER'S** SUIT!
AND YOU RETURNED SAFELY.

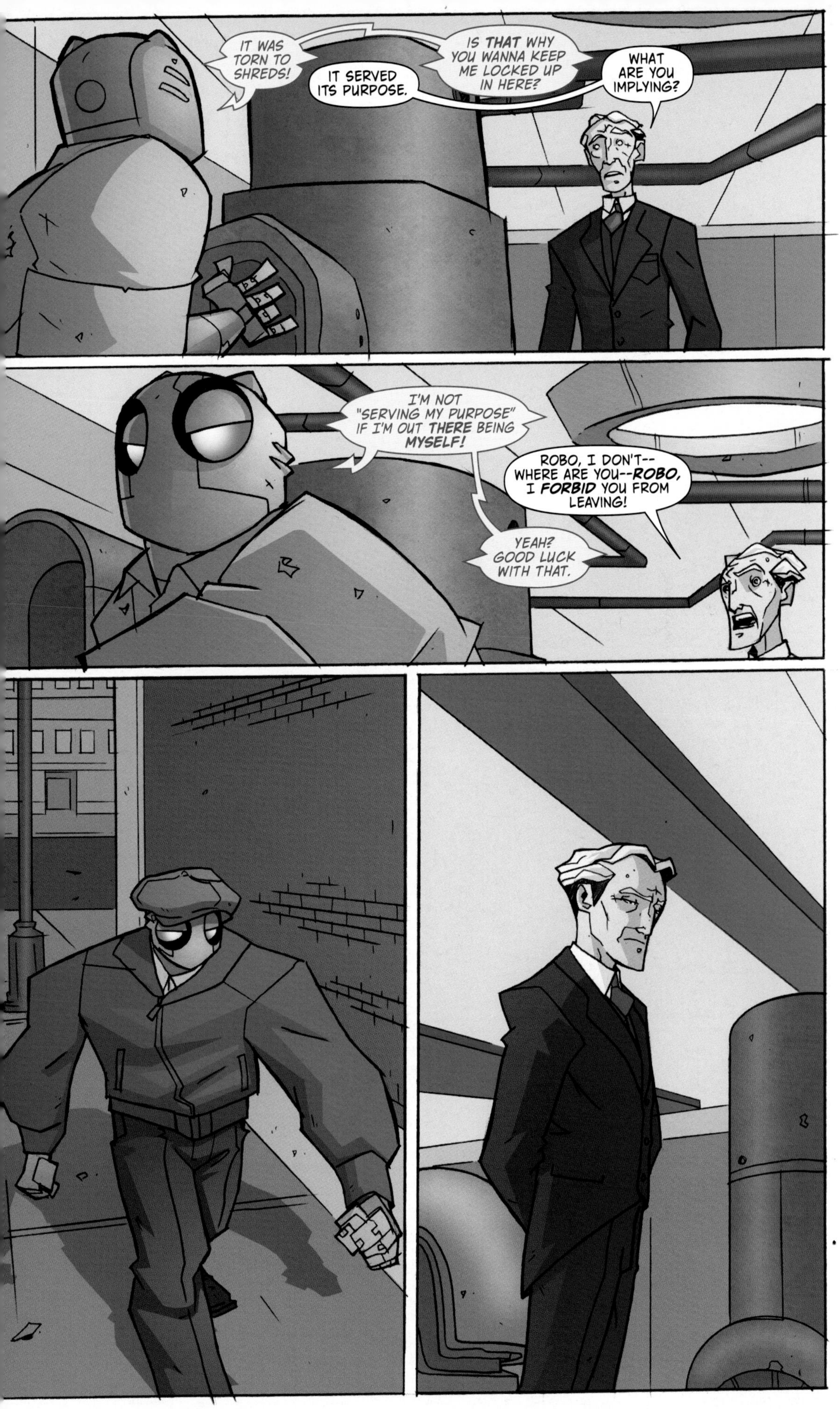
IT WAS TORN TO SHREDS!
IT SERVED ITS PURPOSE.
IS **THAT** WHY YOU WANNA KEEP ME LOCKED UP IN HERE?
WHAT ARE YOU IMPLYING?
I'M NOT "SERVING MY PURPOSE" IF I'M OUT **THERE** BEING **MYSELF!**
ROBO, I DON'T-- WHERE ARE YOU--**ROBO,** I **FORBID** YOU FROM LEAVING!
YEAH? GOOD LUCK WITH THAT.

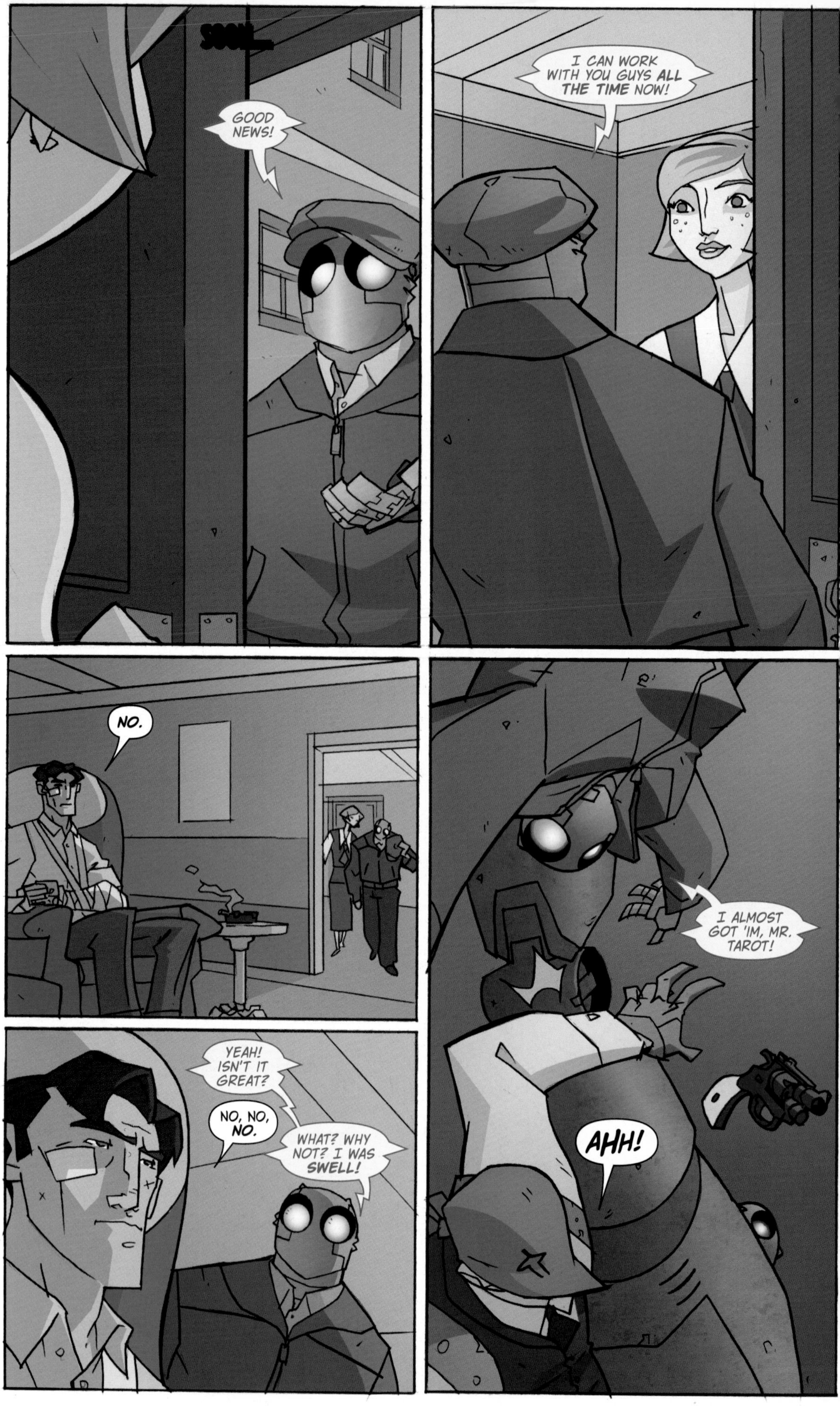
SOON...
GOOD NEWS!
I CAN WORK WITH YOU GUYS ALL THE TIME NOW!
NO.
YEAH! ISN'T IT GREAT?
NO, NO, NO.
WHAT? WHY NOT? I WAS SWELL!
I ALMOST GOT 'IM, MR. TAROT!
AHH!

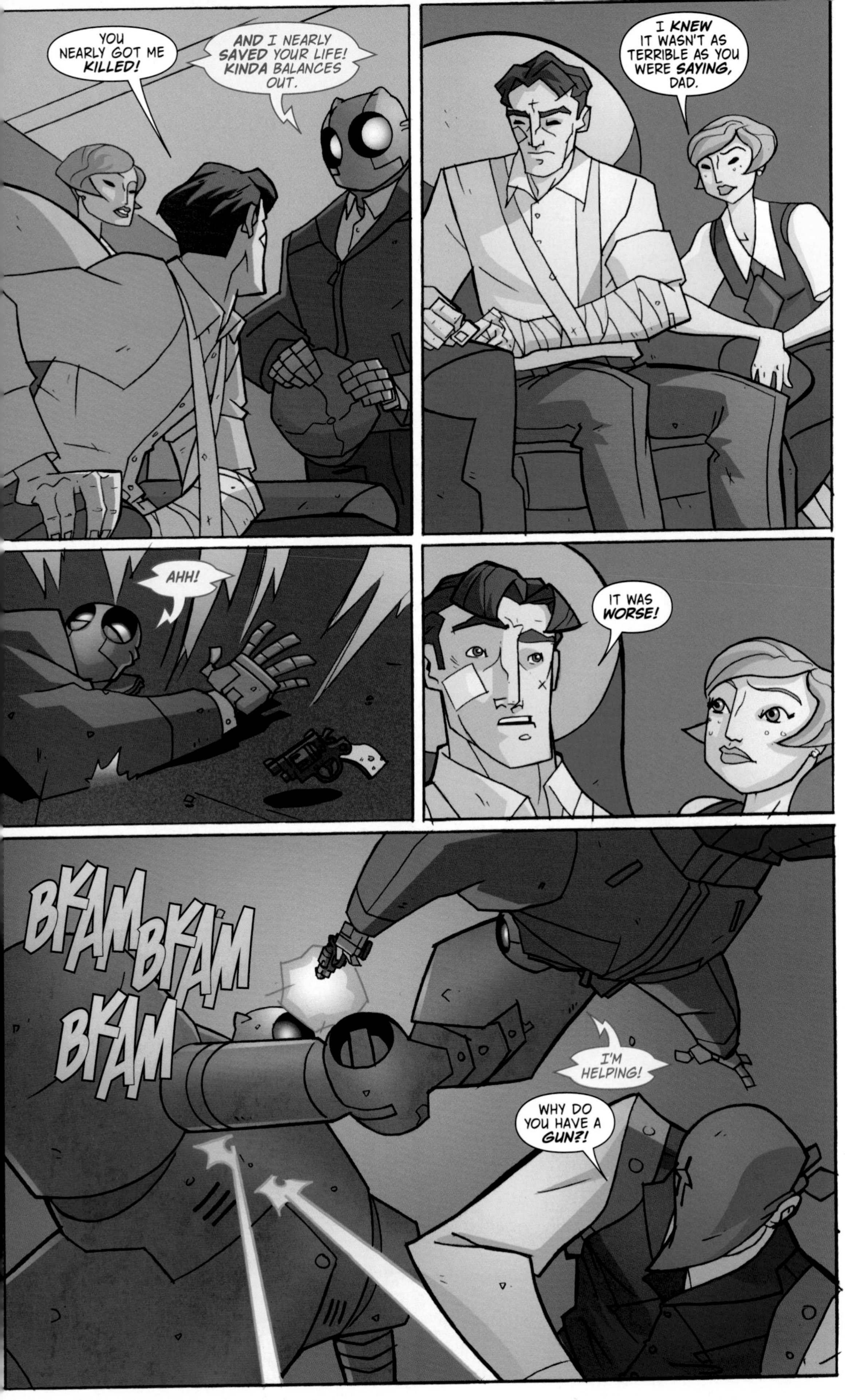

YOU NEARLY GOT ME KILLED!
AND I NEARLY SAVED YOUR LIFE! KINDA BALANCES OUT.
I KNEW IT WASN'T AS TERRIBLE AS YOU WERE SAYING, DAD.
AHH!
IT WAS WORSE!
BKAM BKAM BKAM
I'M HELPING!
WHY DO YOU HAVE A GUN?!

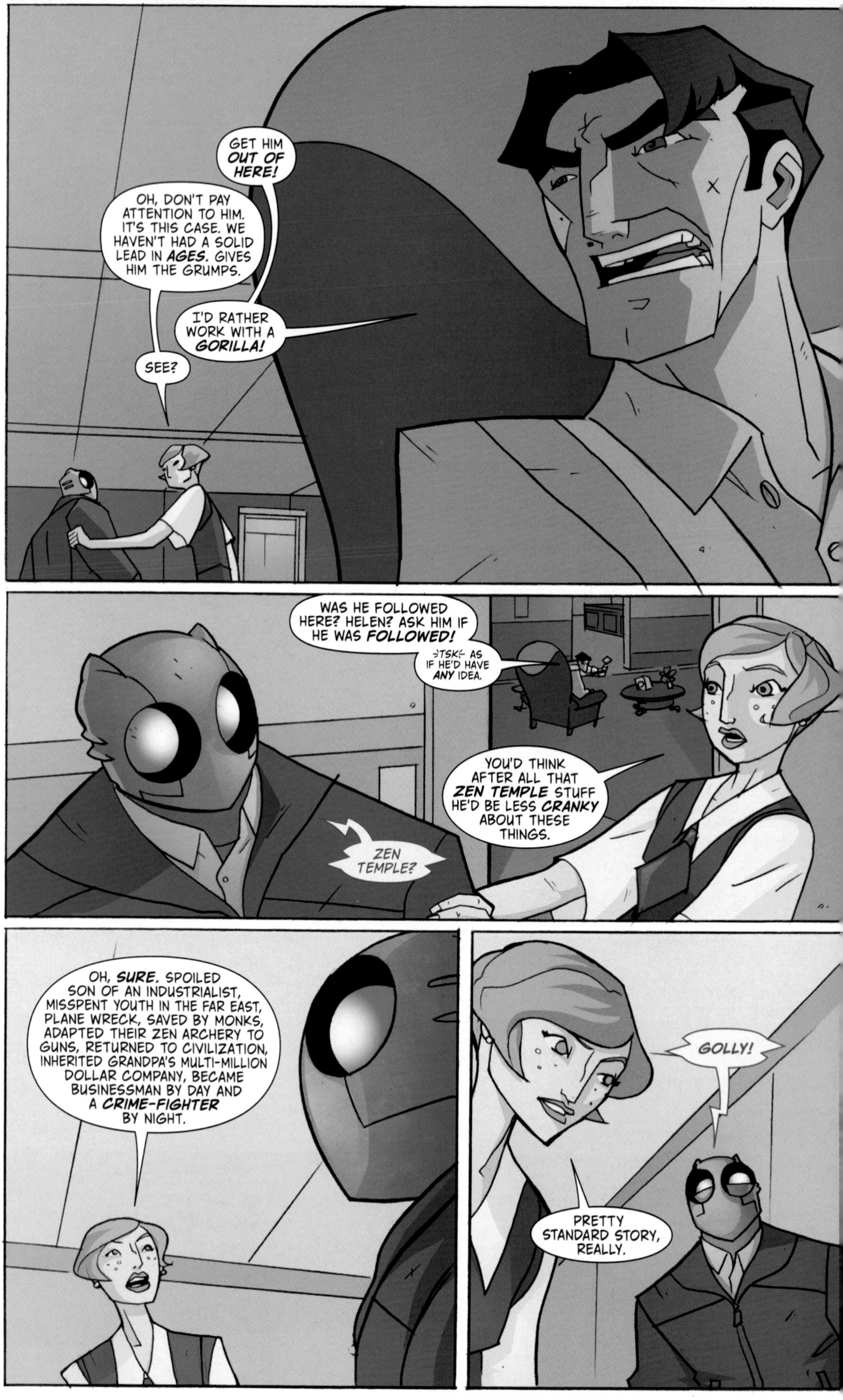
GET HIM OUT OF HERE!
OH, DON'T PAY ATTENTION TO HIM. IT'S THIS CASE. WE HAVEN'T HAD A SOLID LEAD IN AGES. GIVES HIM THE GRUMPS.
I'D RATHER WORK WITH A GORILLA!
SEE?
WAS HE FOLLOWED HERE? HELEN? ASK HIM IF HE WAS FOLLOWED!
TSK AS IF HE'D HAVE ANY IDEA.
YOU'D THINK AFTER ALL THAT ZEN TEMPLE STUFF HE'D BE LESS CRANKY ABOUT THESE THINGS.
ZEN TEMPLE?
OH, SURE. SPOILED SON OF AN INDUSTRIALIST, MISSPENT YOUTH IN THE FAR EAST, PLANE WRECK, SAVED BY MONKS, ADAPTED THEIR ZEN ARCHERY TO GUNS, RETURNED TO CIVILIZATION, INHERITED GRANDPA'S MULTI-MILLION DOLLAR COMPANY, BECAME BUSINESSMAN BY DAY AND A CRIME-FIGHTER BY NIGHT.
GOLLY!
PRETTY STANDARD STORY, REALLY.

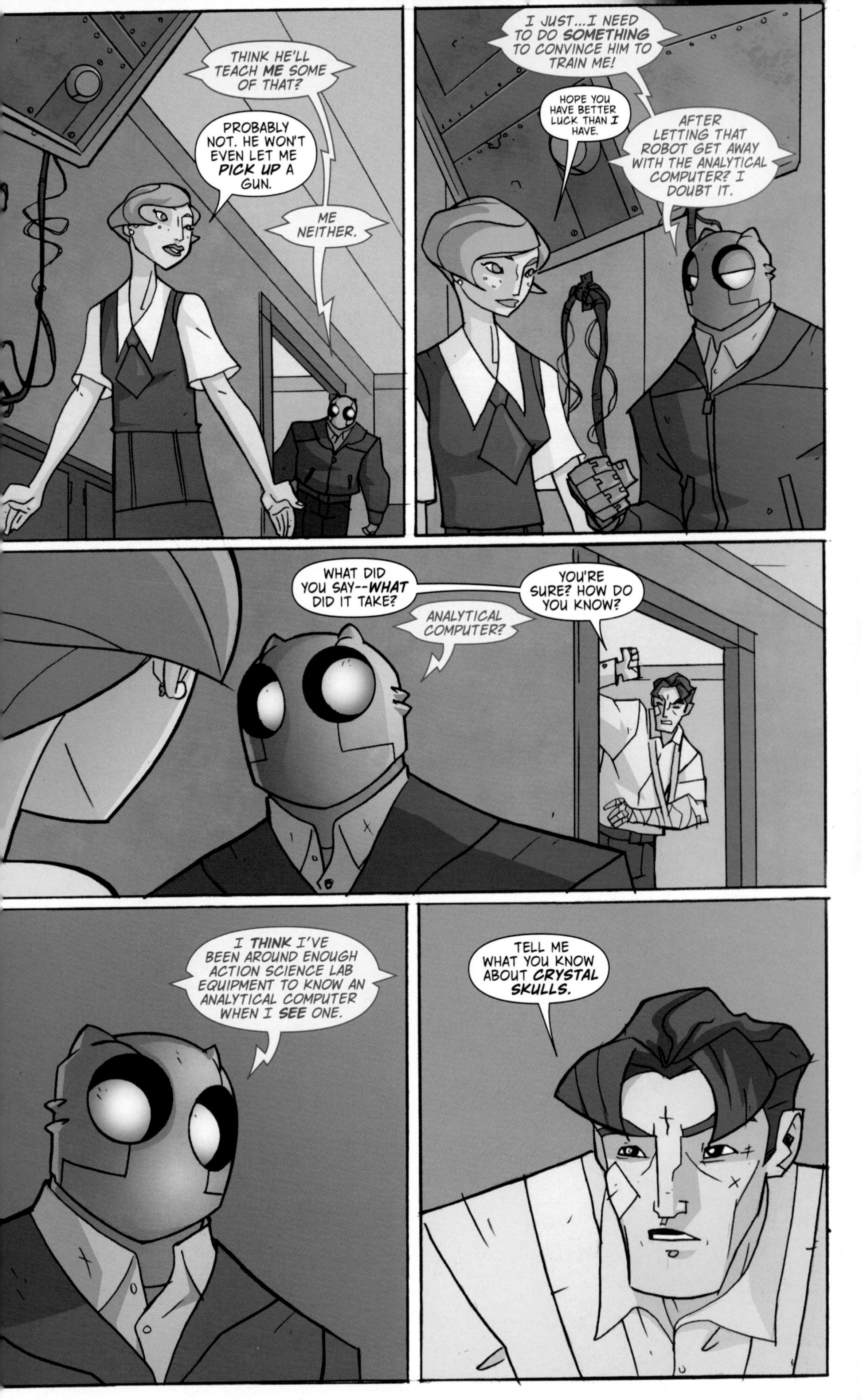
THINK HE'LL TEACH ME SOME OF THAT?
PROBABLY NOT. HE WON'T EVEN LET ME PICK UP A GUN.
ME NEITHER.
I JUST...I NEED TO DO SOMETHING TO CONVINCE HIM TO TRAIN ME!
HOPE YOU HAVE BETTER LUCK THAN I HAVE.
AFTER LETTING THAT ROBOT GET AWAY WITH THE ANALYTICAL COMPUTER? I DOUBT IT.
WHAT DID YOU SAY--WHAT DID IT TAKE?
ANALYTICAL COMPUTER?
YOU'RE SURE? HOW DO YOU KNOW?
I THINK I'VE BEEN AROUND ENOUGH ACTION SCIENCE LAB EQUIPMENT TO KNOW AN ANALYTICAL COMPUTER WHEN I SEE ONE.
TELL ME WHAT YOU KNOW ABOUT CRYSTAL SKULLS.

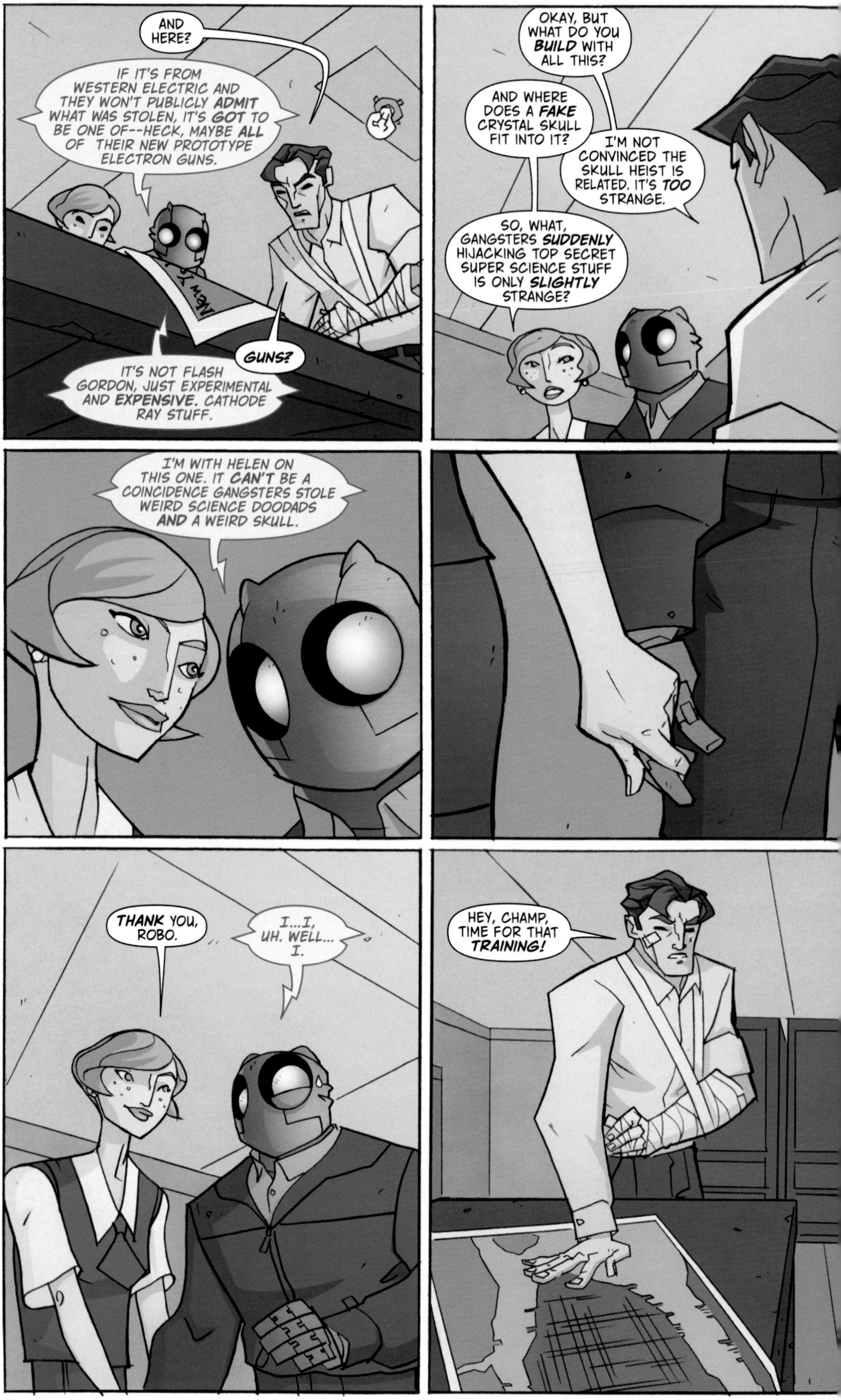
AND HERE?
IF IT'S FROM WESTERN ELECTRIC AND THEY WON'T PUBLICLY ADMIT WHAT WAS STOLEN, IT'S GOT TO BE ONE OF--HECK, MAYBE ALL OF THEIR NEW PROTOTYPE ELECTRON GUNS.
GUNS?
IT'S NOT FLASH GORDON, JUST EXPERIMENTAL AND EXPENSIVE. CATHODE RAY STUFF.
OKAY, BUT WHAT DO YOU BUILD WITH ALL THIS?
AND WHERE DOES A FAKE CRYSTAL SKULL FIT INTO IT?
I'M NOT CONVINCED THE SKULL HEIST IS RELATED. IT'S TOO STRANGE.
SO, WHAT, GANGSTERS SUDDENLY HIJACKING TOP SECRET SUPER SCIENCE STUFF IS ONLY SLIGHTLY STRANGE?
I'M WITH HELEN ON THIS ONE. IT CAN'T BE A COINCIDENCE GANGSTERS STOLE WEIRD SCIENCE DOODADS AND A WEIRD SKULL.
THANK YOU, ROBO.
I...I, UH. WELL... I.
HEY, CHAMP, TIME FOR THAT TRAINING!

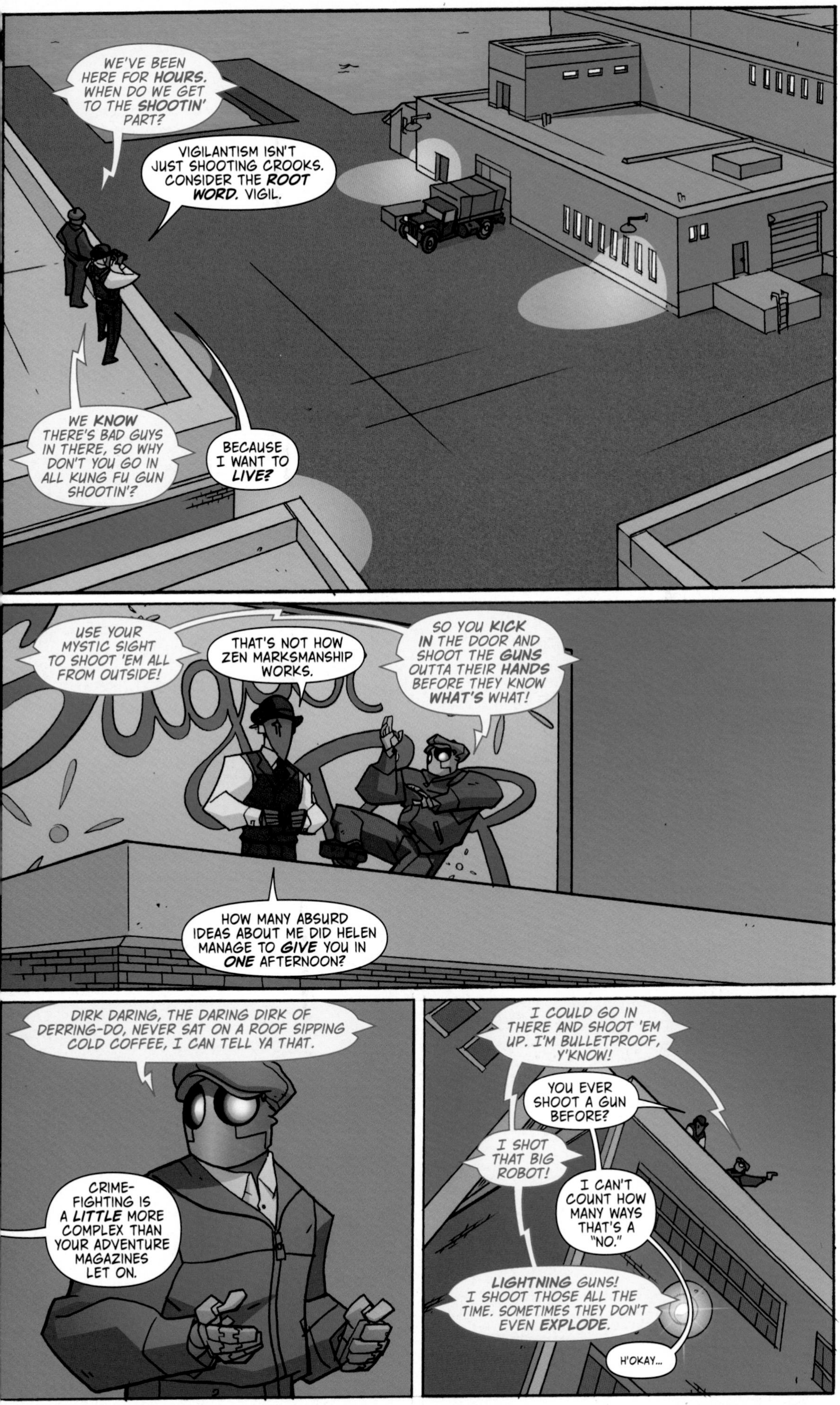
WE'VE BEEN HERE FOR HOURS. WHEN DO WE GET TO THE SHOOTIN' PART?
VIGILANTISM ISN'T JUST SHOOTING CROOKS. CONSIDER THE ROOT WORD. VIGIL.
WE KNOW THERE'S BAD GUYS IN THERE, SO WHY DON'T YOU GO IN ALL KUNG FU GUN SHOOTIN'?
BECAUSE I WANT TO LIVE?
USE YOUR MYSTIC SIGHT TO SHOOT 'EM ALL FROM OUTSIDE!
THAT'S NOT HOW ZEN MARKSMANSHIP WORKS.
SO YOU KICK IN THE DOOR AND SHOOT THE GUNS OUTTA THEIR HANDS BEFORE THEY KNOW WHAT'S WHAT!
HOW MANY ABSURD IDEAS ABOUT ME DID HELEN MANAGE TO GIVE YOU IN ONE AFTERNOON?
DIRK DARING, THE DARING DIRK OF DERRING-DO, NEVER SAT ON A ROOF SIPPING COLD COFFEE, I CAN TELL YA THAT.
CRIME-FIGHTING IS A LITTLE MORE COMPLEX THAN YOUR ADVENTURE MAGAZINES LET ON.
I COULD GO IN THERE AND SHOOT 'EM UP. I'M BULLETPROOF, Y'KNOW!
YOU EVER SHOOT A GUN BEFORE?
I SHOT THAT BIG ROBOT!
I CAN'T COUNT HOW MANY WAYS THAT'S A "NO."
LIGHTNING GUNS! I SHOOT THOSE ALL THE TIME. SOMETIMES THEY DON'T EVEN EXPLODE.
H'OKAY...

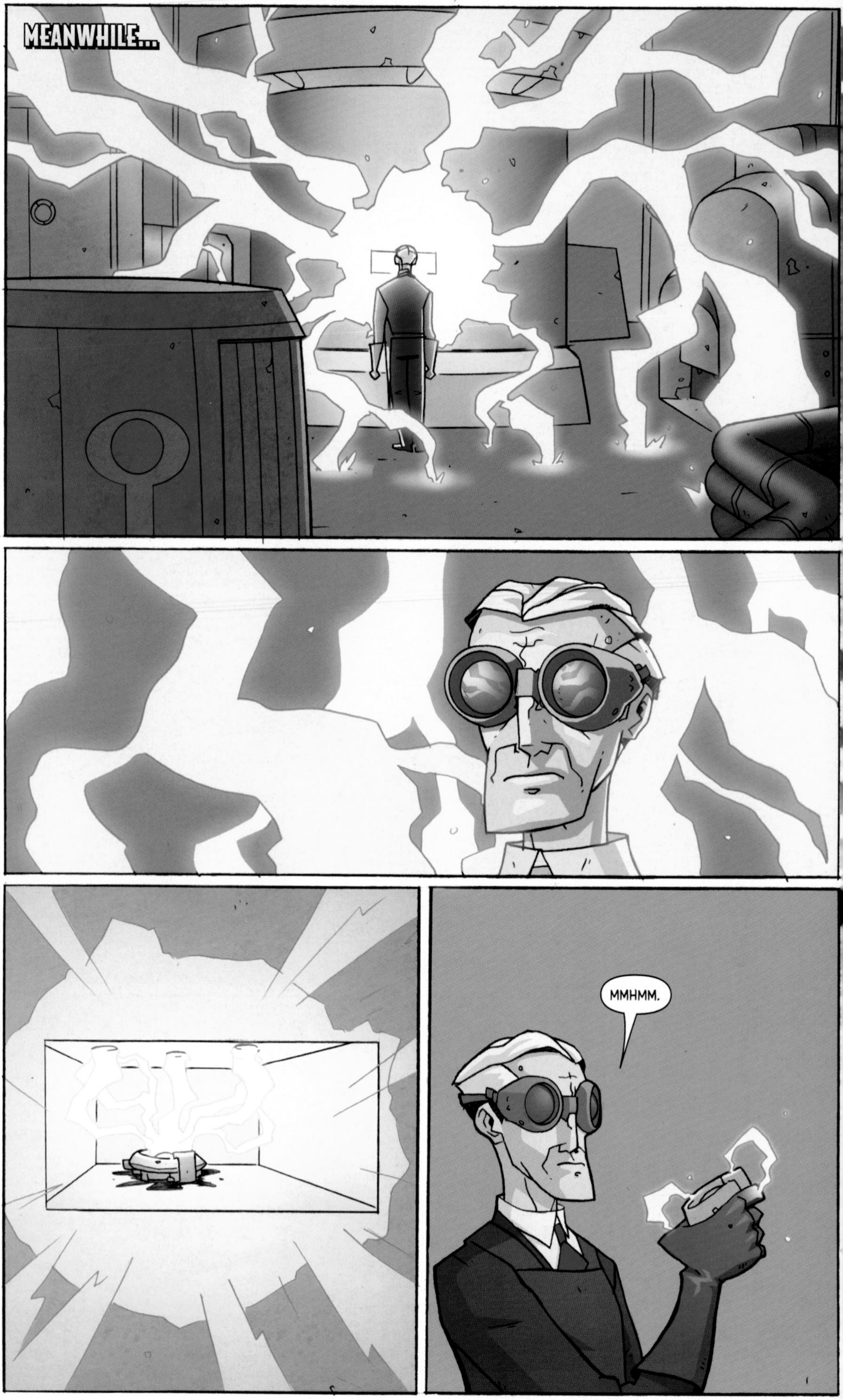
MEANWHILE...
MMHMM.

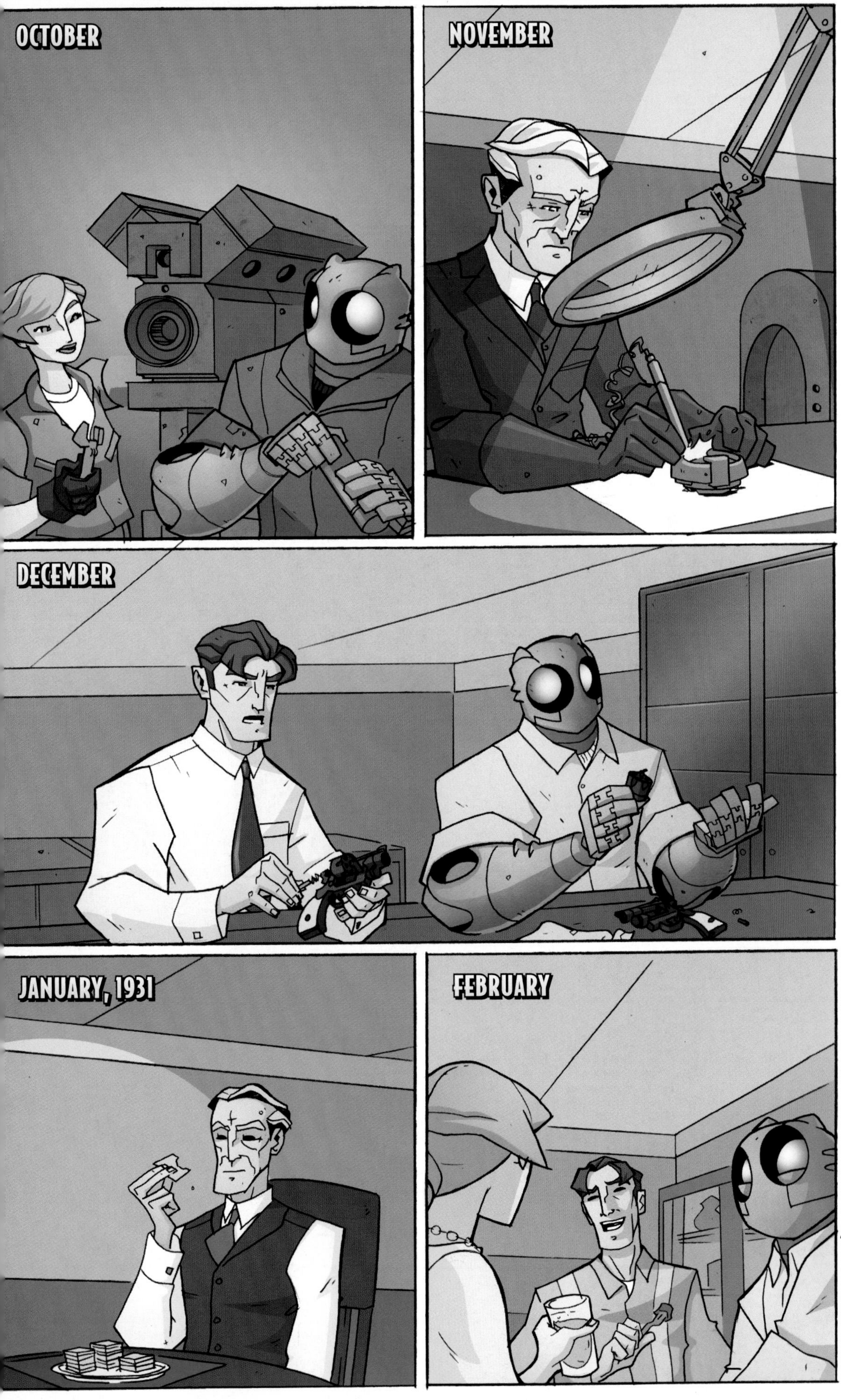
OCTOBER
NOVEMBER
DECEMBER
JANUARY, 1931
FEBRUARY

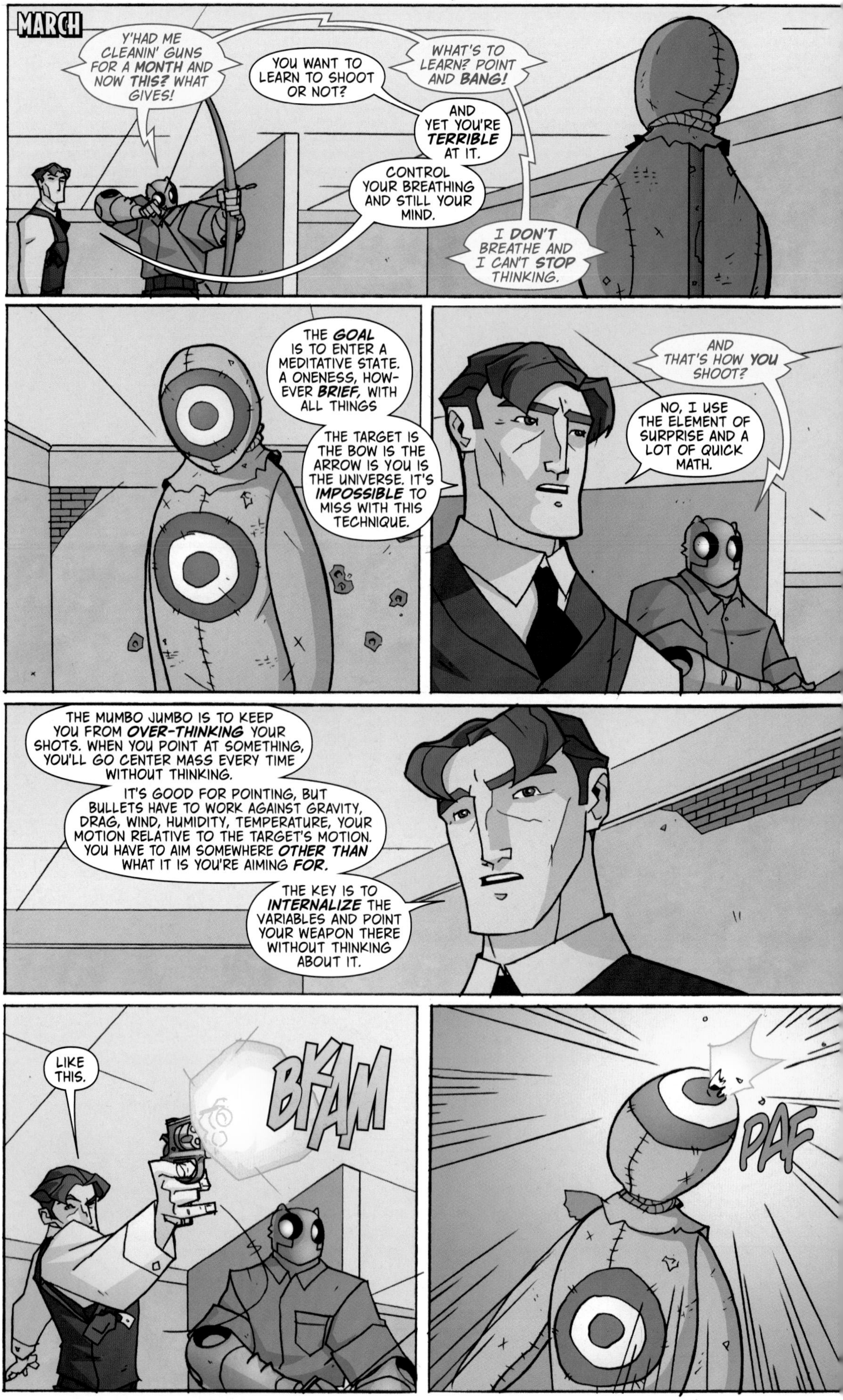
MARCH
Y'HAD ME CLEANIN' GUNS FOR A MONTH AND NOW THIS? WHAT GIVES!
YOU WANT TO LEARN TO SHOOT OR NOT?
WHAT'S TO LEARN? POINT AND BANG!
AND YET YOU'RE TERRIBLE AT IT.
CONTROL YOUR BREATHING AND STILL YOUR MIND.
I DON'T BREATHE AND I CAN'T STOP THINKING.
THE GOAL IS TO ENTER A MEDITATIVE STATE. A ONENESS, HOW-EVER BRIEF, WITH ALL THINGS
THE TARGET IS THE BOW IS THE ARROW IS YOU IS THE UNIVERSE. IT'S IMPOSSIBLE TO MISS WITH THIS TECHNIQUE.
AND THAT'S HOW YOU SHOOT?
NO, I USE THE ELEMENT OF SURPRISE AND A LOT OF QUICK MATH.
THE MUMBO JUMBO IS TO KEEP YOU FROM OVER-THINKING YOUR SHOTS. WHEN YOU POINT AT SOMETHING, YOU'LL GO CENTER MASS EVERY TIME WITHOUT THINKING.
IT'S GOOD FOR POINTING, BUT BULLETS HAVE TO WORK AGAINST GRAVITY, DRAG, WIND, HUMIDITY, TEMPERATURE, YOUR MOTION RELATIVE TO THE TARGET'S MOTION. YOU HAVE TO AIM SOMEWHERE OTHER THAN WHAT IT IS YOU'RE AIMING FOR.
THE KEY IS TO INTERNALIZE THE VARIABLES AND POINT YOUR WEAPON THERE WITHOUT THINKING ABOUT IT.
LIKE THIS.
BKAM
PAF

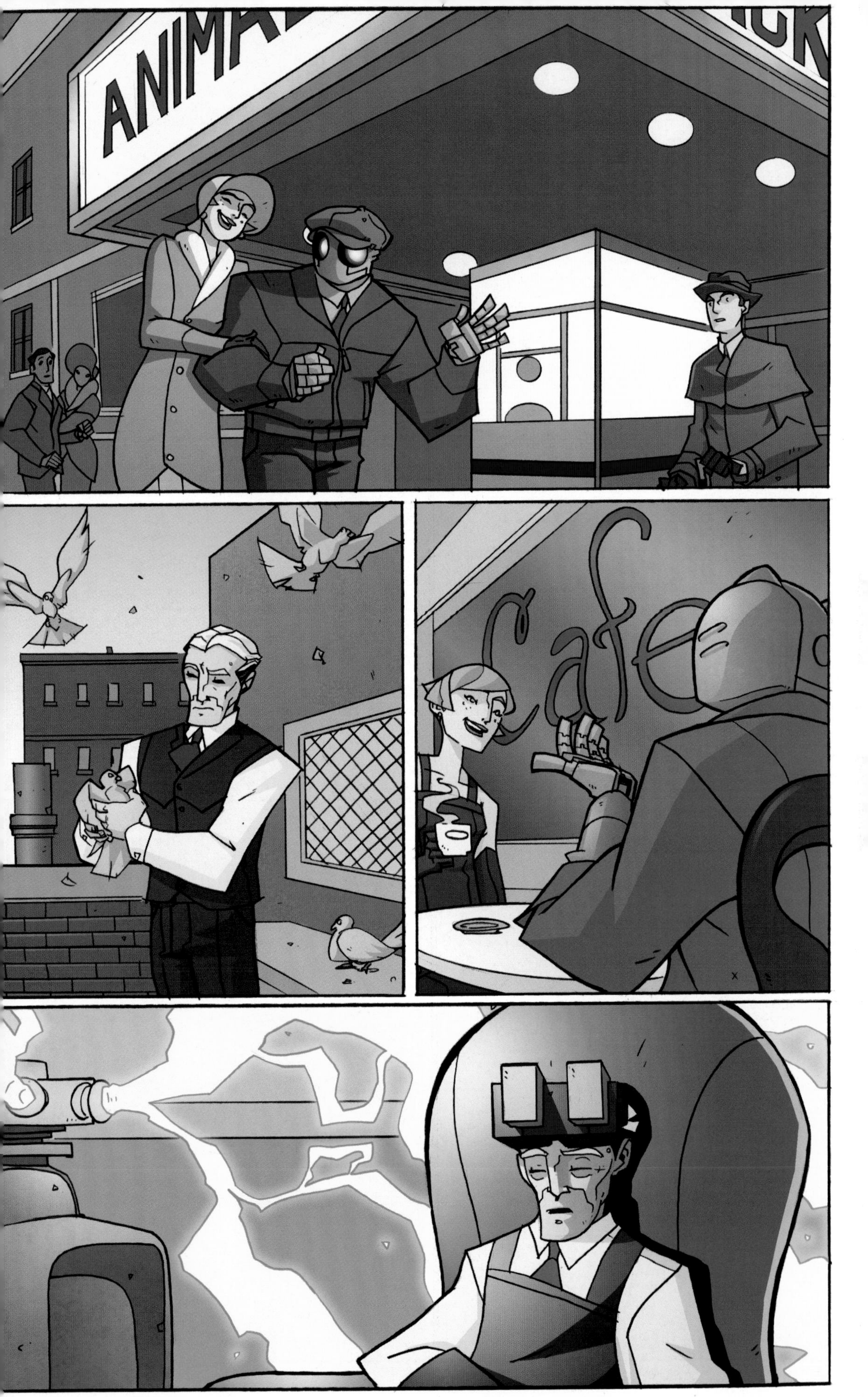
Cafe

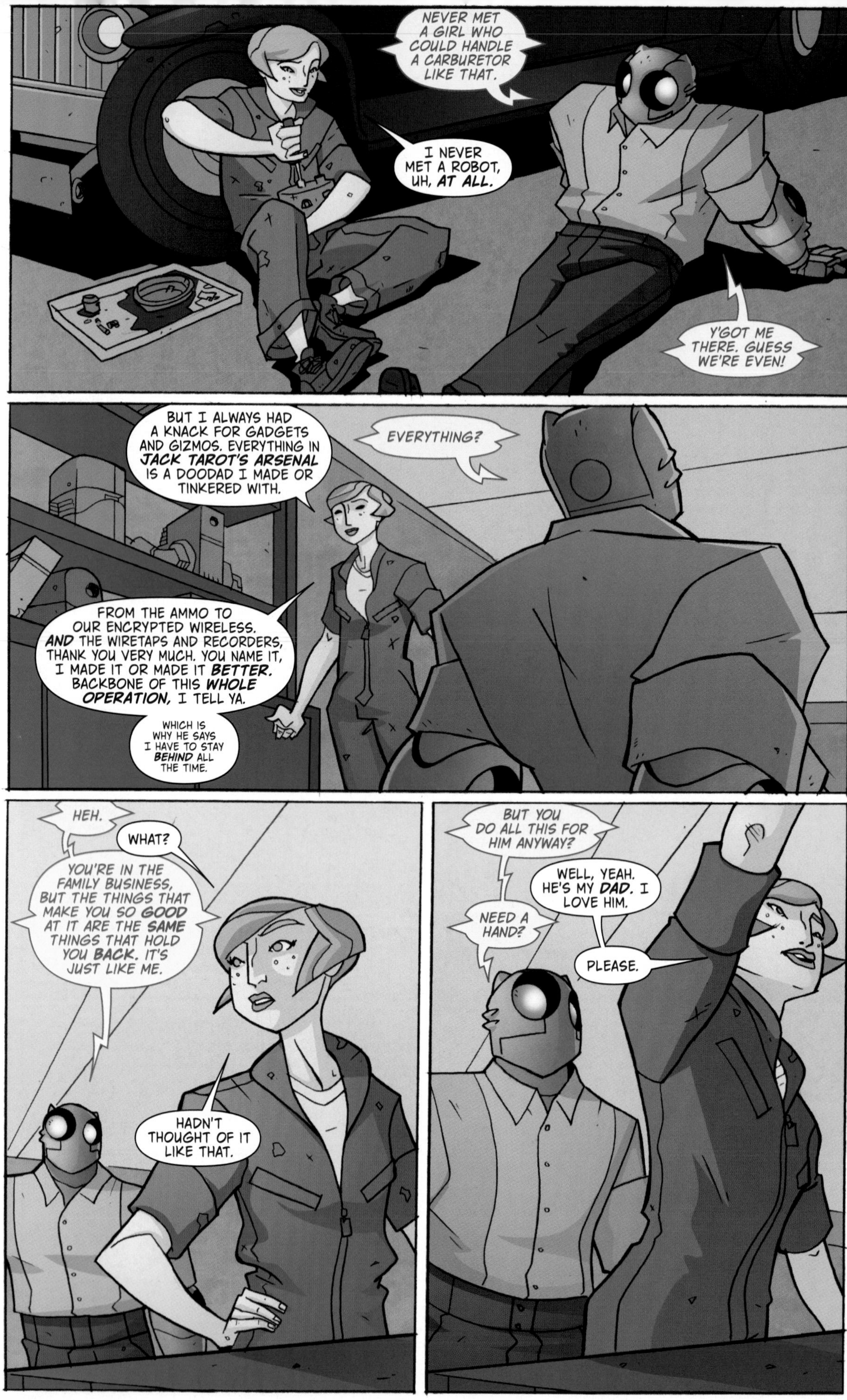
NEVER MET A GIRL WHO COULD HANDLE A CARBURETOR LIKE THAT.
I NEVER MET A ROBOT, UH, AT ALL.
Y'GOT ME THERE. GUESS WE'RE EVEN!
BUT I ALWAYS HAD A KNACK FOR GADGETS AND GIZMOS. EVERYTHING IN JACK TAROT'S ARSENAL IS A DOODAD I MADE OR TINKERED WITH.
EVERYTHING?
FROM THE AMMO TO OUR ENCRYPTED WIRELESS. AND THE WIRETAPS AND RECORDERS, THANK YOU VERY MUCH. YOU NAME IT, I MADE IT OR MADE IT BETTER. BACKBONE OF THIS WHOLE OPERATION, I TELL YA.
WHICH IS WHY HE SAYS I HAVE TO STAY BEHIND ALL THE TIME.
HEH.
WHAT?
YOU'RE IN THE FAMILY BUSINESS, BUT THE THINGS THAT MAKE YOU SO GOOD AT IT ARE THE SAME THINGS THAT HOLD YOU BACK. IT'S JUST LIKE ME.
HADN'T THOUGHT OF IT LIKE THAT.
BUT YOU DO ALL THIS FOR HIM ANYWAY?
WELL, YEAH. HE'S MY DAD. I LOVE HIM.
NEED A HAND?
PLEASE.

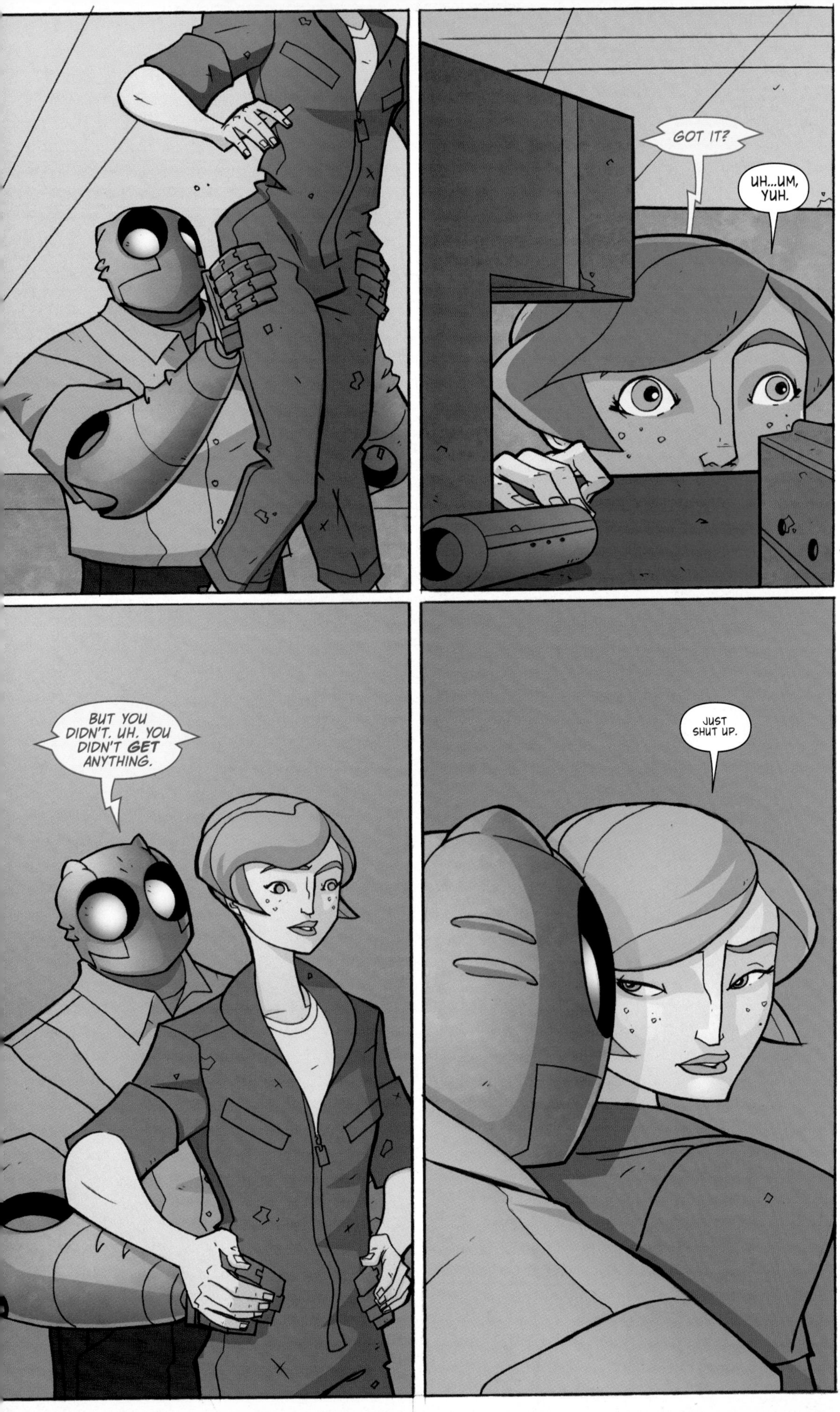
GOT IT?
UH...UM, YUH.
BUT YOU DIDN'T. UH. YOU DIDN'T GET ANYTHING.
JUST SHUT UP.

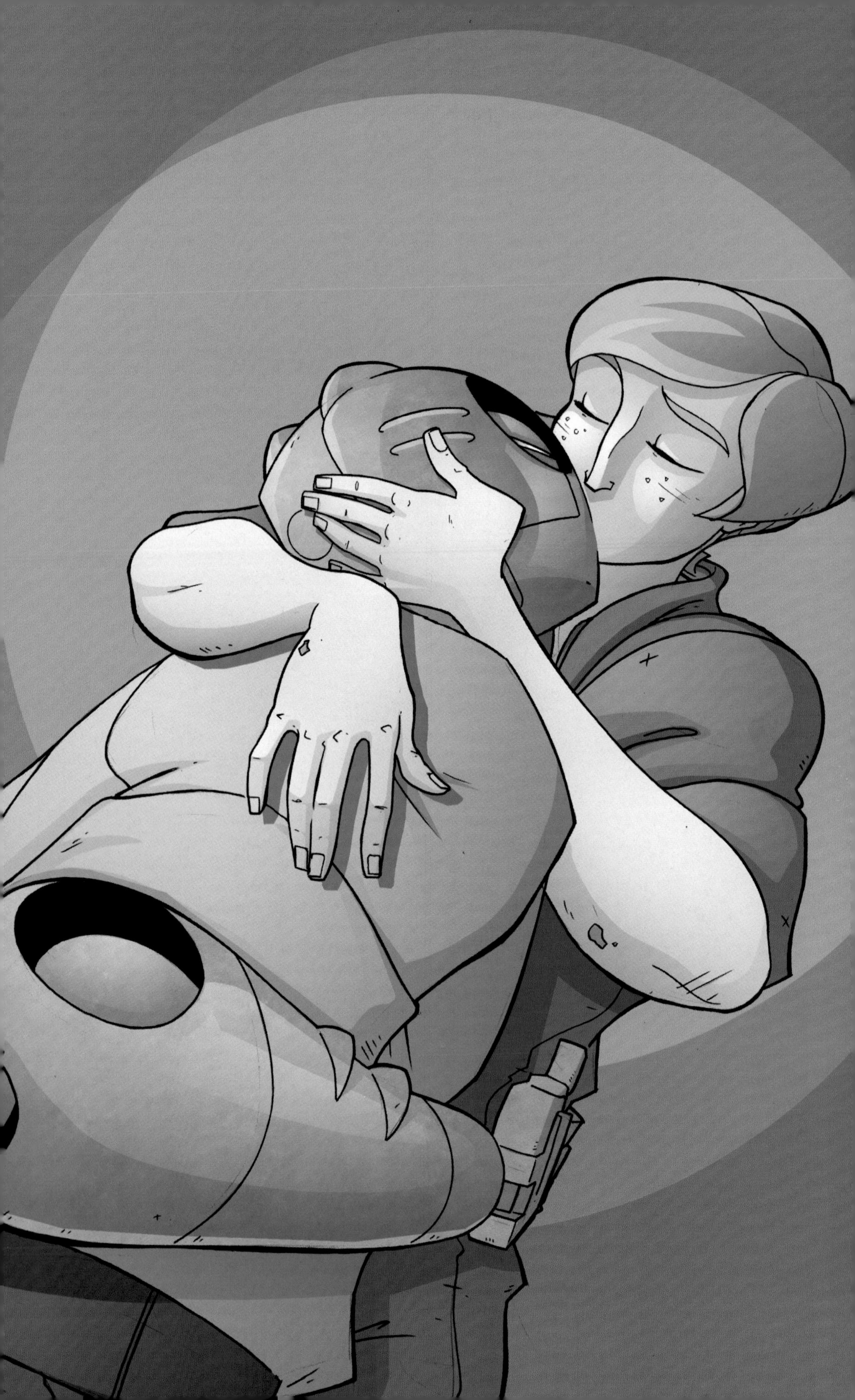

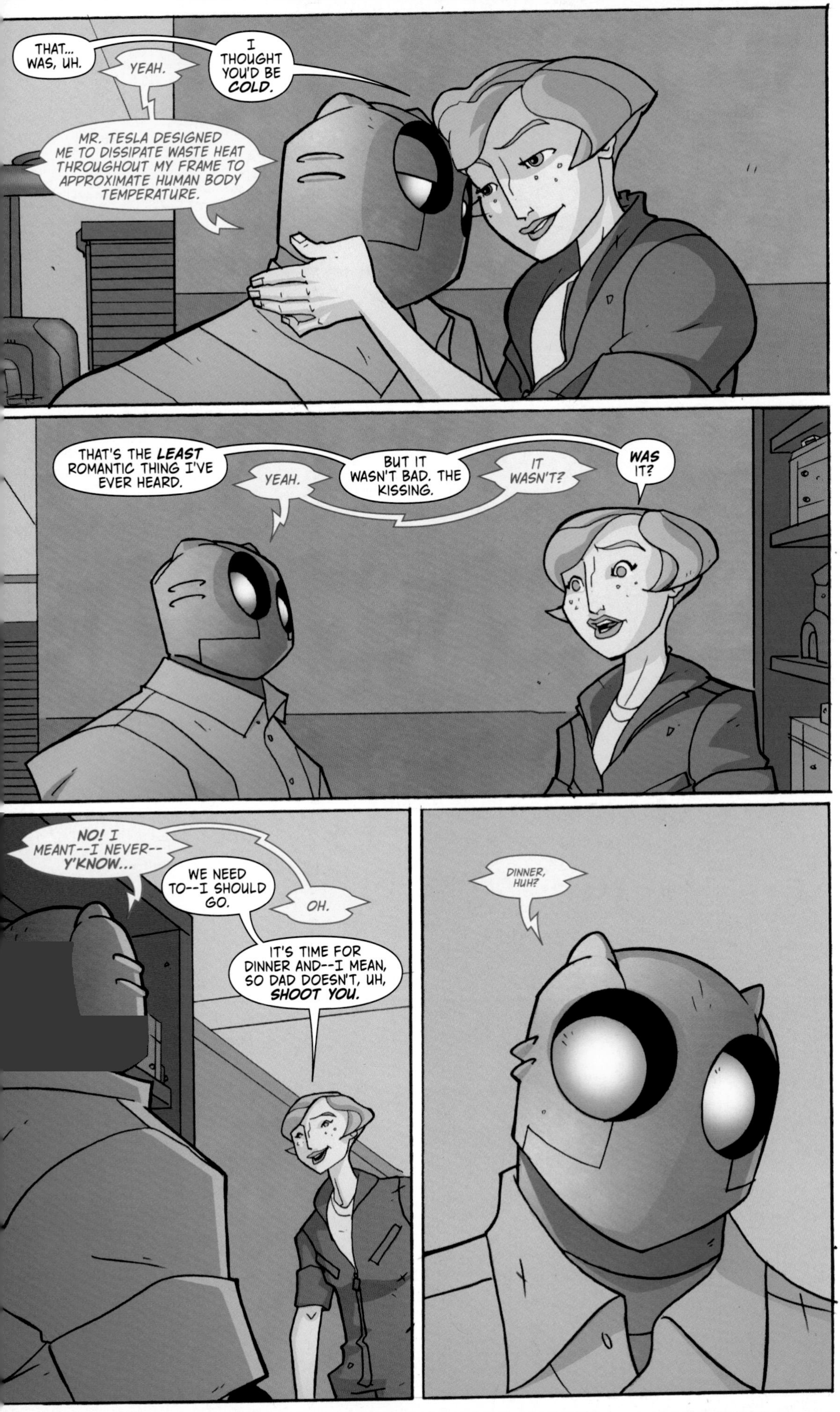

THAT... WAS, UH.
YEAH.
I THOUGHT YOU'D BE **COLD.**
MR. TESLA DESIGNED ME TO DISSIPATE WASTE HEAT THROUGHOUT MY FRAME TO APPROXIMATE HUMAN BODY TEMPERATURE.
THAT'S THE **LEAST** ROMANTIC THING I'VE EVER HEARD.
YEAH.
BUT IT WASN'T BAD. THE KISSING.
IT WASN'T?
WAS IT?
NO! I MEANT--I NEVER-- **Y'KNOW...**
WE NEED TO--I SHOULD GO.
OH.
IT'S TIME FOR DINNER AND--I MEAN, SO DAD DOESN'T, UH, **SHOOT YOU.**
DINNER, HUH?

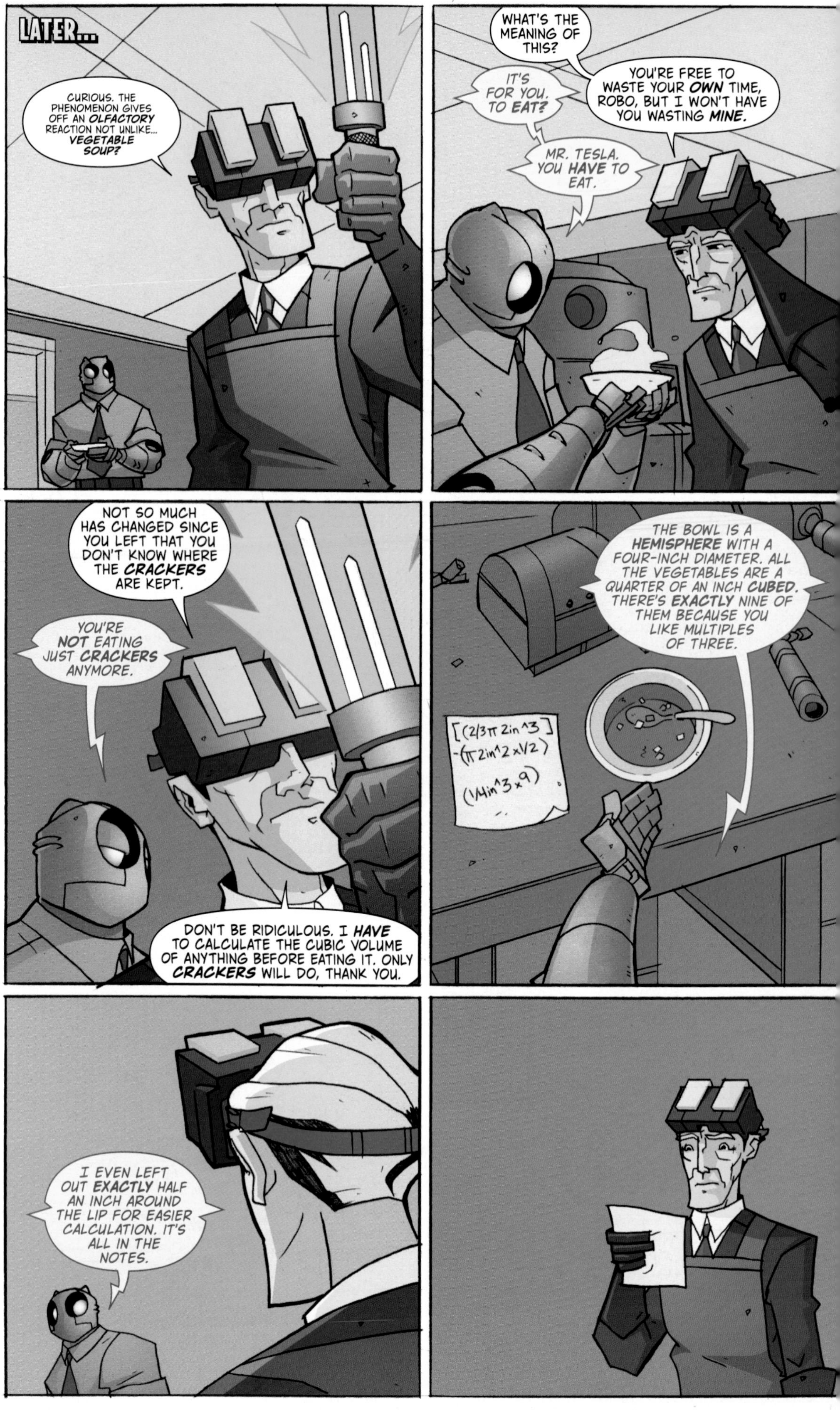
LATER...
CURIOUS. THE PHENOMENON GIVES OFF AN OLFACTORY REACTION NOT UNLIKE... VEGETABLE SOUP?
WHAT'S THE MEANING OF THIS?
IT'S FOR YOU. TO EAT?
YOU'RE FREE TO WASTE YOUR OWN TIME, ROBO, BUT I WON'T HAVE YOU WASTING MINE.
MR. TESLA. YOU HAVE TO EAT.
NOT SO MUCH HAS CHANGED SINCE YOU LEFT THAT YOU DON'T KNOW WHERE THE CRACKERS ARE KEPT.
YOU'RE NOT EATING JUST CRACKERS ANYMORE.
DON'T BE RIDICULOUS. I HAVE TO CALCULATE THE CUBIC VOLUME OF ANYTHING BEFORE EATING IT. ONLY CRACKERS WILL DO, THANK YOU.
THE BOWL IS A HEMISPHERE WITH A FOUR-INCH DIAMETER. ALL THE VEGETABLES ARE A QUARTER OF AN INCH CUBED. THERE'S EXACTLY NINE OF THEM BECAUSE YOU LIKE MULTIPLES OF THREE.
[(2/3π 2in^3]
-(π 2in^2 x1/2)
(1/4in^3 x9)
I EVEN LEFT OUT EXACTLY HALF AN INCH AROUND THE LIP FOR EASIER CALCULATION. IT'S ALL IN THE NOTES.

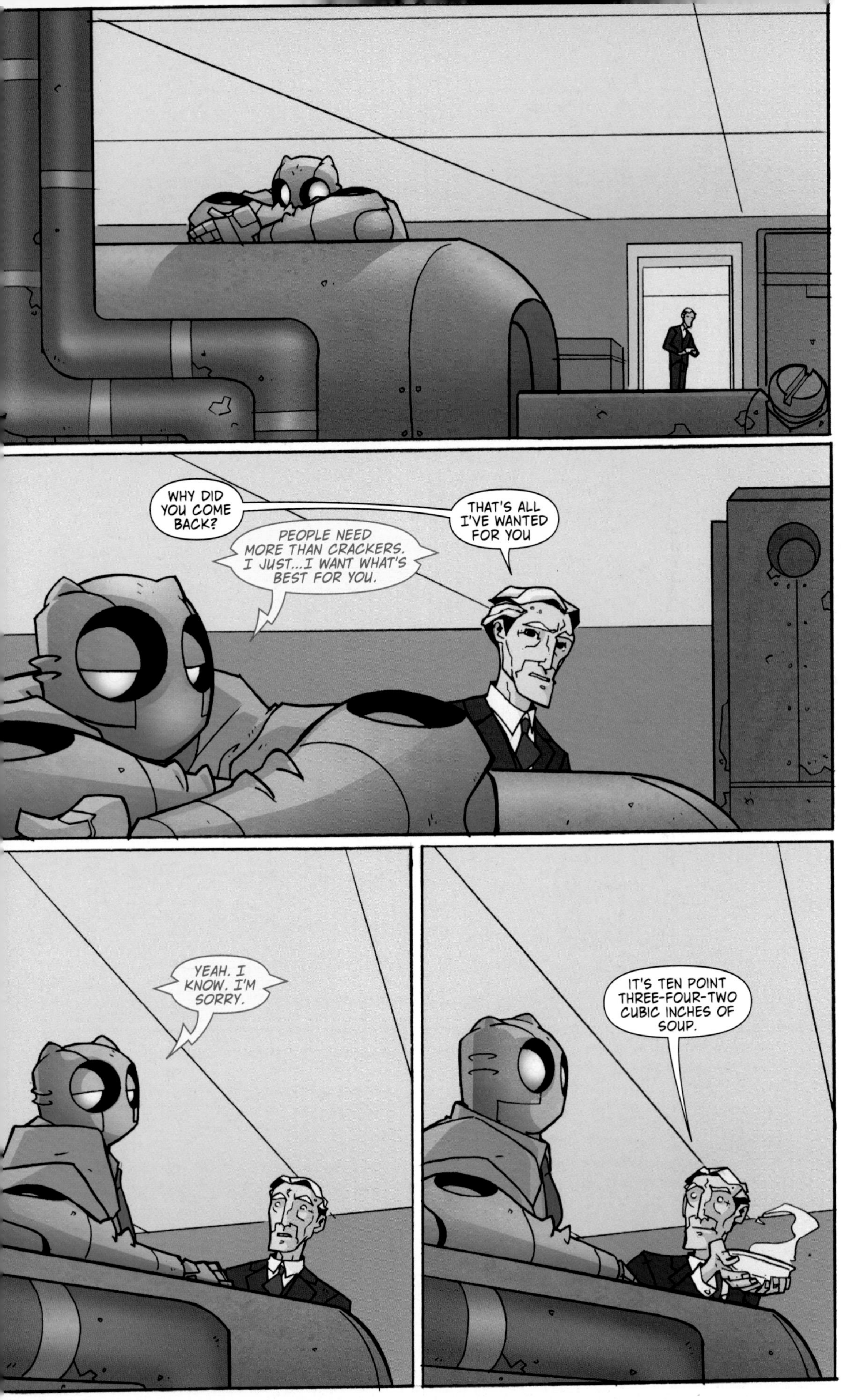
WHY DID YOU COME BACK?
PEOPLE NEED MORE THAN CRACKERS. I JUST...I WANT WHAT'S BEST FOR YOU.
THAT'S ALL I'VE WANTED FOR YOU
YEAH. I KNOW. I'M SORRY.
IT'S TEN POINT THREE-FOUR-TWO CUBIC INCHES OF SOUP.

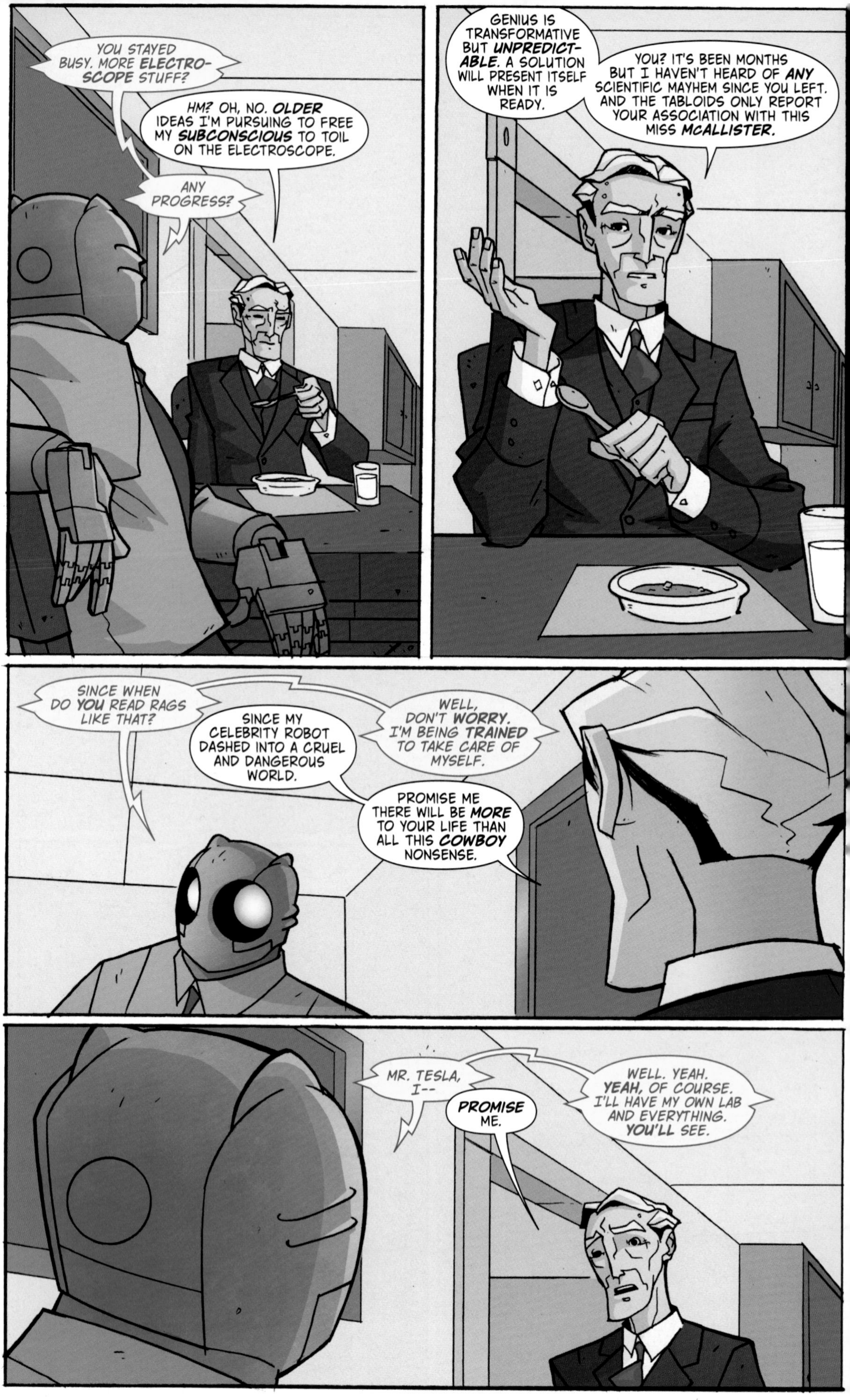
YOU STAYED BUSY. MORE ELECTRO-SCOPE STUFF?
HM? OH, NO. OLDER IDEAS I'M PURSUING TO FREE MY SUBCONSCIOUS TO TOIL ON THE ELECTROSCOPE.
ANY PROGRESS?
GENIUS IS TRANSFORMATIVE BUT UNPREDICT-ABLE. A SOLUTION WILL PRESENT ITSELF WHEN IT IS READY.
YOU? IT'S BEEN MONTHS BUT I HAVEN'T HEARD OF ANY SCIENTIFIC MAYHEM SINCE YOU LEFT. AND THE TABLOIDS ONLY REPORT YOUR ASSOCIATION WITH THIS MISS McALLISTER.
SINCE WHEN DO YOU READ RAGS LIKE THAT?
SINCE MY CELEBRITY ROBOT DASHED INTO A CRUEL AND DANGEROUS WORLD.
WELL, DON'T WORRY. I'M BEING TRAINED TO TAKE CARE OF MYSELF.
PROMISE ME THERE WILL BE MORE TO YOUR LIFE THAN ALL THIS COWBOY NONSENSE.
MR. TESLA, I--
PROMISE ME.
WELL. YEAH. YEAH, OF COURSE. I'LL HAVE MY OWN LAB AND EVERYTHING. YOU'LL SEE.

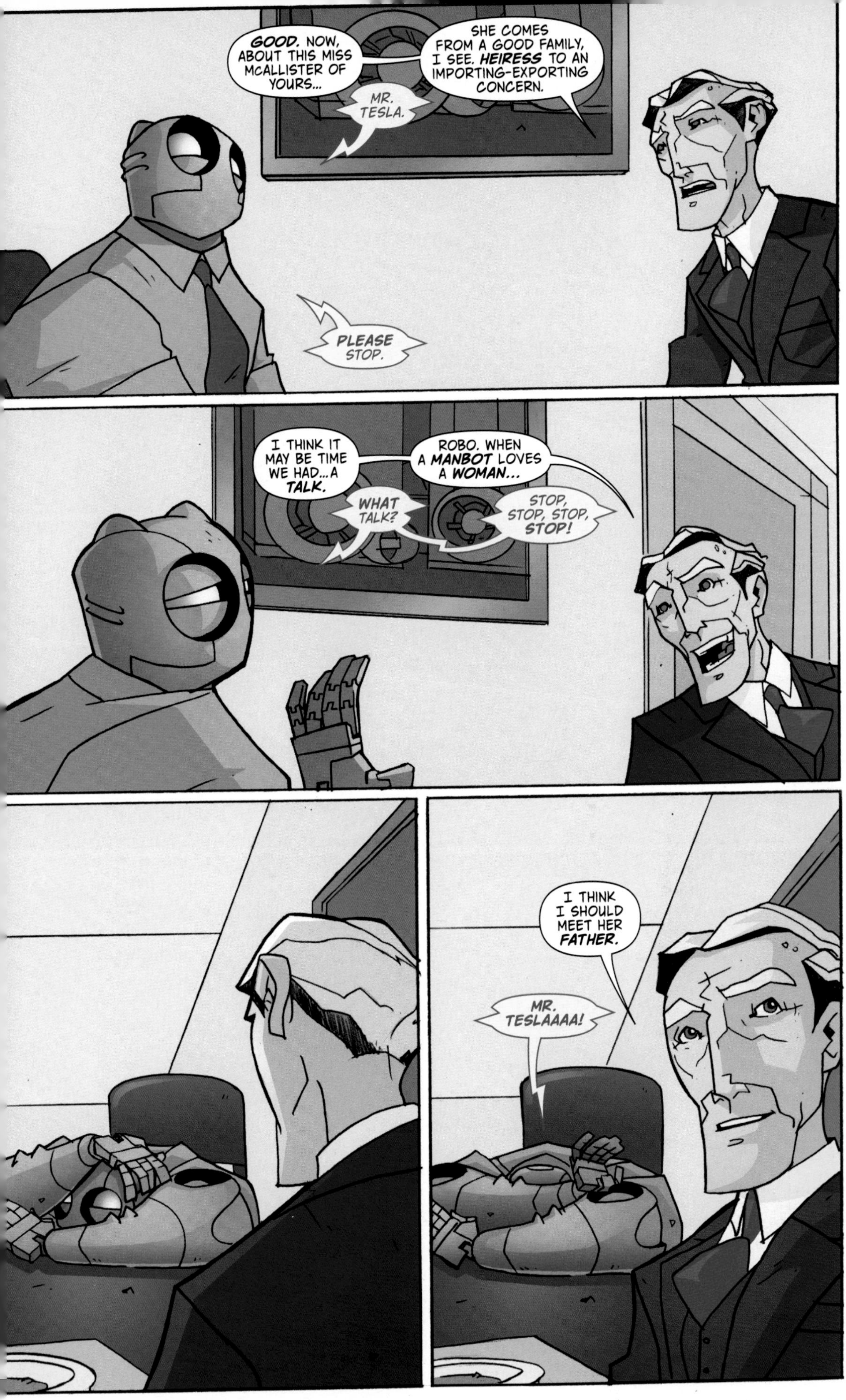
GOOD. NOW, ABOUT THIS MISS McALLISTER OF YOURS...
SHE COMES FROM A GOOD FAMILY, I SEE. HEIRESS TO AN IMPORTING-EXPORTING CONCERN.
MR. TESLA.
PLEASE STOP.
I THINK IT MAY BE TIME WE HAD...A TALK.
ROBO. WHEN A MANBOT LOVES A WOMAN...
WHAT TALK?
STOP, STOP, STOP, STOP!
I THINK I SHOULD MEET HER FATHER.
MR. TESLAAAA!

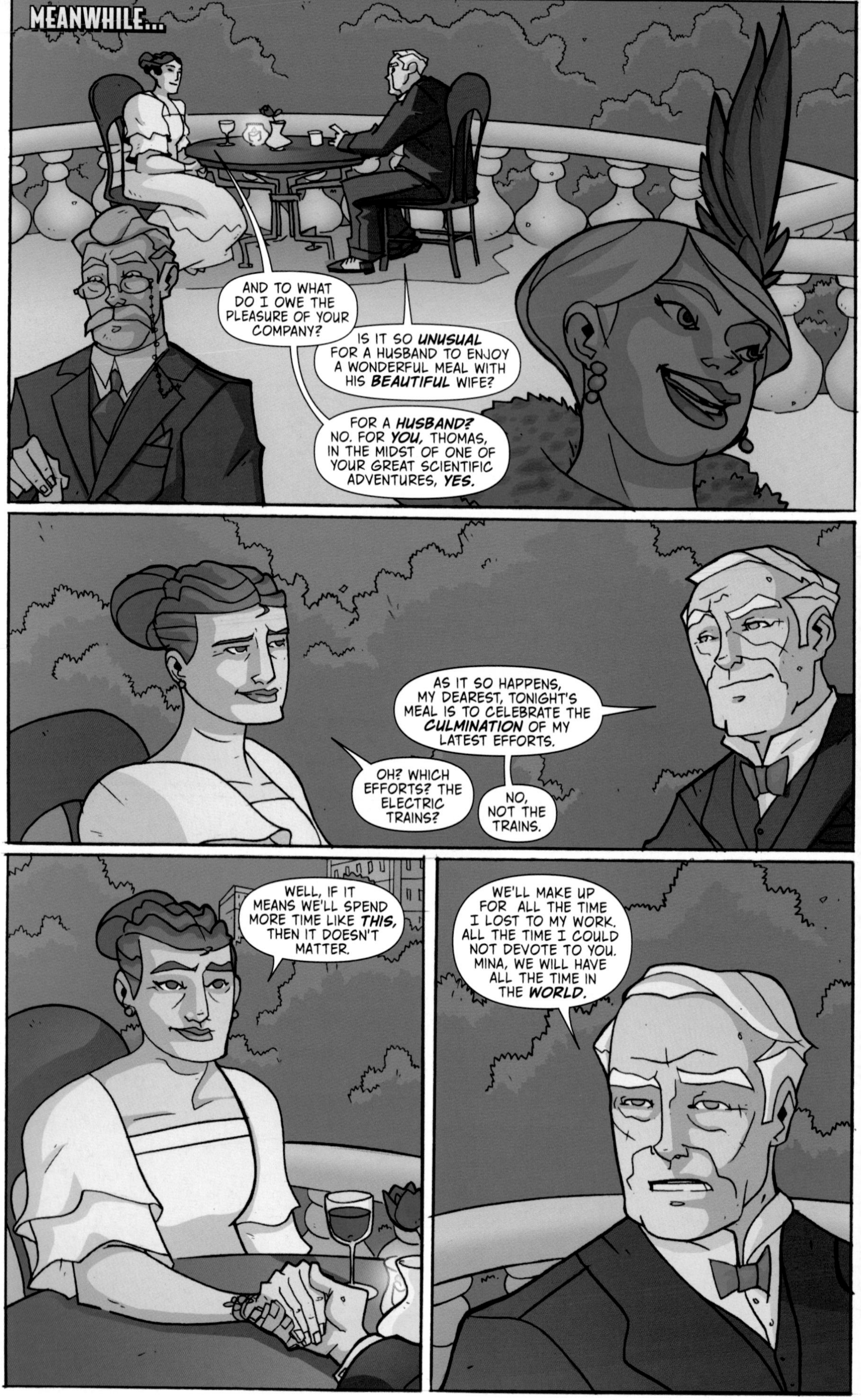
MEANWHILE...
AND TO WHAT DO I OWE THE PLEASURE OF YOUR COMPANY?
IS IT SO UNUSUAL FOR A HUSBAND TO ENJOY A WONDERFUL MEAL WITH HIS BEAUTIFUL WIFE?
FOR A HUSBAND? NO. FOR YOU, THOMAS, IN THE MIDST OF ONE OF YOUR GREAT SCIENTIFIC ADVENTURES, YES.
AS IT SO HAPPENS, MY DEAREST, TONIGHT'S MEAL IS TO CELEBRATE THE CULMINATION OF MY LATEST EFFORTS.
OH? WHICH EFFORTS? THE ELECTRIC TRAINS?
NO, NOT THE TRAINS.
WELL, IF IT MEANS WE'LL SPEND MORE TIME LIKE THIS, THEN IT DOESN'T MATTER.
WE'LL MAKE UP FOR ALL THE TIME I LOST TO MY WORK. ALL THE TIME I COULD NOT DEVOTE TO YOU. MINA, WE WILL HAVE ALL THE TIME IN THE WORLD.

THE WIZARD OF MENLO PARK

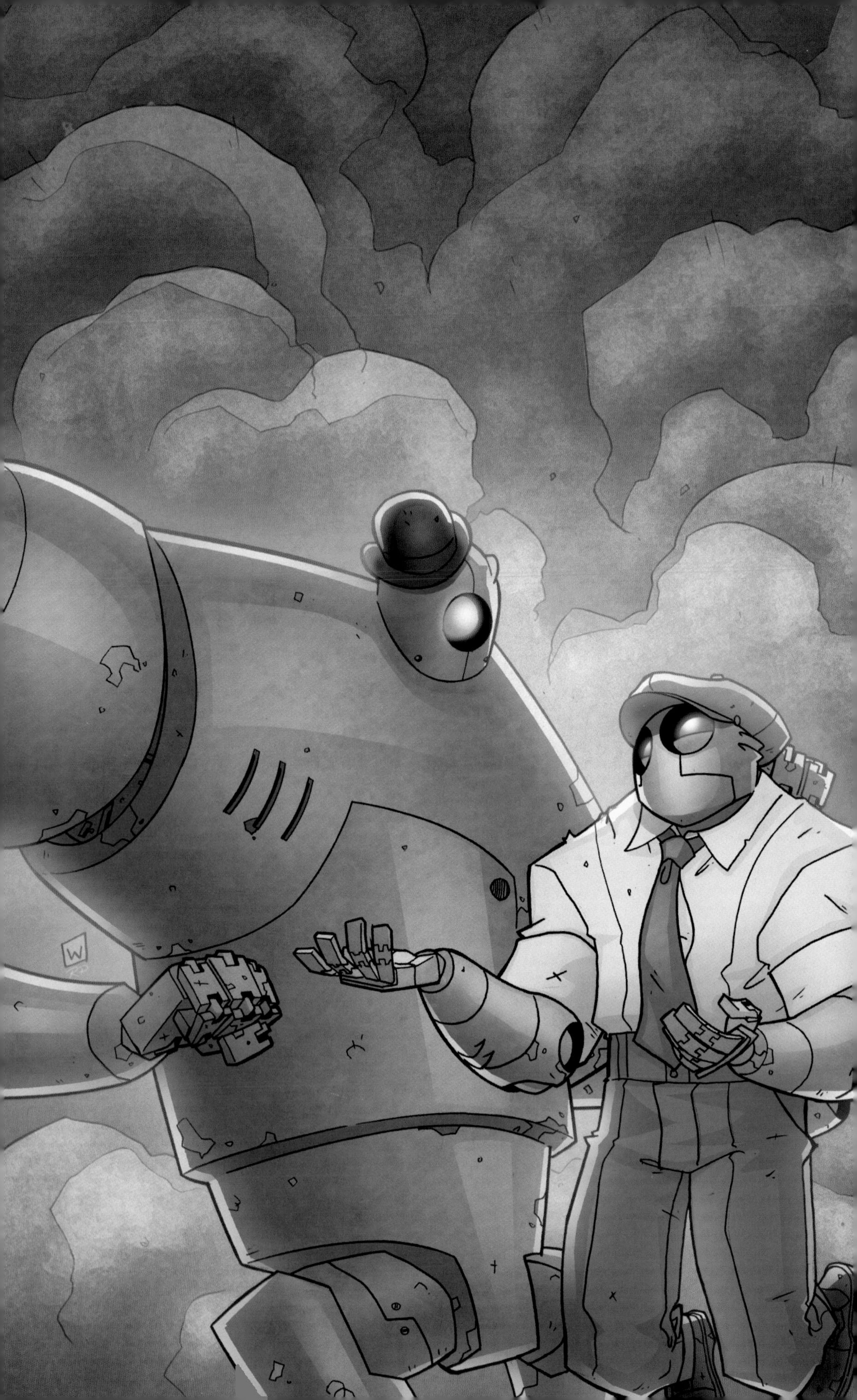

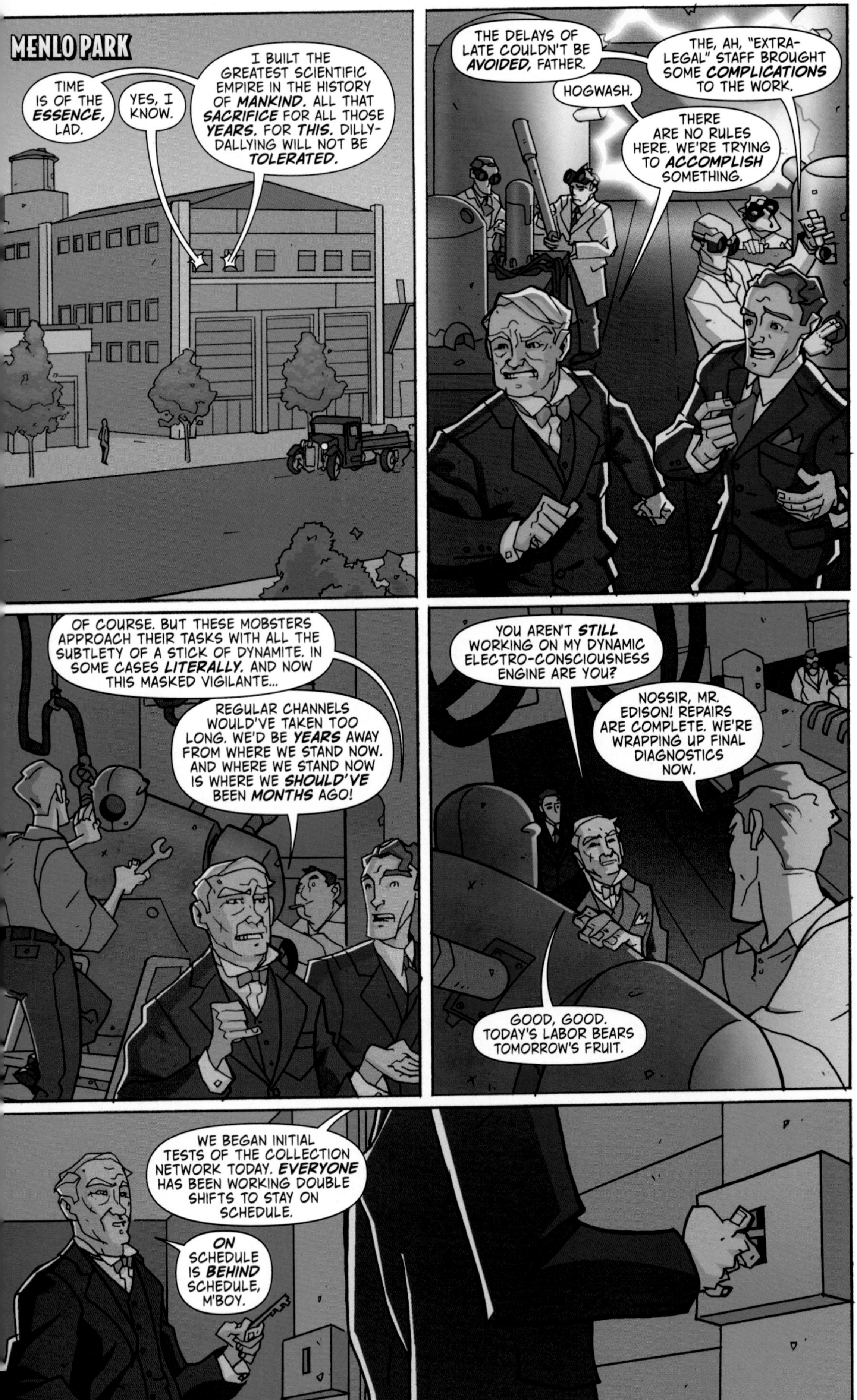
MENLO PARK
TIME IS OF THE ESSENCE, LAD.
YES, I KNOW.
I BUILT THE GREATEST SCIENTIFIC EMPIRE IN THE HISTORY OF MANKIND. ALL THAT SACRIFICE FOR ALL THOSE YEARS. FOR THIS. DILLY-DALLYING WILL NOT BE TOLERATED.
THE DELAYS OF LATE COULDN'T BE AVOIDED, FATHER.
THE, AH, "EXTRA-LEGAL" STAFF BROUGHT SOME COMPLICATIONS TO THE WORK.
HOGWASH.
THERE ARE NO RULES HERE. WE'RE TRYING TO ACCOMPLISH SOMETHING.
OF COURSE. BUT THESE MOBSTERS APPROACH THEIR TASKS WITH ALL THE SUBTLETY OF A STICK OF DYNAMITE. IN SOME CASES LITERALLY. AND NOW THIS MASKED VIGILANTE...
REGULAR CHANNELS WOULD'VE TAKEN TOO LONG. WE'D BE YEARS AWAY FROM WHERE WE STAND NOW. AND WHERE WE STAND NOW IS WHERE WE SHOULD'VE BEEN MONTHS AGO!
YOU AREN'T STILL WORKING ON MY DYNAMIC ELECTRO-CONSCIOUSNESS ENGINE ARE YOU?
NOSSIR, MR. EDISON! REPAIRS ARE COMPLETE. WE'RE WRAPPING UP FINAL DIAGNOSTICS NOW.
GOOD, GOOD. TODAY'S LABOR BEARS TOMORROW'S FRUIT.
WE BEGAN INITIAL TESTS OF THE COLLECTION NETWORK TODAY. EVERYONE HAS BEEN WORKING DOUBLE SHIFTS TO STAY ON SCHEDULE.
ON SCHEDULE IS BEHIND SCHEDULE, M'BOY.

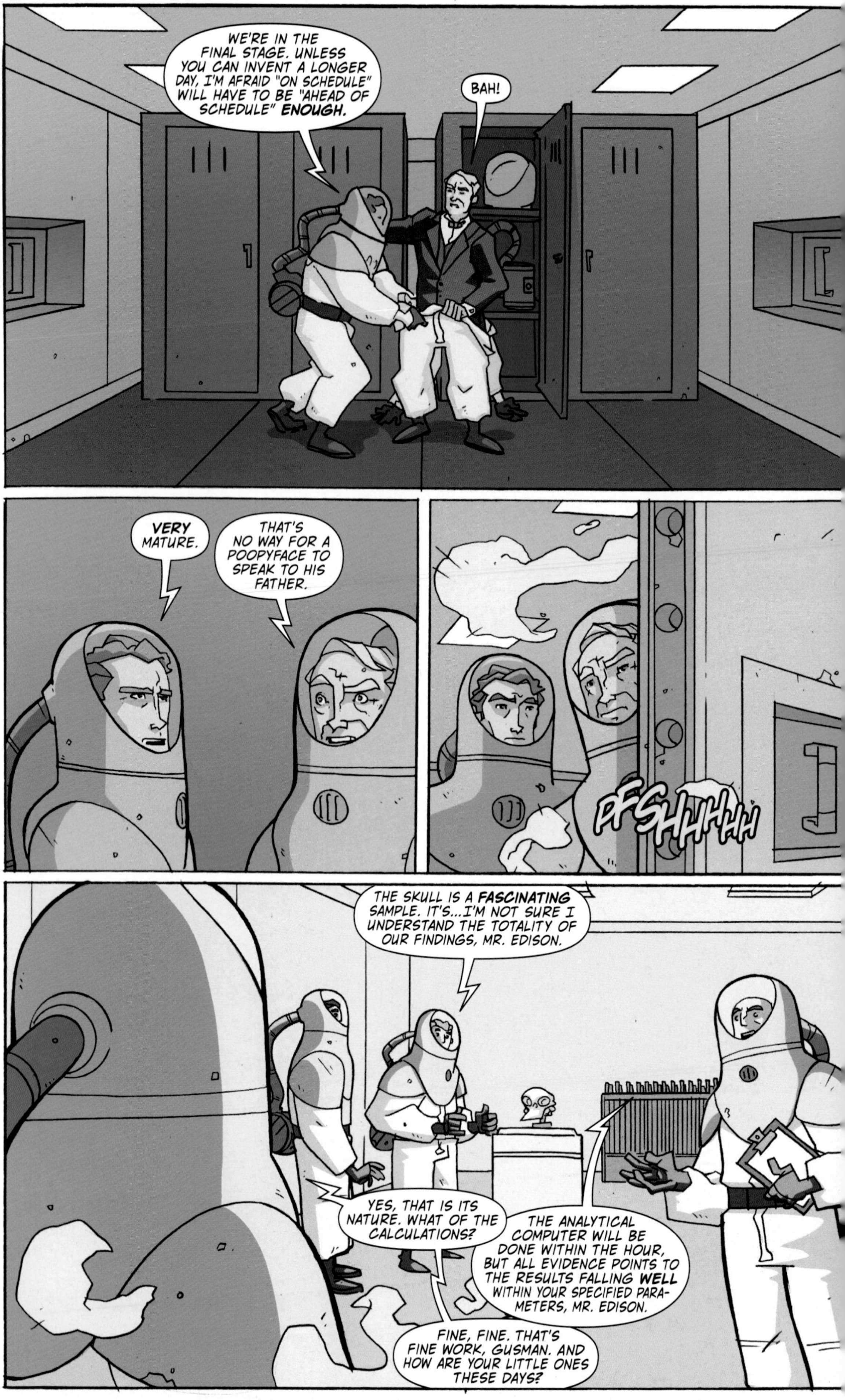
WE'RE IN THE FINAL STAGE. UNLESS YOU CAN INVENT A LONGER DAY, I'M AFRAID "ON SCHEDULE" WILL HAVE TO BE "AHEAD OF SCHEDULE" ENOUGH.
BAH!
VERY MATURE.
THAT'S NO WAY FOR A POOPYFACE TO SPEAK TO HIS FATHER.
PFSHHHHH
THE SKULL IS A FASCINATING SAMPLE. IT'S...I'M NOT SURE I UNDERSTAND THE TOTALITY OF OUR FINDINGS, MR. EDISON.
YES, THAT IS ITS NATURE. WHAT OF THE CALCULATIONS?
THE ANALYTICAL COMPUTER WILL BE DONE WITHIN THE HOUR, BUT ALL EVIDENCE POINTS TO THE RESULTS FALLING WELL WITHIN YOUR SPECIFIED PARA-METERS, MR. EDISON.
FINE, FINE. THAT'S FINE WORK, GUSMAN. AND HOW ARE YOUR LITTLE ONES THESE DAYS?

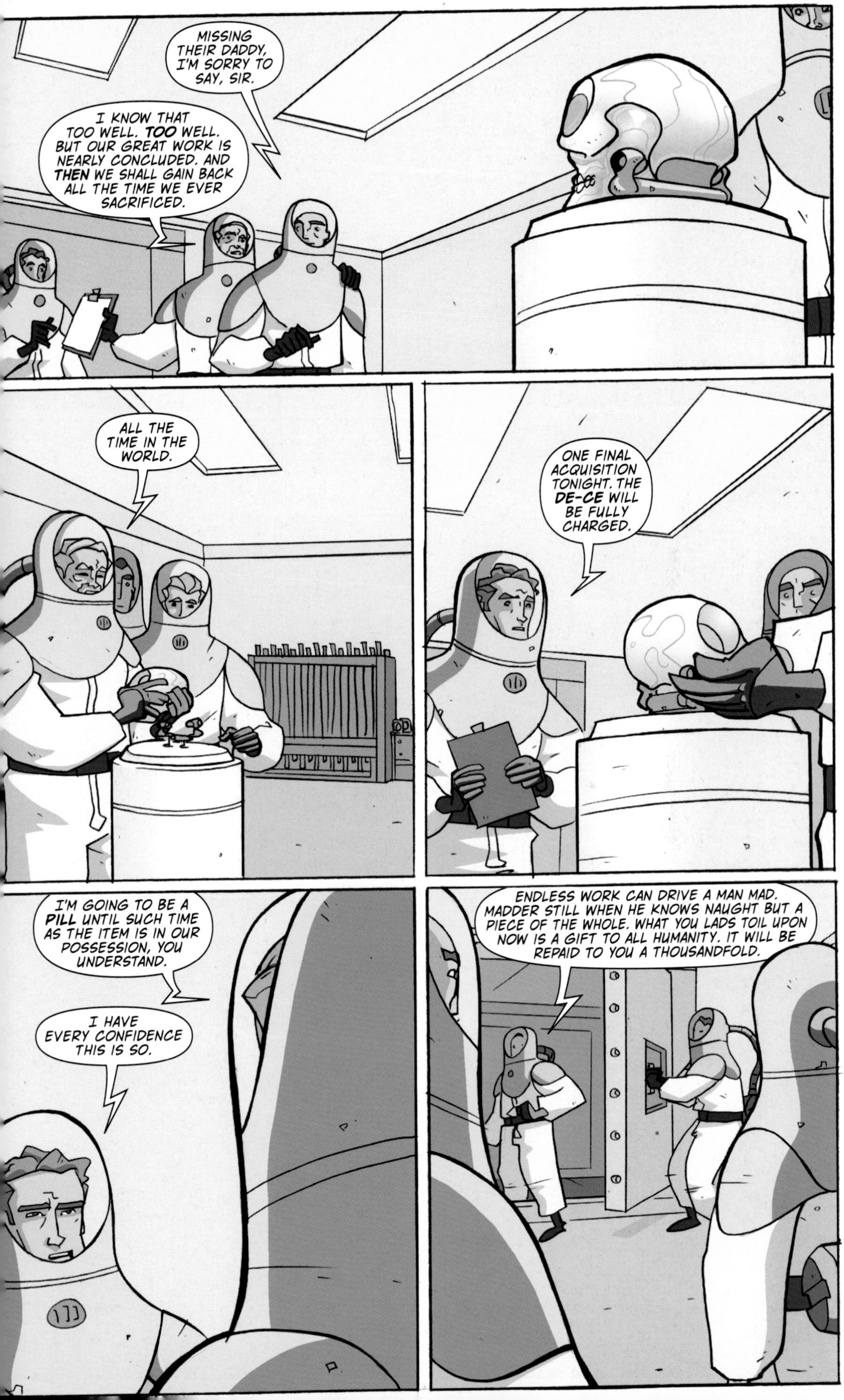
MISSING THEIR DADDY, I'M SORRY TO SAY, SIR.
I KNOW THAT TOO WELL. **TOO** WELL. BUT OUR GREAT WORK IS NEARLY CONCLUDED. AND **THEN** WE SHALL GAIN BACK ALL THE TIME WE EVER SACRIFICED.
ALL THE TIME IN THE WORLD.
ONE FINAL ACQUISITION TONIGHT. THE **DE-CE** WILL BE FULLY CHARGED.
I'M GOING TO BE A **PILL** UNTIL SUCH TIME AS THE ITEM IS IN OUR POSSESSION, YOU UNDERSTAND.
I HAVE EVERY CONFIDENCE THIS IS SO.
ENDLESS WORK CAN DRIVE A MAN MAD. MADDER STILL WHEN HE KNOWS NAUGHT BUT A PIECE OF THE WHOLE. WHAT YOU LADS TOIL UPON NOW IS A GIFT TO ALL HUMANITY. IT WILL BE REPAID TO YOU A THOUSANDFOLD.

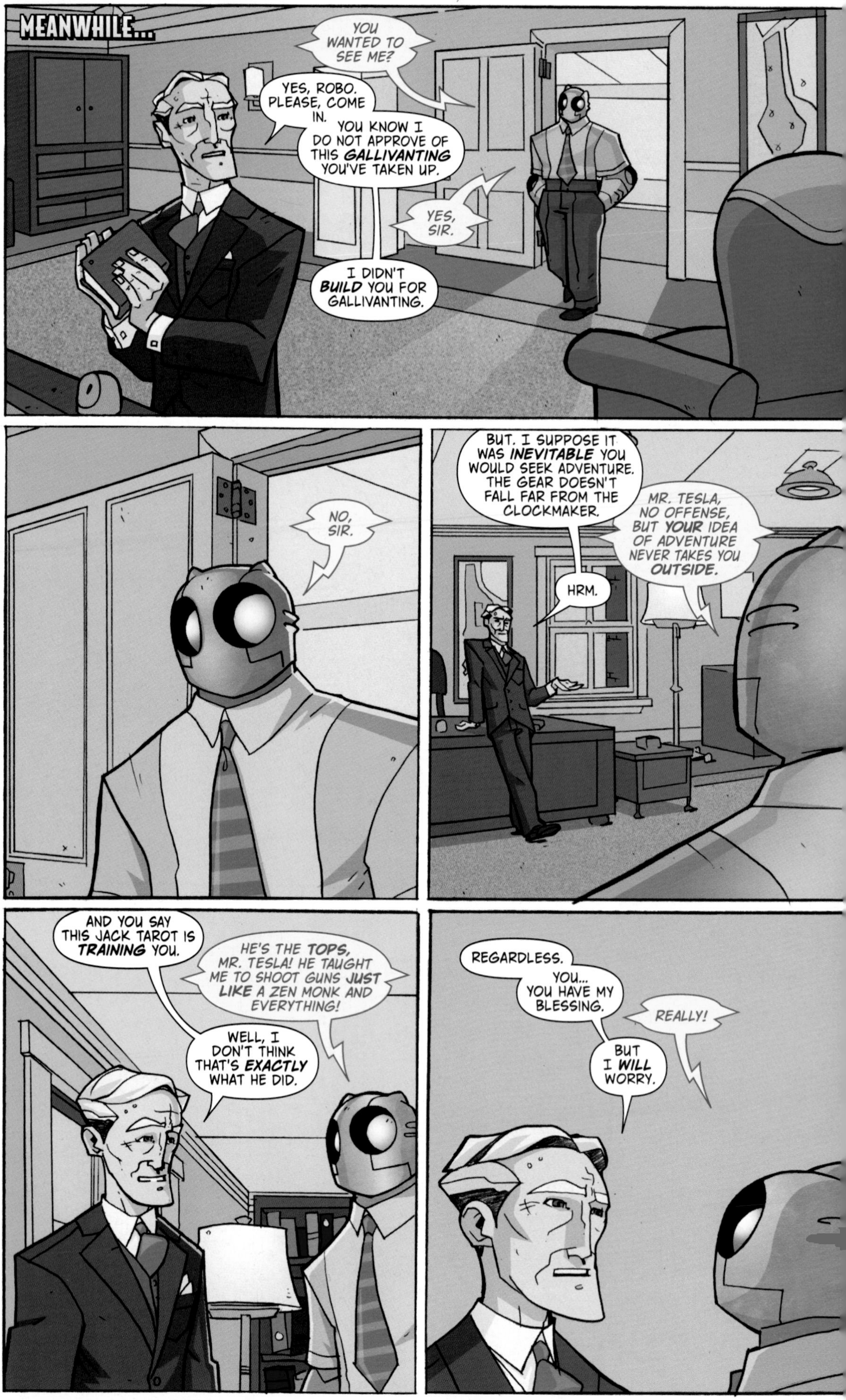
MEANWHILE...
YOU WANTED TO SEE ME?
YES, ROBO. PLEASE, COME IN.
YOU KNOW I DO NOT APPROVE OF THIS **GALLIVANTING** YOU'VE TAKEN UP.
YES, SIR.
I DIDN'T **BUILD** YOU FOR GALLIVANTING.
NO, SIR.
BUT. I SUPPOSE IT WAS **INEVITABLE** YOU WOULD SEEK ADVENTURE. THE GEAR DOESN'T FALL FAR FROM THE CLOCKMAKER.
MR. TESLA, NO OFFENSE, BUT **YOUR** IDEA OF ADVENTURE NEVER TAKES YOU **OUTSIDE.**
HRM.
AND YOU SAY THIS JACK TAROT IS **TRAINING** YOU.
HE'S THE **TOPS,** MR. TESLA! HE TAUGHT ME TO SHOOT GUNS **JUST LIKE** A ZEN MONK AND EVERYTHING!
WELL, I DON'T THINK THAT'S **EXACTLY** WHAT HE DID.
REGARDLESS.
YOU... YOU HAVE MY BLESSING.
REALLY!
BUT I **WILL** WORRY.

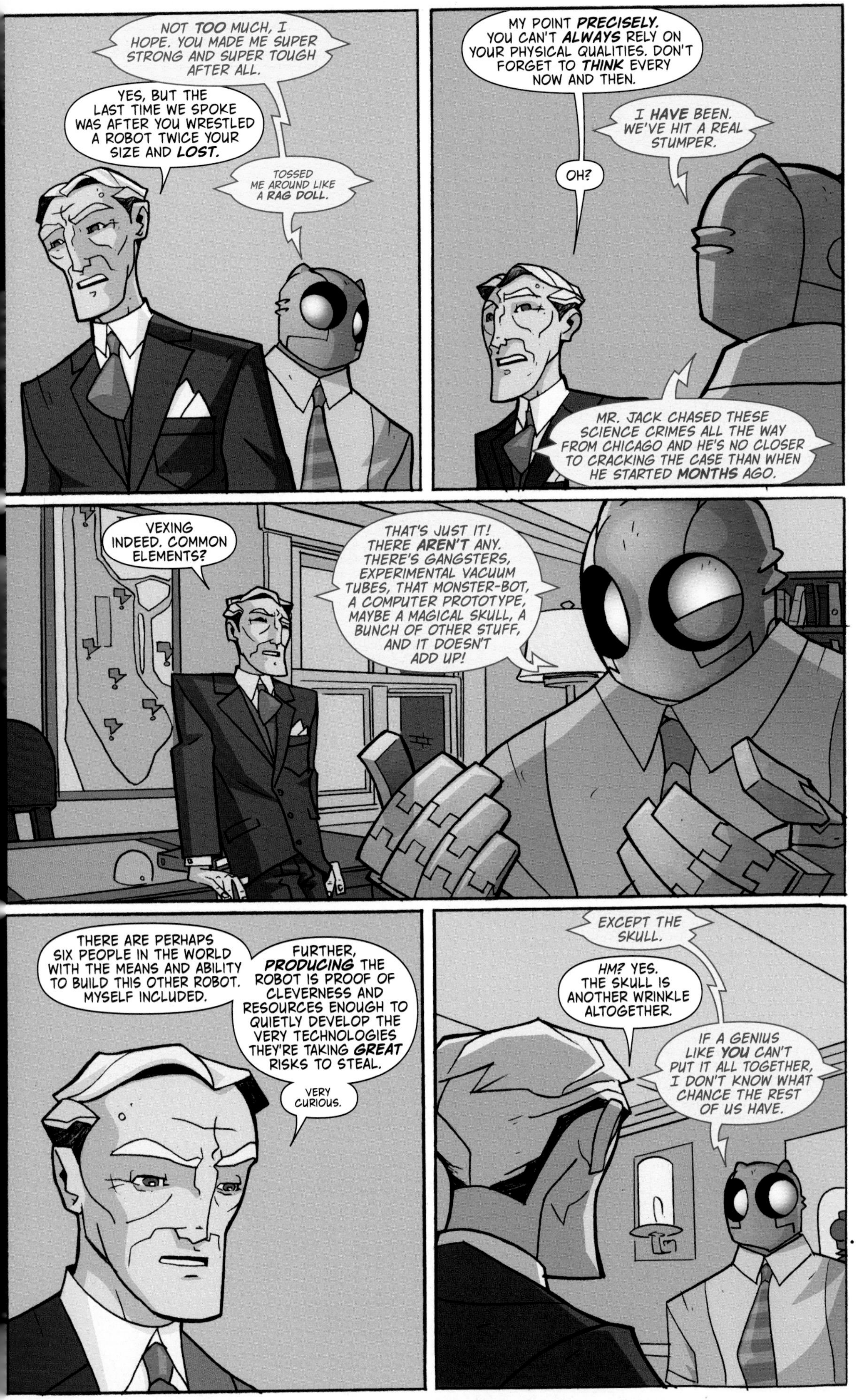
NOT TOO MUCH, I HOPE. YOU MADE ME SUPER STRONG AND SUPER TOUGH AFTER ALL.
YES, BUT THE LAST TIME WE SPOKE WAS AFTER YOU WRESTLED A ROBOT TWICE YOUR SIZE AND LOST.
TOSSED ME AROUND LIKE A RAG DOLL.
MY POINT PRECISELY. YOU CAN'T ALWAYS RELY ON YOUR PHYSICAL QUALITIES. DON'T FORGET TO THINK EVERY NOW AND THEN.
I HAVE BEEN. WE'VE HIT A REAL STUMPER.
OH?
MR. JACK CHASED THESE SCIENCE CRIMES ALL THE WAY FROM CHICAGO AND HE'S NO CLOSER TO CRACKING THE CASE THAN WHEN HE STARTED MONTHS AGO.
VEXING INDEED. COMMON ELEMENTS?
THAT'S JUST IT! THERE AREN'T ANY. THERE'S GANGSTERS, EXPERIMENTAL VACUUM TUBES, THAT MONSTER-BOT, A COMPUTER PROTOTYPE, MAYBE A MAGICAL SKULL, A BUNCH OF OTHER STUFF, AND IT DOESN'T ADD UP!
THERE ARE PERHAPS SIX PEOPLE IN THE WORLD WITH THE MEANS AND ABILITY TO BUILD THIS OTHER ROBOT. MYSELF INCLUDED.
FURTHER, PRODUCING THE ROBOT IS PROOF OF CLEVERNESS AND RESOURCES ENOUGH TO QUIETLY DEVELOP THE VERY TECHNOLOGIES THEY'RE TAKING GREAT RISKS TO STEAL.
VERY CURIOUS.
EXCEPT THE SKULL.
HM? YES. THE SKULL IS ANOTHER WRINKLE ALTOGETHER.
IF A GENIUS LIKE YOU CAN'T PUT IT ALL TOGETHER, I DON'T KNOW WHAT CHANCE THE REST OF US HAVE.

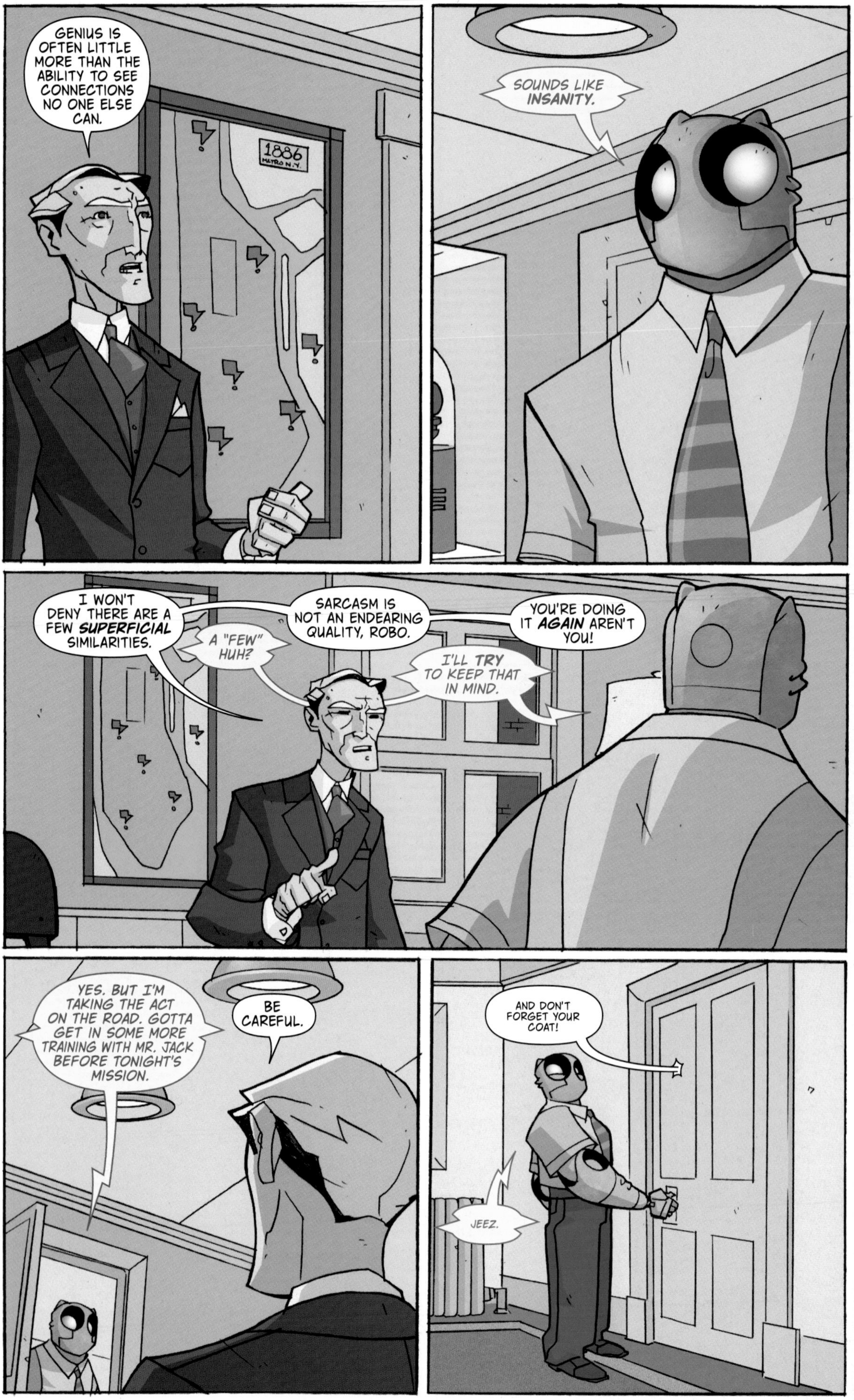
GENIUS IS OFTEN LITTLE MORE THAN THE ABILITY TO SEE CONNECTIONS NO ONE ELSE CAN.
1886 METRO N.Y.
SOUNDS LIKE **INSANITY.**
I WON'T DENY THERE ARE A FEW **SUPERFICIAL** SIMILARITIES.
A "FEW" HUH?
SARCASM IS NOT AN ENDEARING QUALITY, ROBO.
I'LL **TRY** TO KEEP THAT IN MIND.
YOU'RE DOING IT **AGAIN** AREN'T YOU!
YES. BUT I'M TAKING THE ACT ON THE ROAD. GOTTA GET IN SOME MORE TRAINING WITH MR. JACK BEFORE TONIGHT'S MISSION.
BE CAREFUL.
AND DON'T FORGET YOUR COAT!
JEEZ.

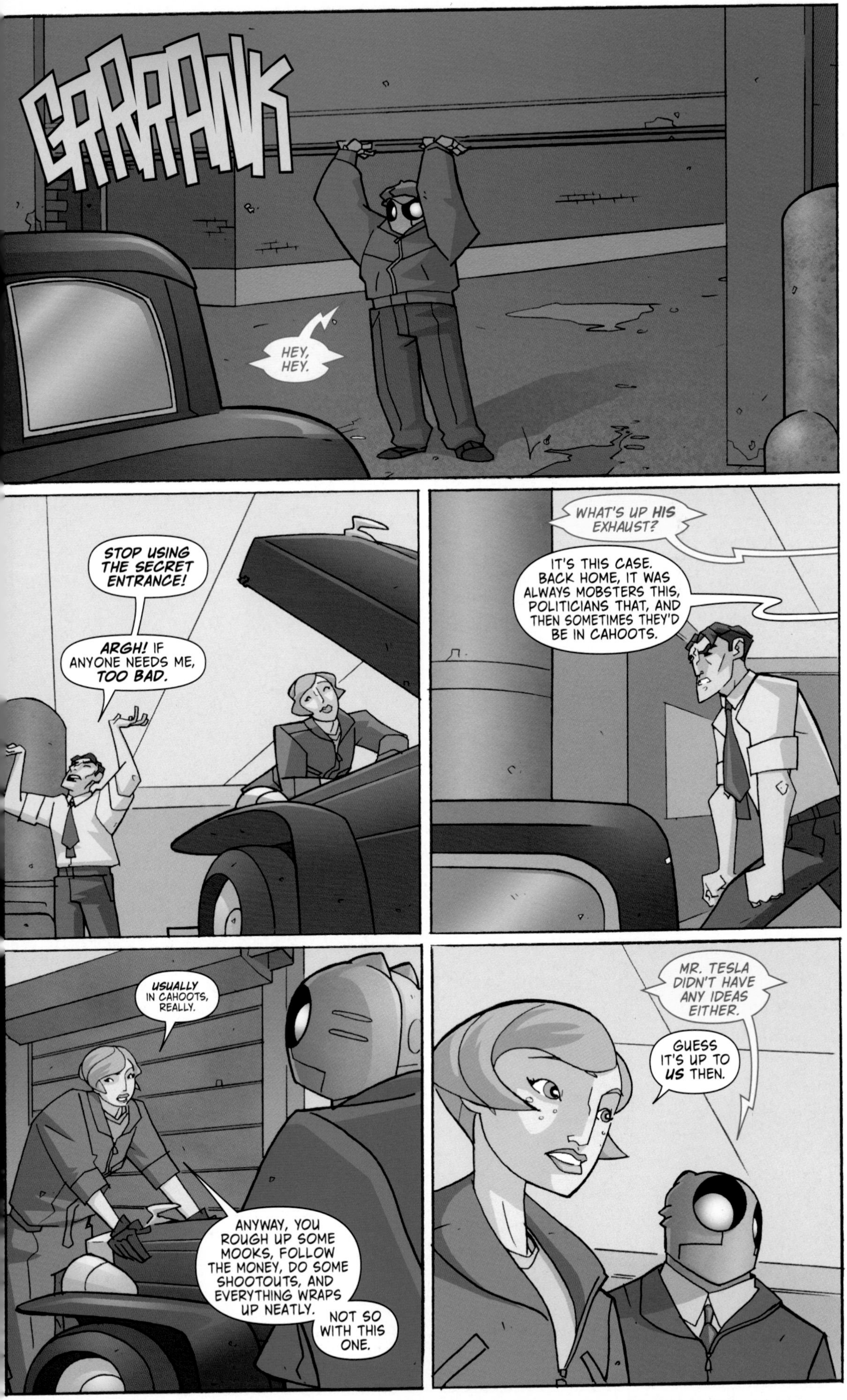
GRRRANK
HEY, HEY.
STOP USING THE SECRET ENTRANCE!
ARGH! IF ANYONE NEEDS ME, TOO BAD.
WHAT'S UP HIS EXHAUST?
IT'S THIS CASE. BACK HOME, IT WAS ALWAYS MOBSTERS THIS, POLITICIANS THAT, AND THEN SOMETIMES THEY'D BE IN CAHOOTS.
USUALLY IN CAHOOTS, REALLY.
ANYWAY, YOU ROUGH UP SOME MOOKS, FOLLOW THE MONEY, DO SOME SHOOTOUTS, AND EVERYTHING WRAPS UP NEATLY.
NOT SO WITH THIS ONE.
MR. TESLA DIDN'T HAVE ANY IDEAS EITHER.
GUESS IT'S UP TO US THEN.

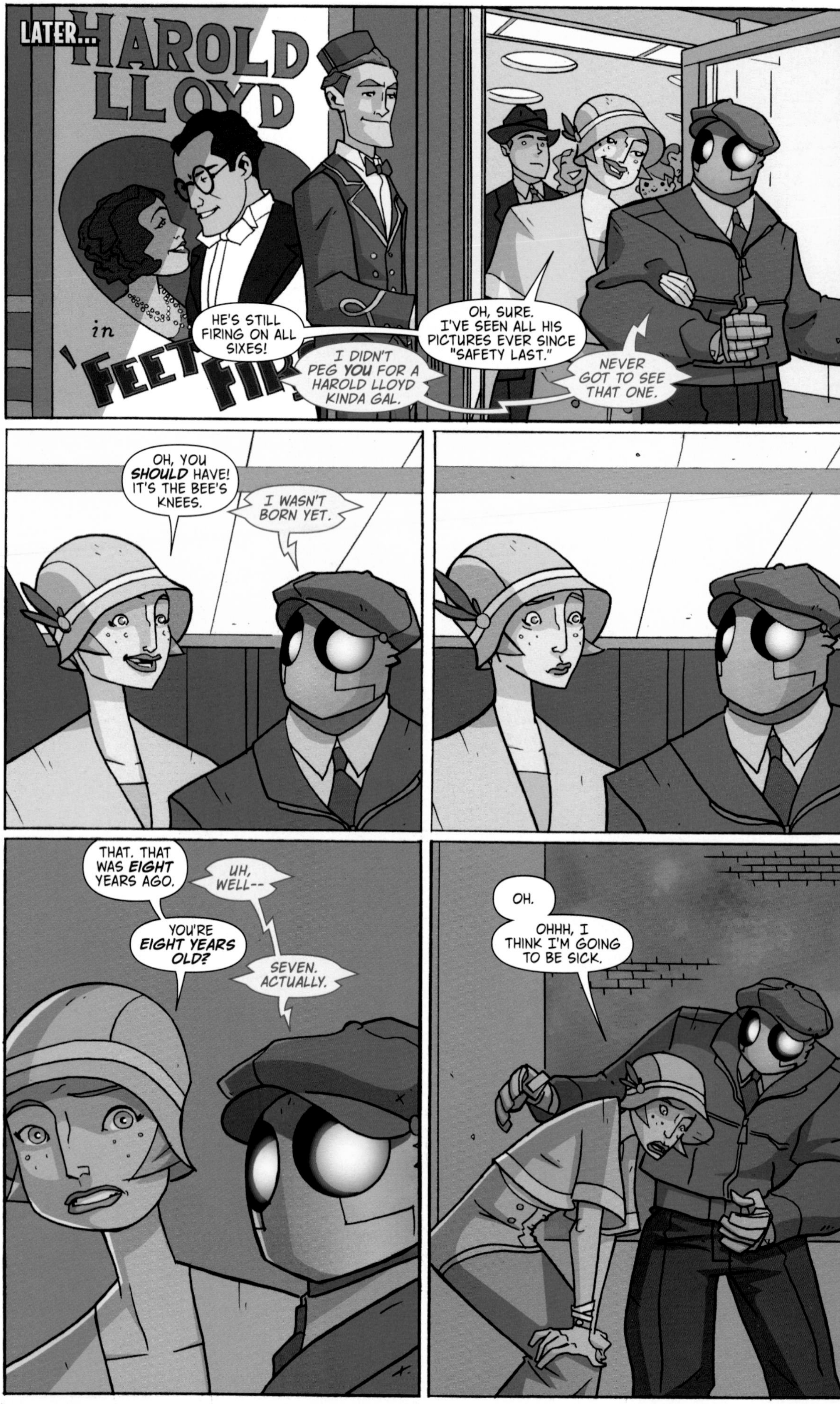
LATER...
HAROLD LLOYD
in
'FEET FIR
HE'S STILL FIRING ON ALL SIXES!
OH, SURE. I'VE SEEN ALL HIS PICTURES EVER SINCE "SAFETY LAST."
I DIDN'T PEG YOU FOR A HAROLD LLOYD KINDA GAL.
NEVER GOT TO SEE THAT ONE.
OH, YOU SHOULD HAVE! IT'S THE BEE'S KNEES.
I WASN'T BORN YET.
THAT. THAT WAS EIGHT YEARS AGO.
UH, WELL--
YOU'RE EIGHT YEARS OLD?
SEVEN. ACTUALLY.
OH.
OHHH, I THINK I'M GOING TO BE SICK.

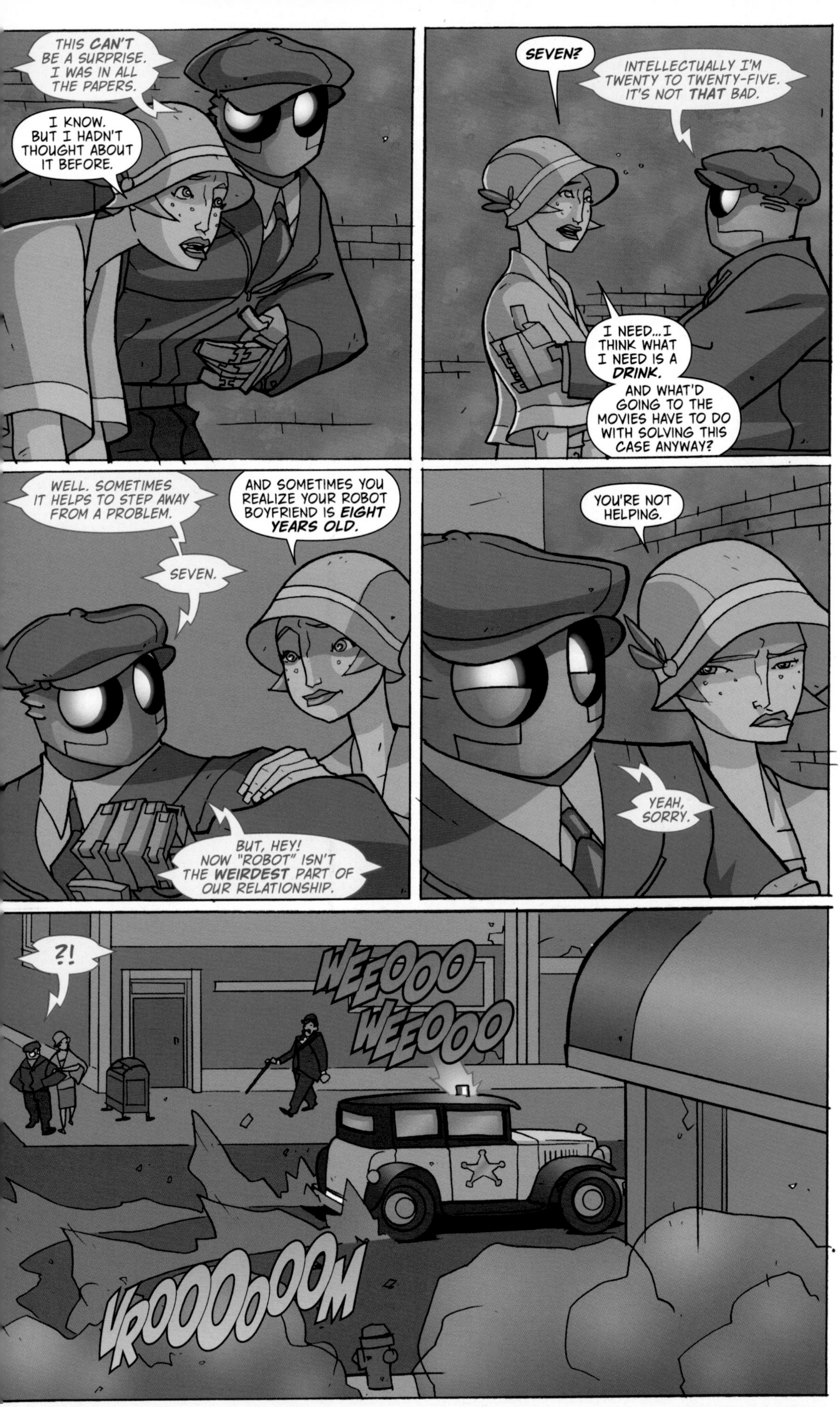
THIS CAN'T BE A SURPRISE. I WAS IN ALL THE PAPERS.
I KNOW. BUT I HADN'T THOUGHT ABOUT IT BEFORE.
SEVEN?
INTELLECTUALLY I'M TWENTY TO TWENTY-FIVE. IT'S NOT THAT BAD.
I NEED... I THINK WHAT I NEED IS A DRINK.
AND WHAT'D GOING TO THE MOVIES HAVE TO DO WITH SOLVING THIS CASE ANYWAY?
WELL. SOMETIMES IT HELPS TO STEP AWAY FROM A PROBLEM.
AND SOMETIMES YOU REALIZE YOUR ROBOT BOYFRIEND IS EIGHT YEARS OLD.
SEVEN.
BUT, HEY! NOW "ROBOT" ISN'T THE WEIRDEST PART OF OUR RELATIONSHIP.
YOU'RE NOT HELPING.
YEAH, SORRY.
?!
WEEOOO WEEOOO
VROOOOOOOM

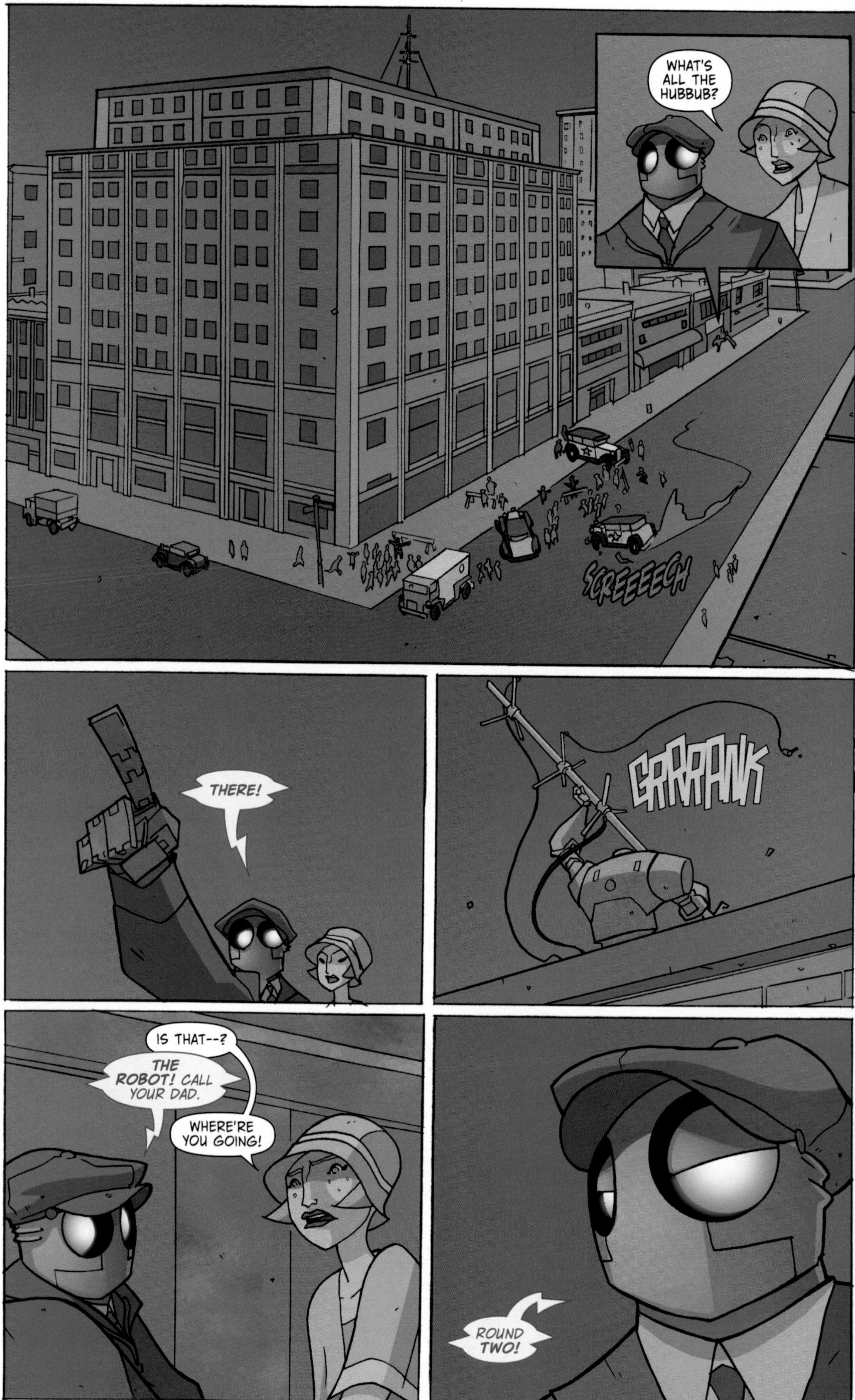
WHAT'S ALL THE HUBBUB?
SCREEEEECH
THERE!
GRRRANK
IS THAT--?
THE ROBOT! CALL YOUR DAD.
WHERE'RE YOU GOING!
ROUND TWO!

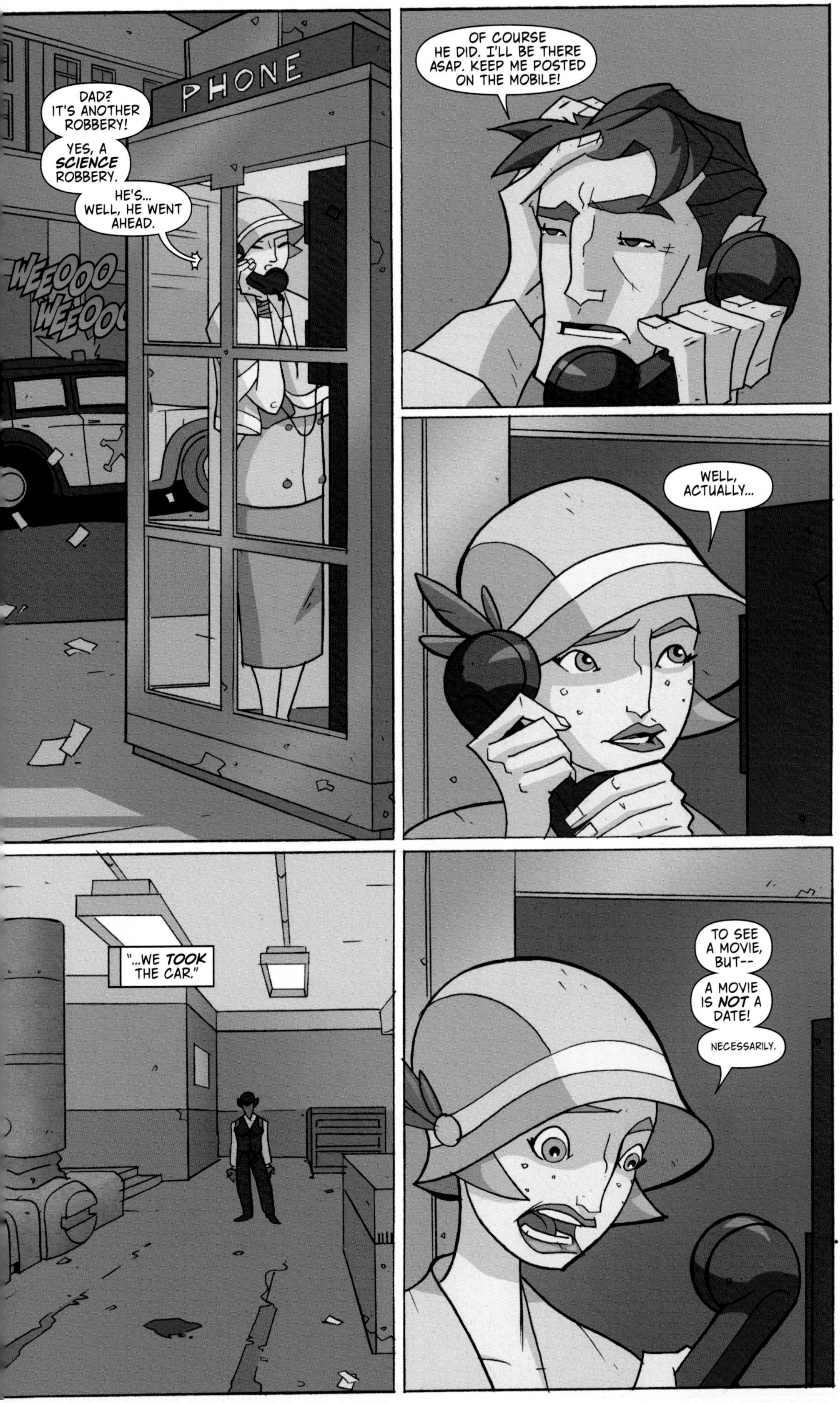
PHONE
DAD? IT'S ANOTHER ROBBERY!
YES, A **SCIENCE** ROBBERY.
HE'S... WELL, HE WENT AHEAD.
WEEOOO WEEOOO
OF COURSE HE DID. I'LL BE THERE ASAP. KEEP ME POSTED ON THE MOBILE!
WELL, ACTUALLY...
"...WE **TOOK** THE CAR."
TO SEE A MOVIE, BUT--
A MOVIE IS **NOT** A DATE!
NECESSARILY.

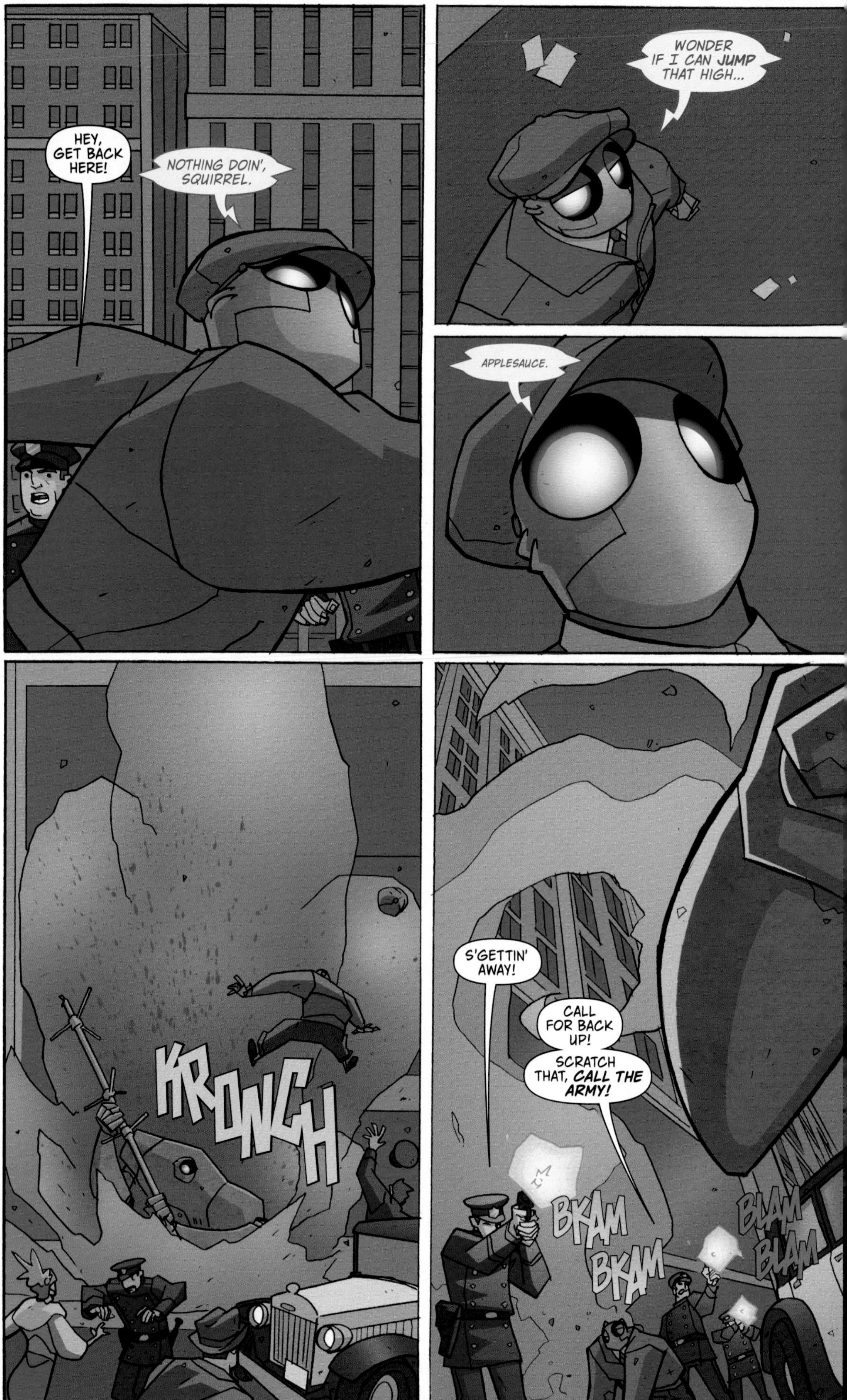
HEY, GET BACK HERE!
NOTHING DOIN', SQUIRREL.
WONDER IF I CAN JUMP THAT HIGH...
APPLESAUCE.
KRONCH
S'GETTIN' AWAY!
CALL FOR BACK UP!
SCRATCH THAT, CALL THE ARMY!
BKAM
BKAM
BLAM
BLAM

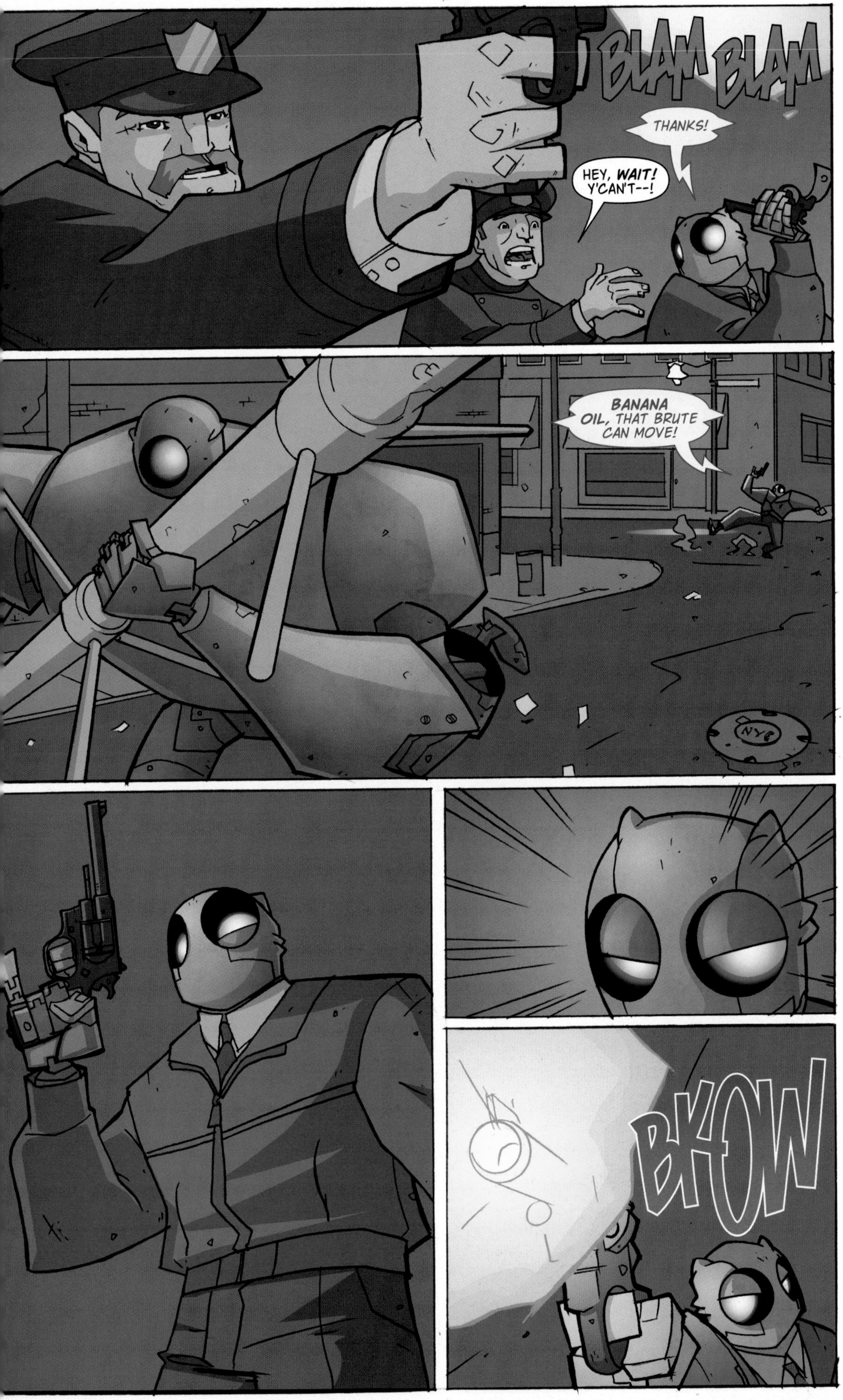
BLAM BLAM
THANKS!
HEY, WAIT! Y'CAN'T--!
BANANA OIL, THAT BRUTE CAN MOVE!
BKOW

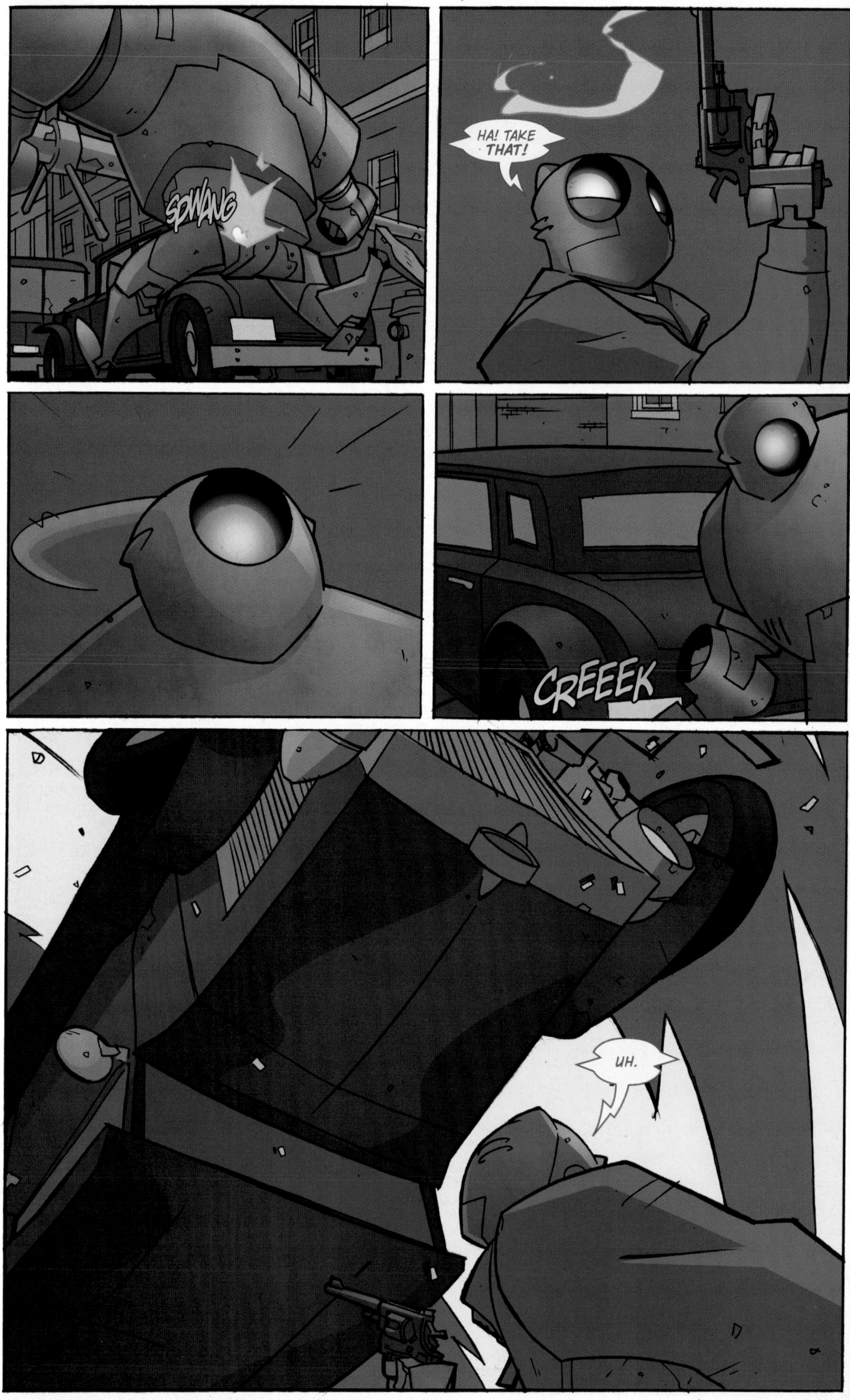
SPWANG
HA! TAKE THAT!
CREEEK
UH.

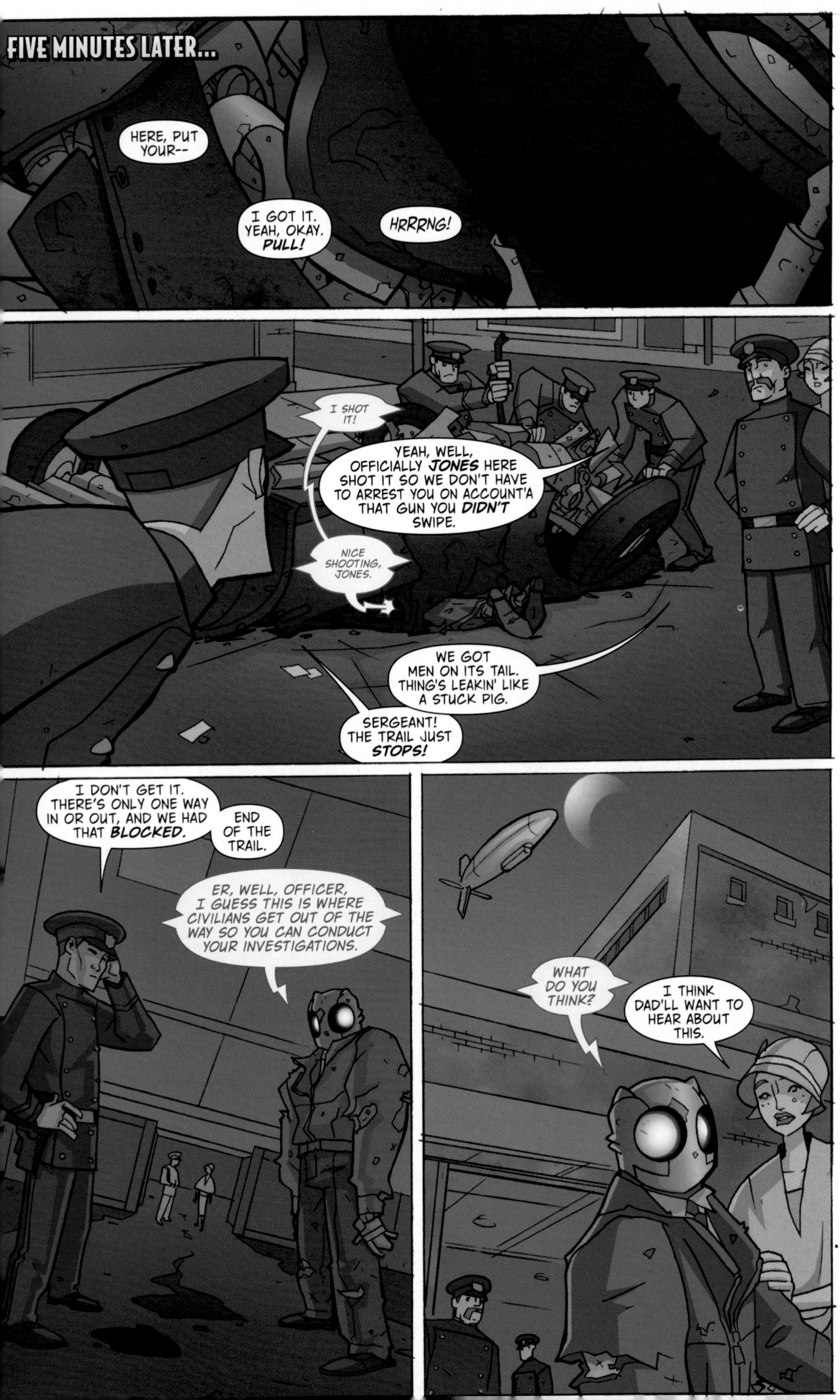
FIVE MINUTES LATER...
HERE, PUT YOUR--
I GOT IT. YEAH, OKAY. PULL!
HRRRNG!
I SHOT IT!
YEAH, WELL, OFFICIALLY JONES HERE SHOT IT SO WE DON'T HAVE TO ARREST YOU ON ACCOUNT'A THAT GUN YOU DIDN'T SWIPE.
NICE SHOOTING, JONES.
WE GOT MEN ON ITS TAIL. THING'S LEAKIN' LIKE A STUCK PIG.
SERGEANT! THE TRAIL JUST STOPS!
I DON'T GET IT. THERE'S ONLY ONE WAY IN OR OUT, AND WE HAD THAT BLOCKED.
END OF THE TRAIL.
ER, WELL, OFFICER, I GUESS THIS IS WHERE CIVILIANS GET OUT OF THE WAY SO YOU CAN CONDUCT YOUR INVESTIGATIONS.
WHAT DO YOU THINK?
I THINK DAD'LL WANT TO HEAR ABOUT THIS.

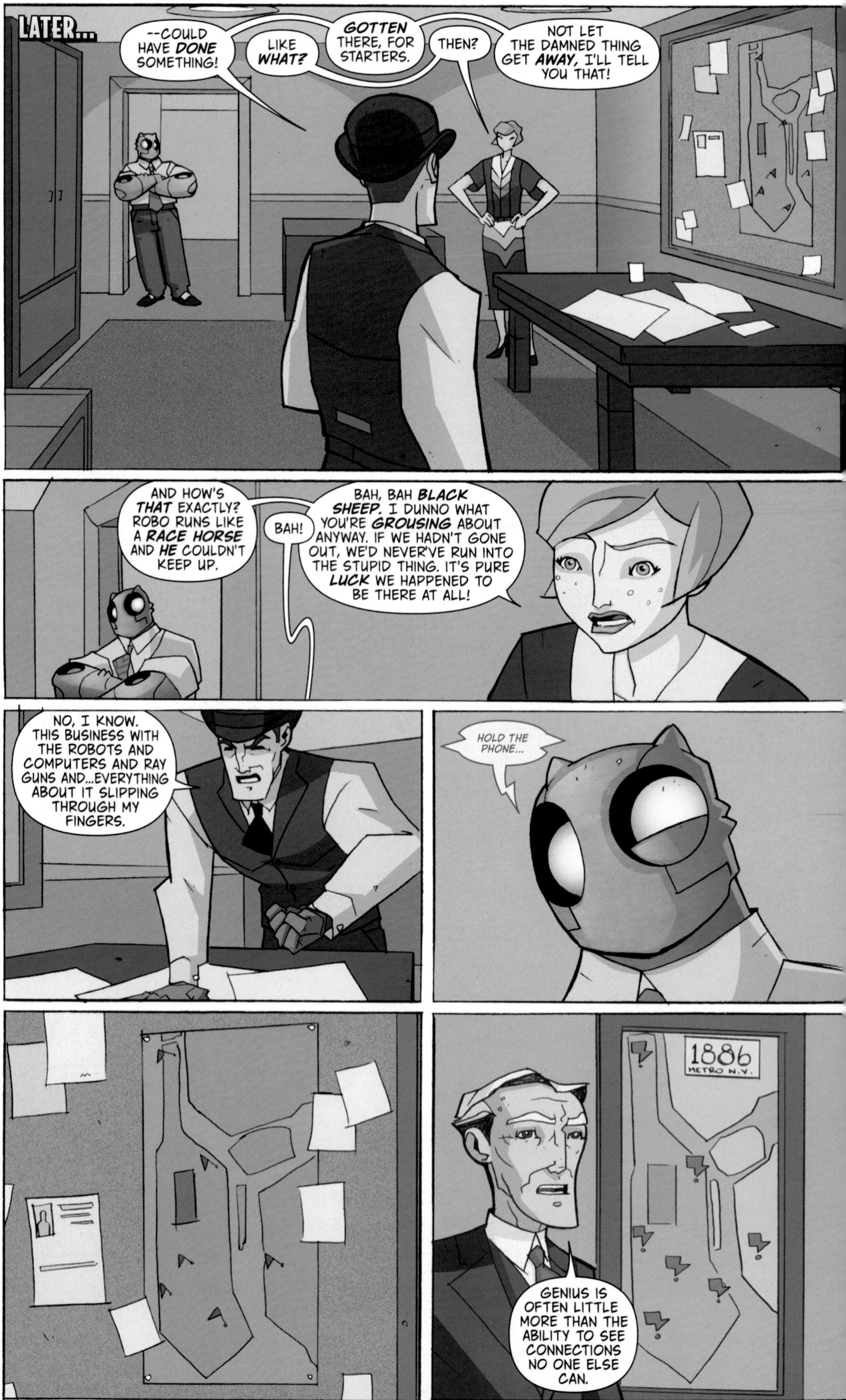
LATER...
--COULD HAVE DONE SOMETHING!
LIKE WHAT?
GOTTEN THERE, FOR STARTERS.
THEN?
NOT LET THE DAMNED THING GET AWAY, I'LL TELL YOU THAT!
AND HOW'S THAT EXACTLY? ROBO RUNS LIKE A RACE HORSE AND HE COULDN'T KEEP UP.
BAH!
BAH, BAH BLACK SHEEP. I DUNNO WHAT YOU'RE GROUSING ABOUT ANYWAY. IF WE HADN'T GONE OUT, WE'D NEVER'VE RUN INTO THE STUPID THING. IT'S PURE LUCK WE HAPPENED TO BE THERE AT ALL!
NO, I KNOW. THIS BUSINESS WITH THE ROBOTS AND COMPUTERS AND RAY GUNS AND...EVERYTHING ABOUT IT SLIPPING THROUGH MY FINGERS.
HOLD THE PHONE...
1886
METRO N.Y.
GENIUS IS OFTEN LITTLE MORE THAN THE ABILITY TO SEE CONNECTIONS NO ONE ELSE CAN.

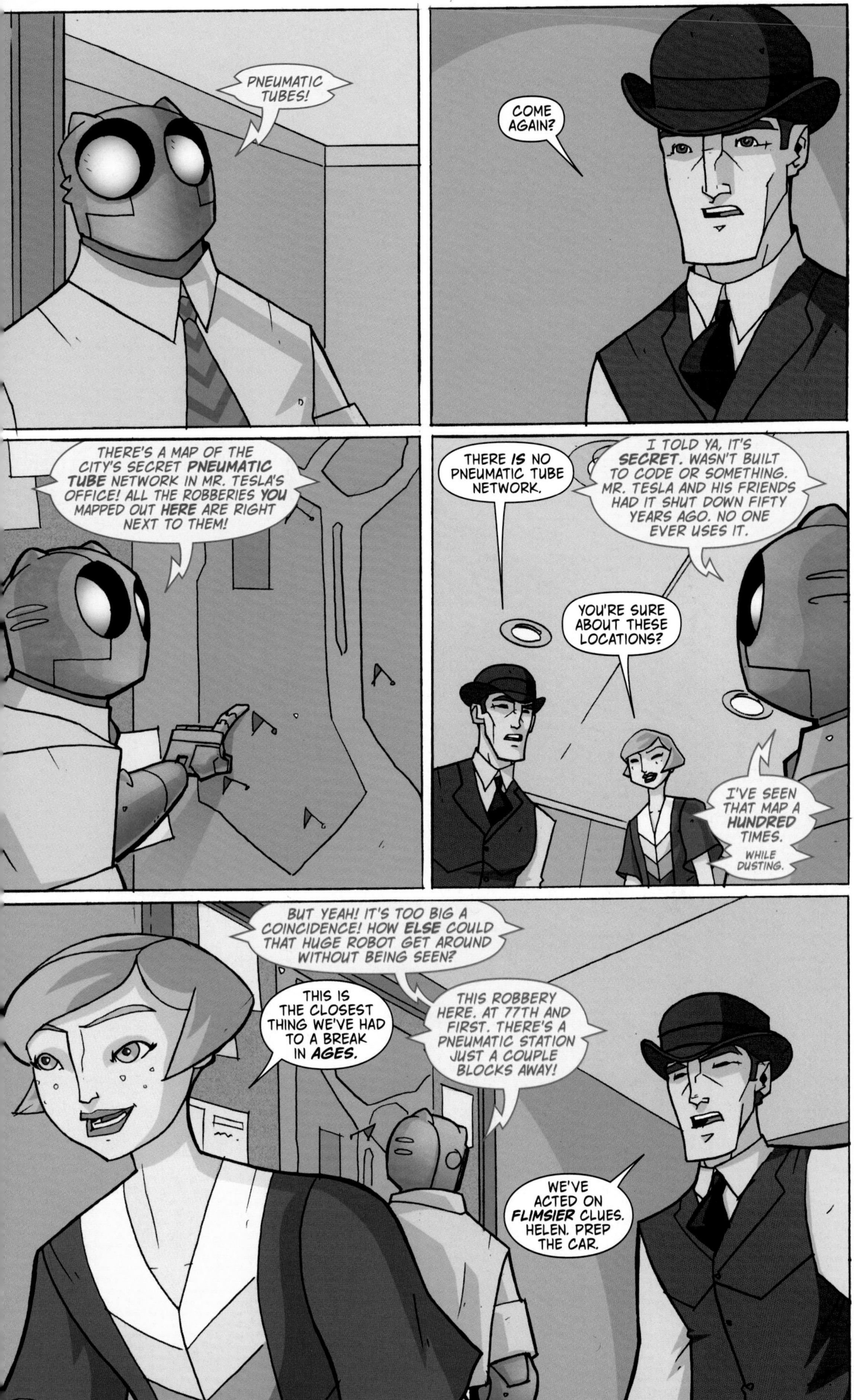
PNEUMATIC TUBES!
COME AGAIN?
THERE'S A MAP OF THE CITY'S SECRET PNEUMATIC TUBE NETWORK IN MR. TESLA'S OFFICE! ALL THE ROBBERIES YOU MAPPED OUT HERE ARE RIGHT NEXT TO THEM!
THERE IS NO PNEUMATIC TUBE NETWORK.
I TOLD YA, IT'S SECRET. WASN'T BUILT TO CODE OR SOMETHING. MR. TESLA AND HIS FRIENDS HAD IT SHUT DOWN FIFTY YEARS AGO. NO ONE EVER USES IT.
YOU'RE SURE ABOUT THESE LOCATIONS?
I'VE SEEN THAT MAP A HUNDRED TIMES.
WHILE DUSTING.
BUT YEAH! IT'S TOO BIG A COINCIDENCE! HOW ELSE COULD THAT HUGE ROBOT GET AROUND WITHOUT BEING SEEN?
THIS IS THE CLOSEST THING WE'VE HAD TO A BREAK IN AGES.
THIS ROBBERY HERE. AT 77TH AND FIRST. THERE'S A PNEUMATIC STATION JUST A COUPLE BLOCKS AWAY!
WE'VE ACTED ON FLIMSIER CLUES. HELEN. PREP THE CAR.

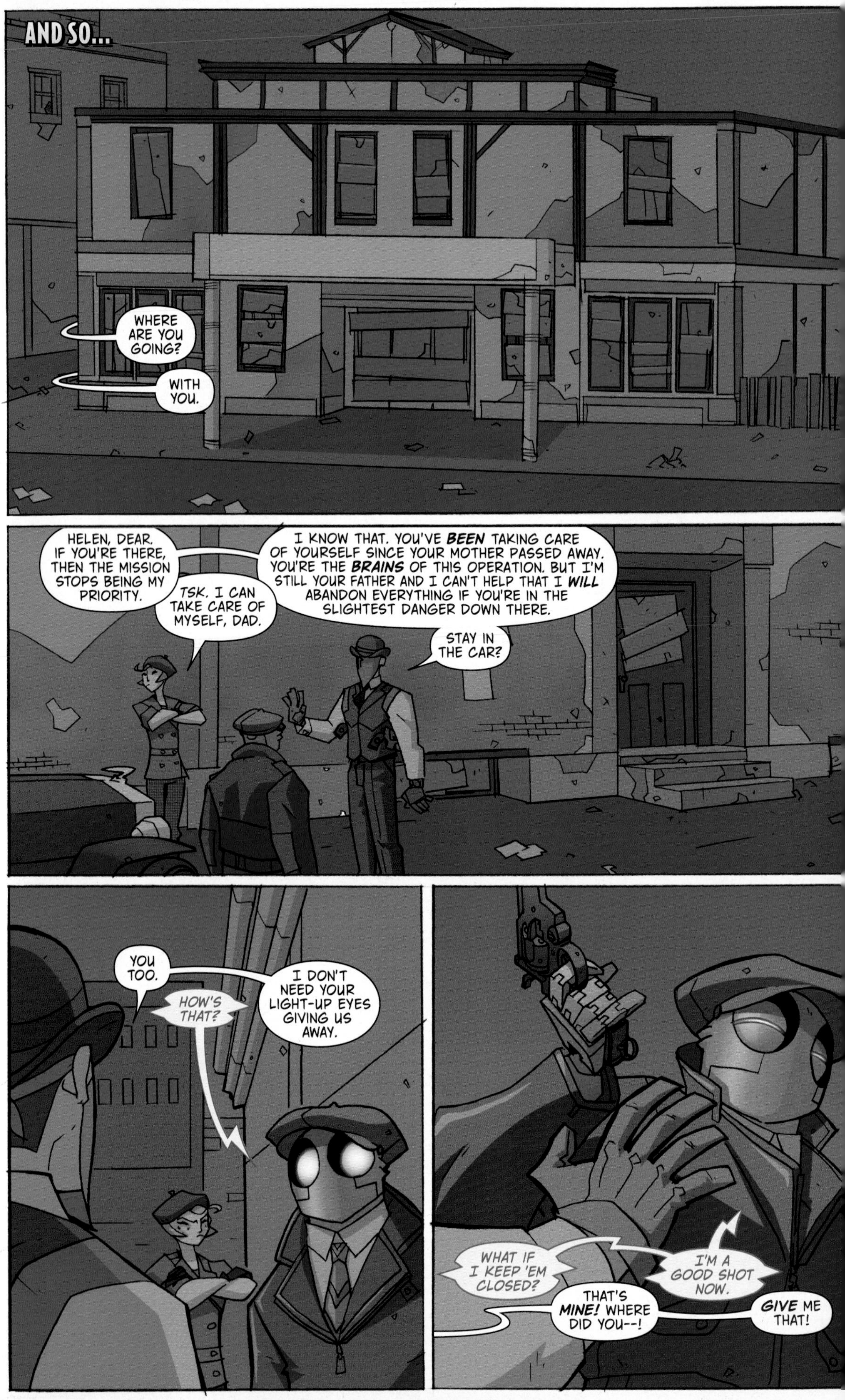
AND SO...
WHERE ARE YOU GOING?
WITH YOU.
HELEN, DEAR. IF YOU'RE THERE, THEN THE MISSION STOPS BEING MY PRIORITY.
TSK. I CAN TAKE CARE OF MYSELF, DAD.
I KNOW THAT. YOU'VE **BEEN** TAKING CARE OF YOURSELF SINCE YOUR MOTHER PASSED AWAY. YOU'RE THE **BRAINS** OF THIS OPERATION. BUT I'M STILL YOUR FATHER AND I CAN'T HELP THAT I ***WILL*** ABANDON EVERYTHING IF YOU'RE IN THE SLIGHTEST DANGER DOWN THERE.
STAY IN THE CAR?
YOU TOO.
I DON'T NEED YOUR LIGHT-UP EYES GIVING US AWAY.
HOW'S THAT?
WHAT IF I KEEP 'EM CLOSED?
I'M A GOOD SHOT NOW.
THAT'S ***MINE!*** WHERE DID YOU--!
GIVE ME THAT!

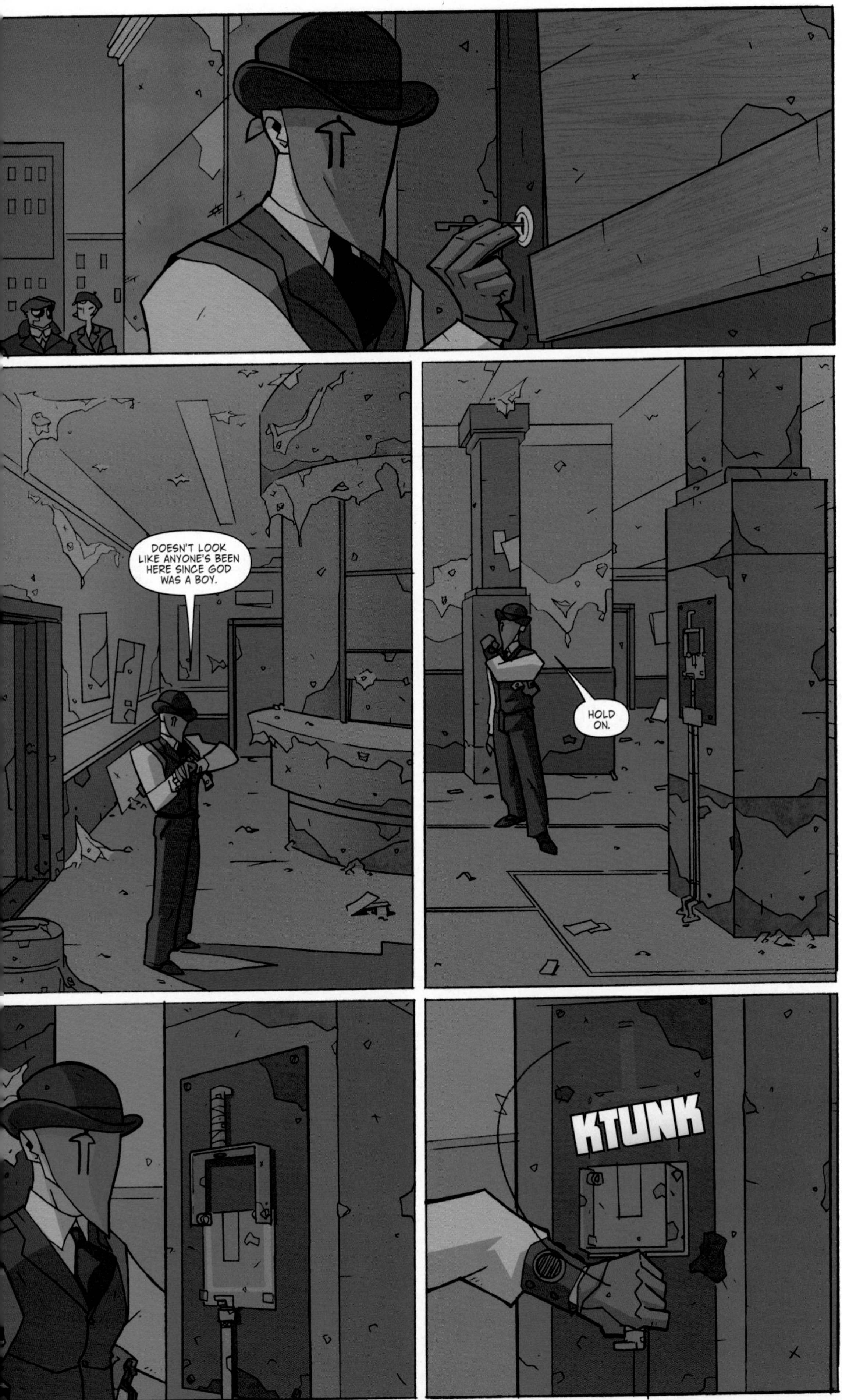
DOESN'T LOOK LIKE ANYONE'S BEEN HERE SINCE GOD WAS A BOY.
HOLD ON.
KTUNK

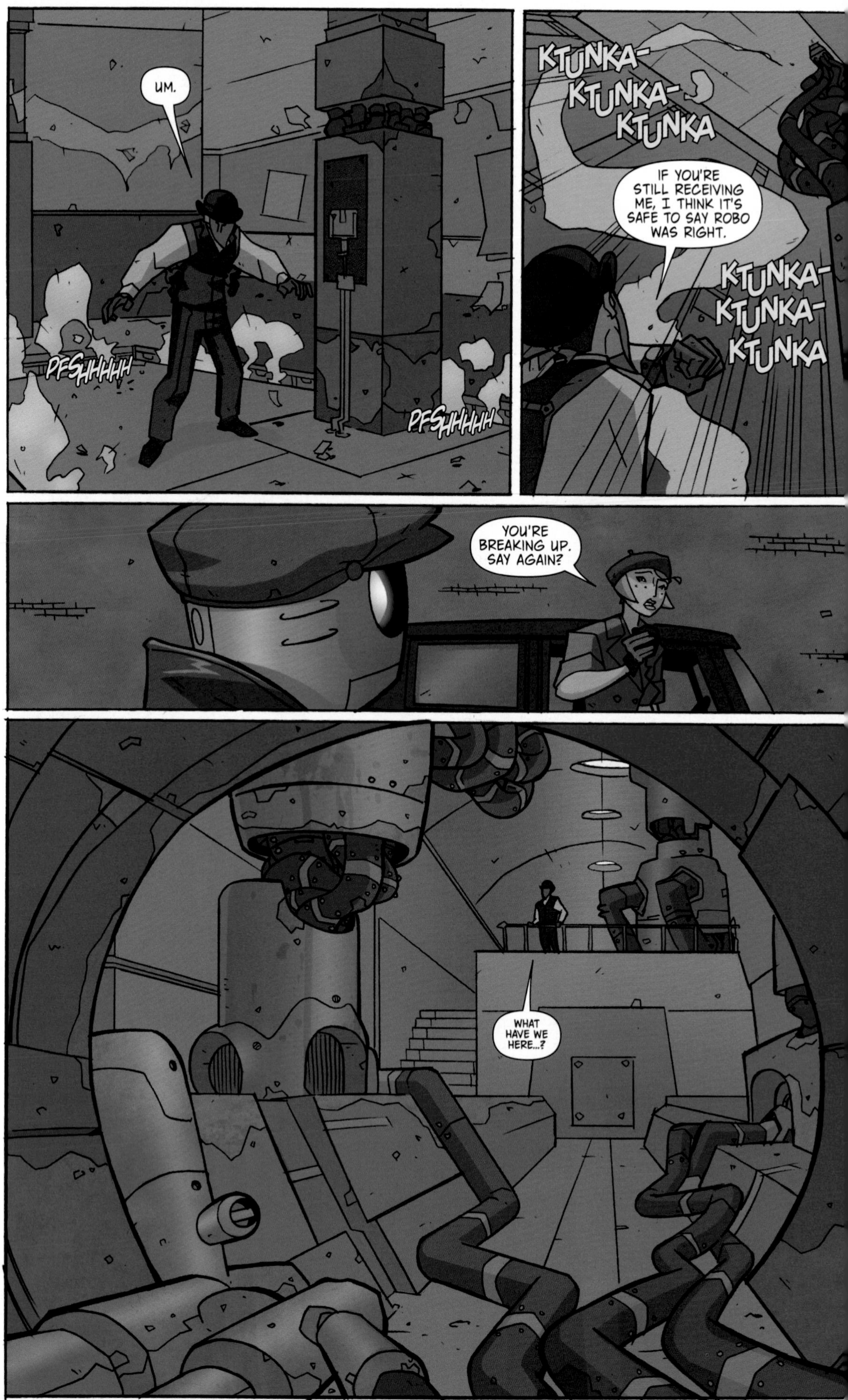
UM.
PFSHHHHH
PFSHHHHH
KTUNKA-KTUNKA-KTUNKA
IF YOU'RE STILL RECEIVING ME, I THINK IT'S SAFE TO SAY ROBO WAS RIGHT.
KTUNKA-KTUNKA-KTUNKA
YOU'RE BREAKING UP. SAY AGAIN?
WHAT HAVE WE HERE...?

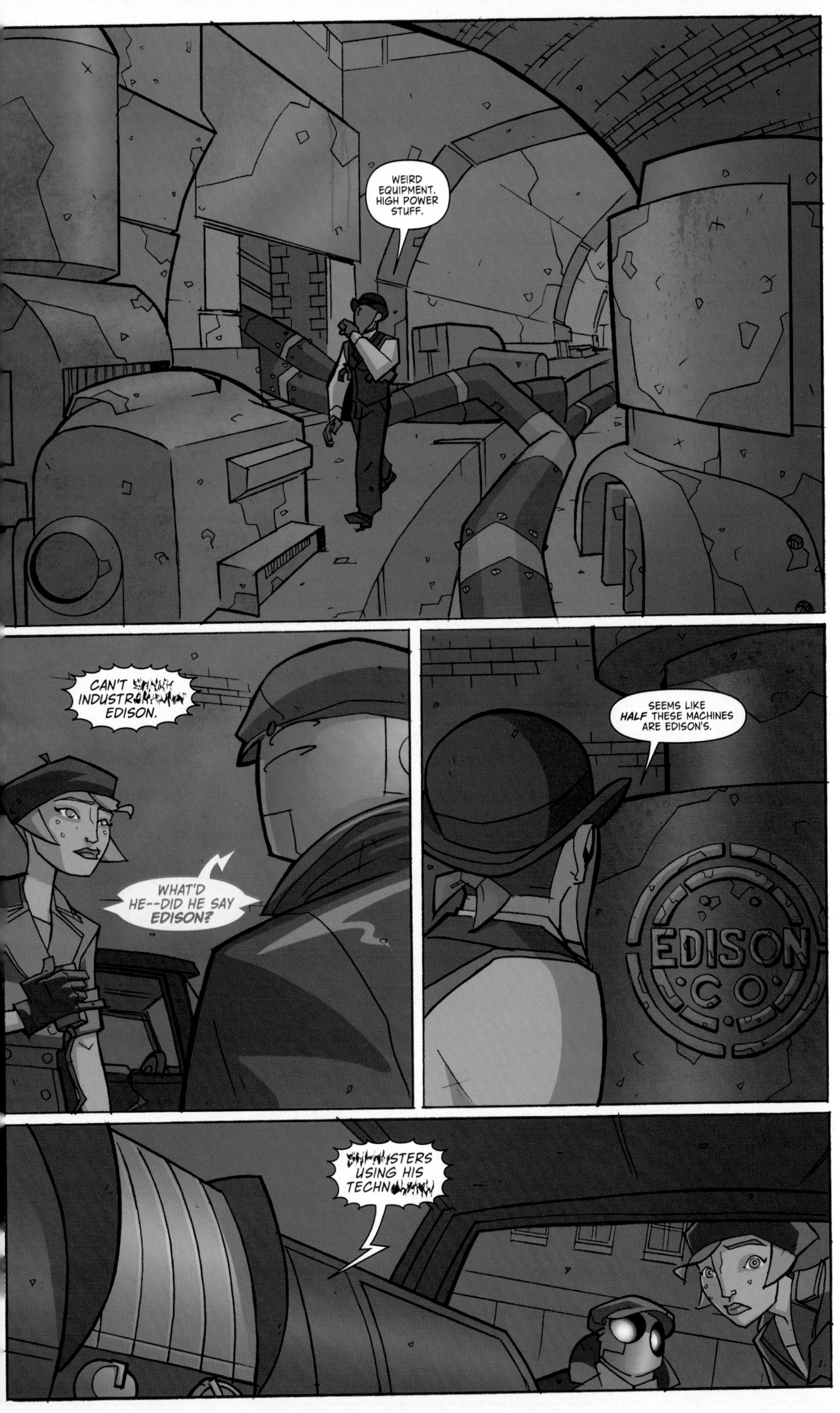
WEIRD EQUIPMENT. HIGH POWER STUFF.
CAN'T INDUSTR EDISON.
WHAT'D HE--DID HE SAY EDISON?
SEEMS LIKE HALF THESE MACHINES ARE EDISON'S.
EDISON C.O
STERS USING HIS TECHN

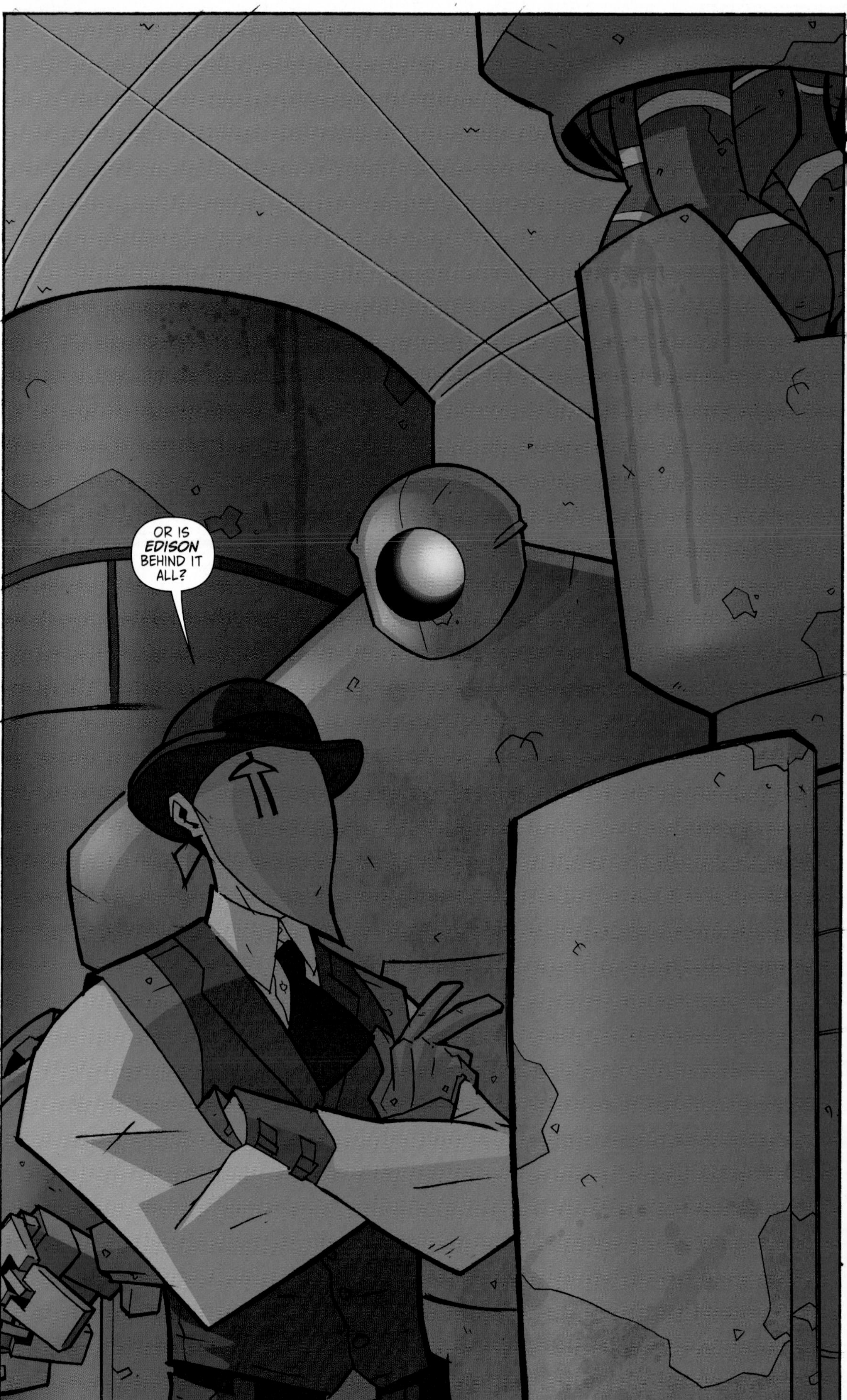
OR IS EDISON BEHIND IT ALL?

THE WAR OF THE CURRENTS

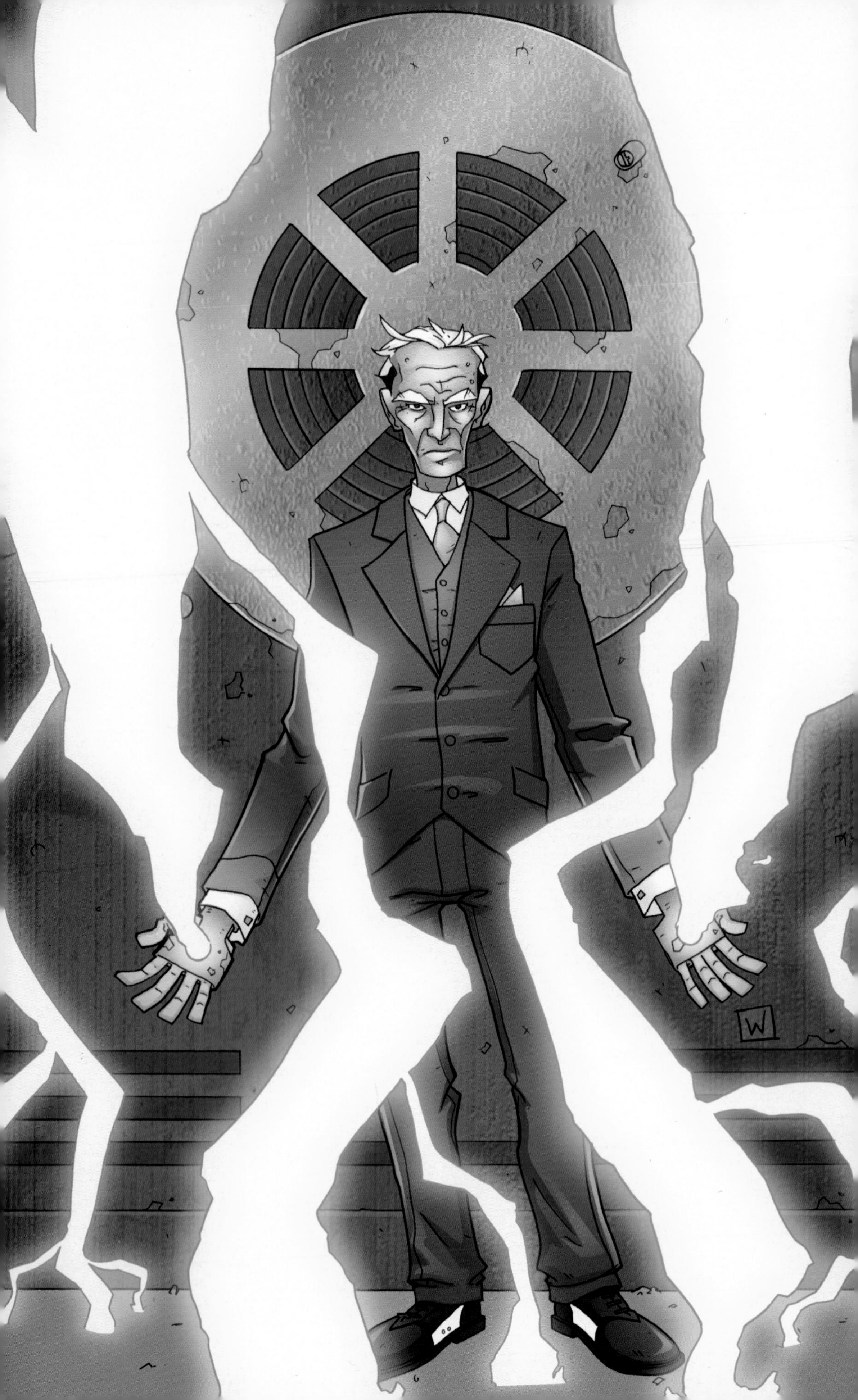

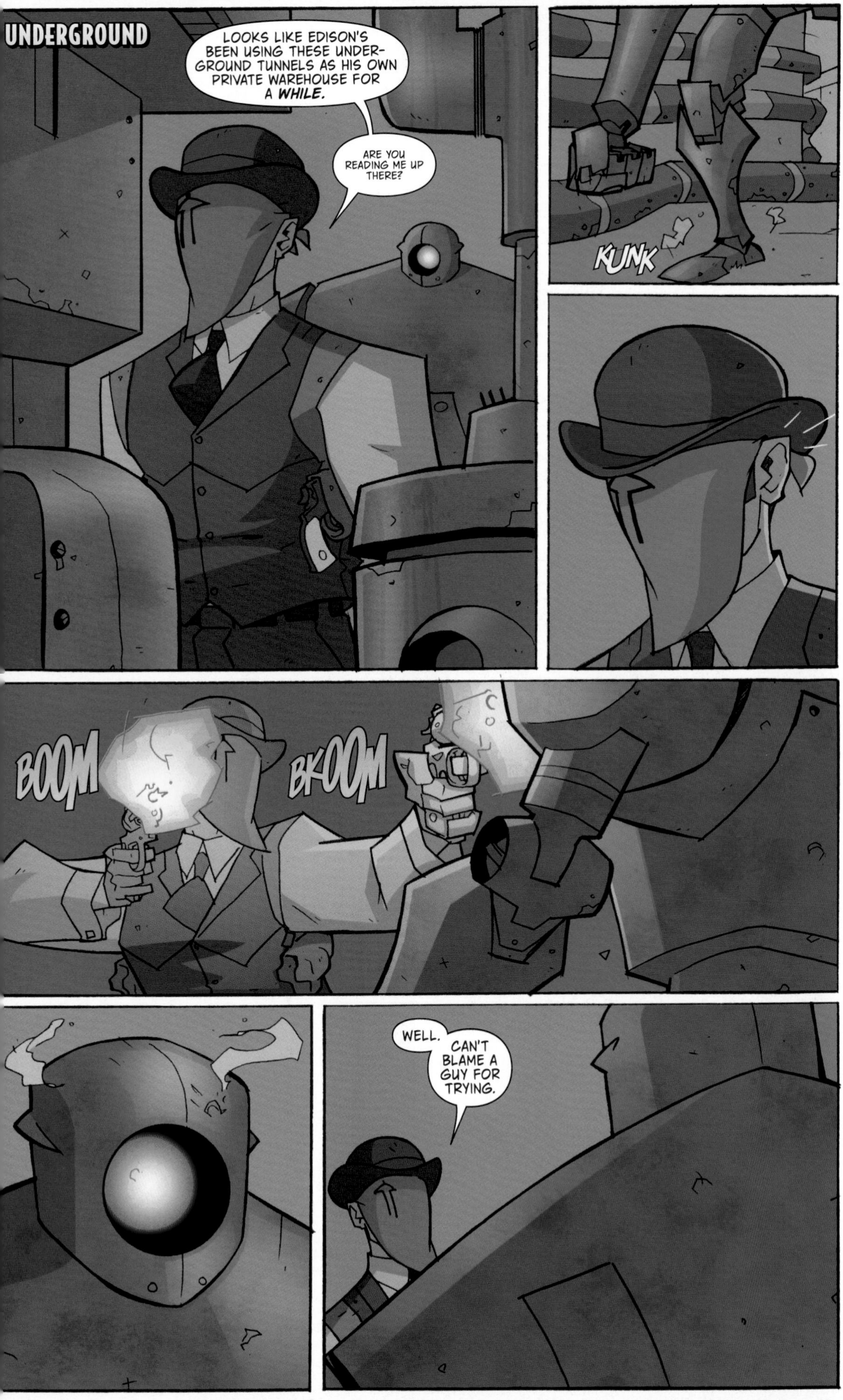
UNDERGROUND
LOOKS LIKE EDISON'S BEEN USING THESE UNDERGROUND TUNNELS AS HIS OWN PRIVATE WAREHOUSE FOR A *WHILE.*
ARE YOU READING ME UP THERE?
KUNK
BOOM
BKOOM
WELL.
CAN'T BLAME A GUY FOR TRYING.

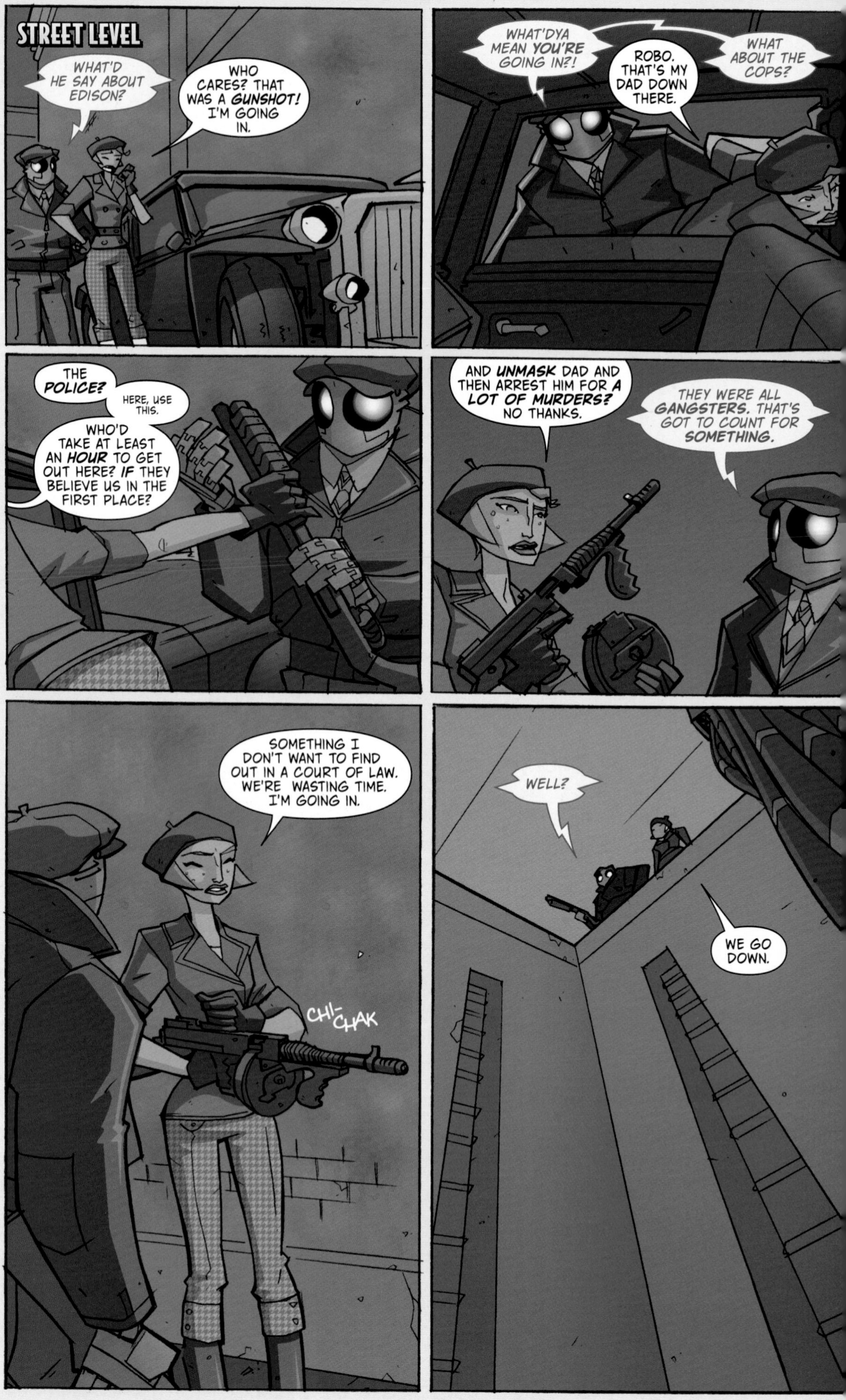
STREET LEVEL
WHAT'D HE SAY ABOUT EDISON?
WHO CARES? THAT WAS A GUNSHOT! I'M GOING IN.
WHAT'DYA MEAN YOU'RE GOING IN?!
ROBO. THAT'S MY DAD DOWN THERE.
WHAT ABOUT THE COPS?
THE POLICE?
HERE, USE THIS.
WHO'D TAKE AT LEAST AN HOUR TO GET OUT HERE? IF THEY BELIEVE US IN THE FIRST PLACE?
AND UNMASK DAD AND THEN ARREST HIM FOR A LOT OF MURDERS? NO THANKS.
THEY WERE ALL GANGSTERS. THAT'S GOT TO COUNT FOR SOMETHING.
SOMETHING I DON'T WANT TO FIND OUT IN A COURT OF LAW. WE'RE WASTING TIME. I'M GOING IN.
CHI-CHAK
WELL?
WE GO DOWN.

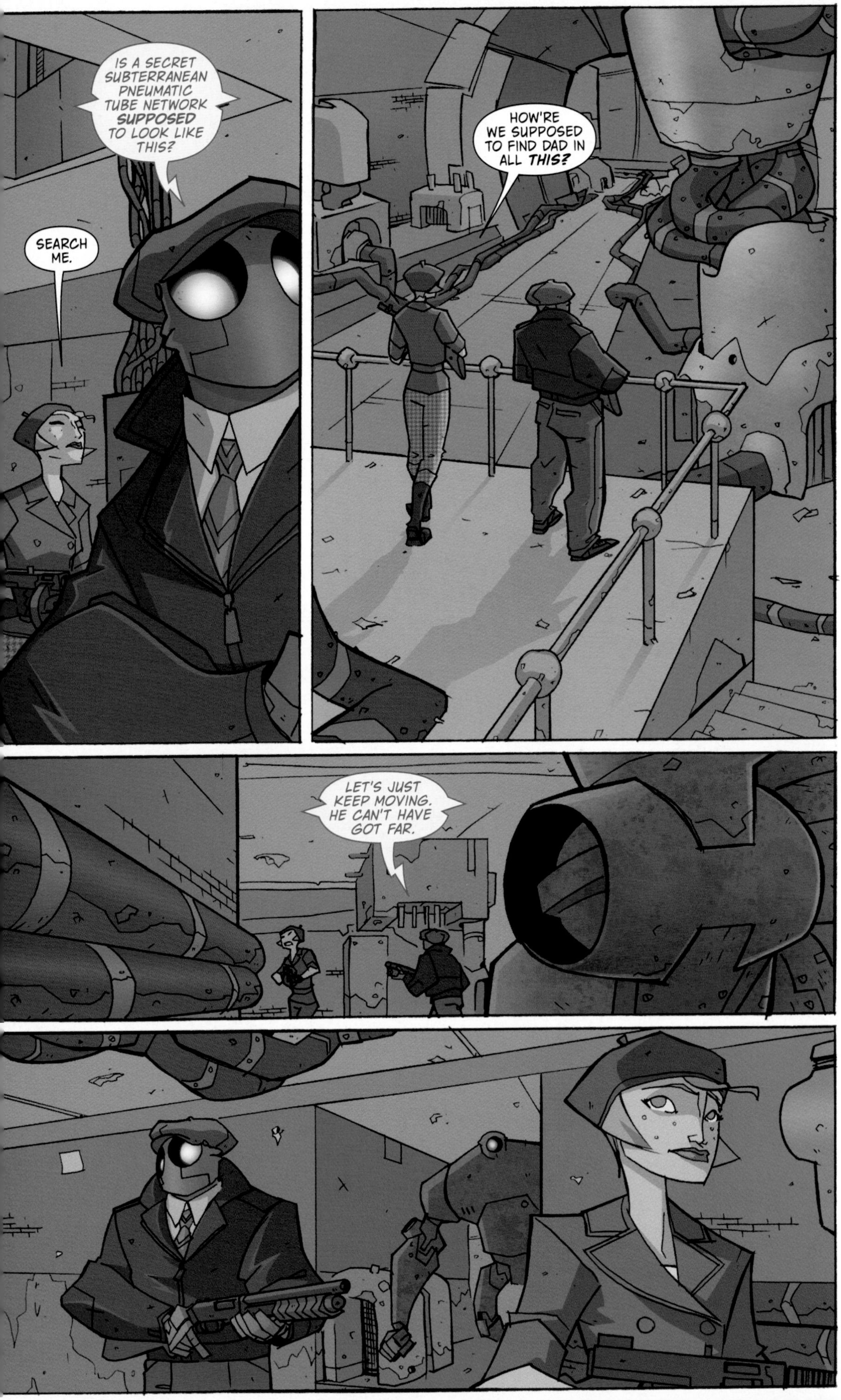
IS A SECRET SUBTERRANEAN PNEUMATIC TUBE NETWORK SUPPOSED TO LOOK LIKE THIS?
SEARCH ME.
HOW'RE WE SUPPOSED TO FIND DAD IN ALL THIS?
LET'S JUST KEEP MOVING. HE CAN'T HAVE GOT FAR.

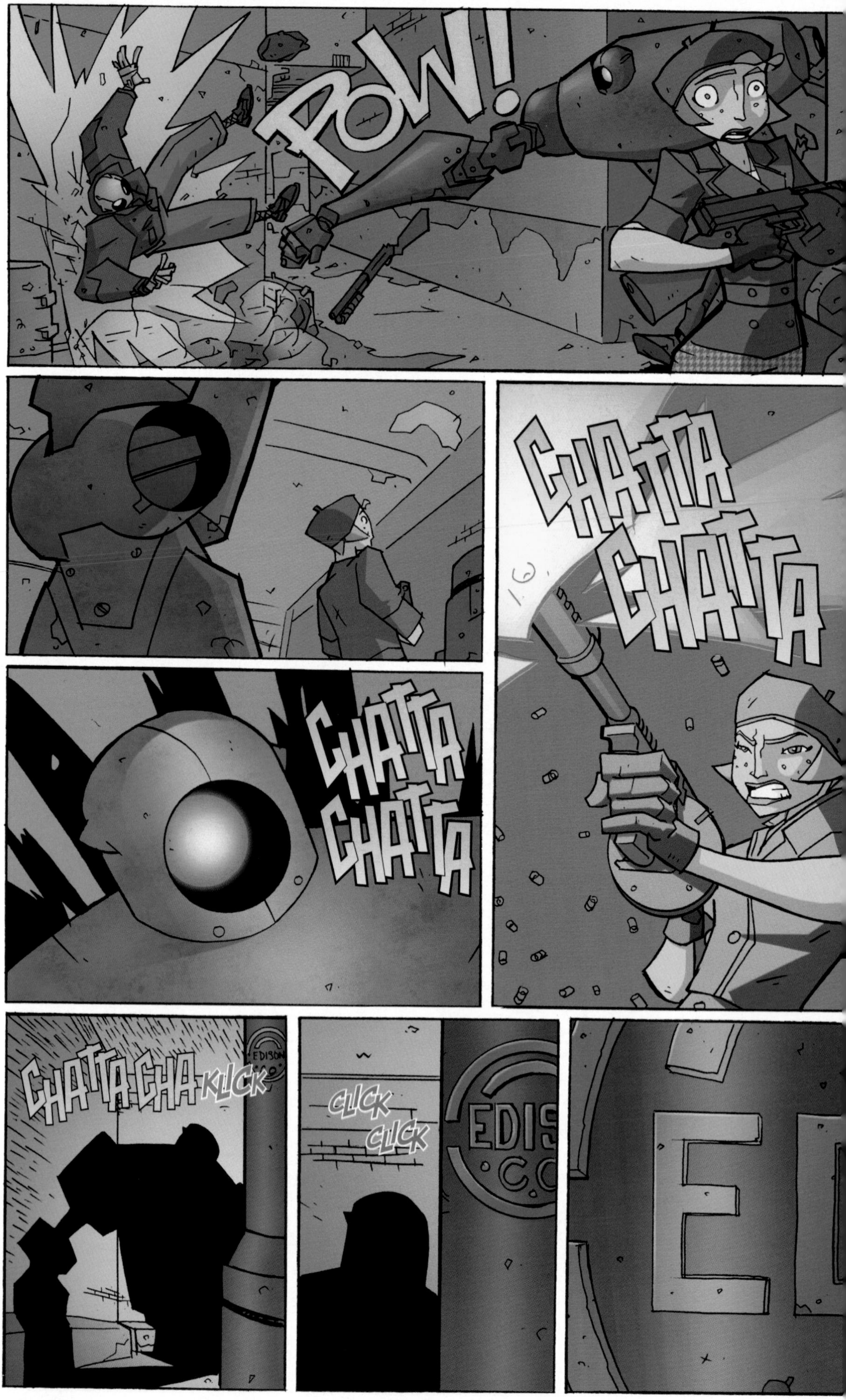
POW!
CHATTA
CHATTA
CHATTA
CHATTA
CHATTA CHA KLICK
EDISON
CLICK
CLICK
EDIS
C.O
E

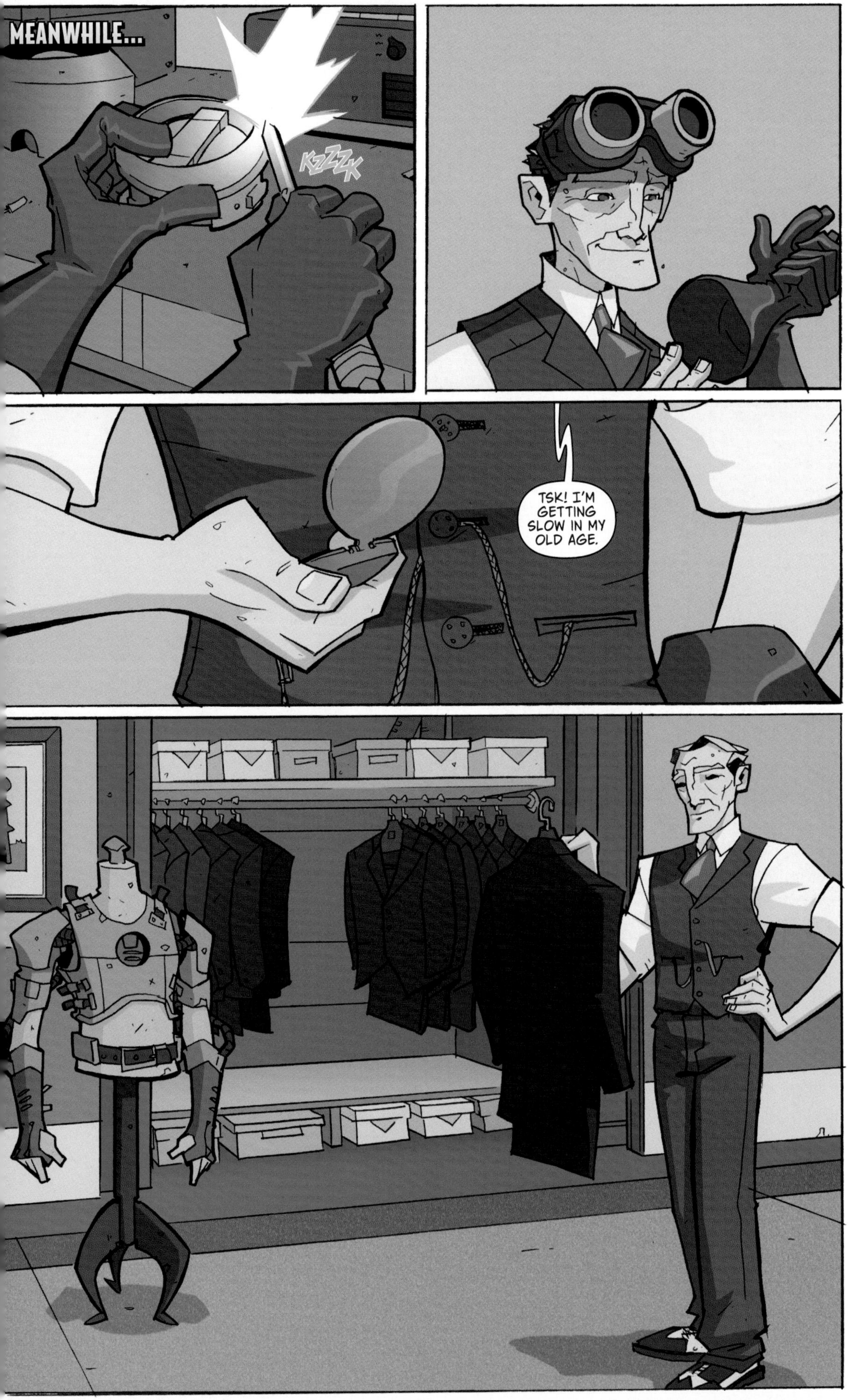
MEANWHILE...
KZZZK
TSK! I'M GETTING SLOW IN MY OLD AGE.

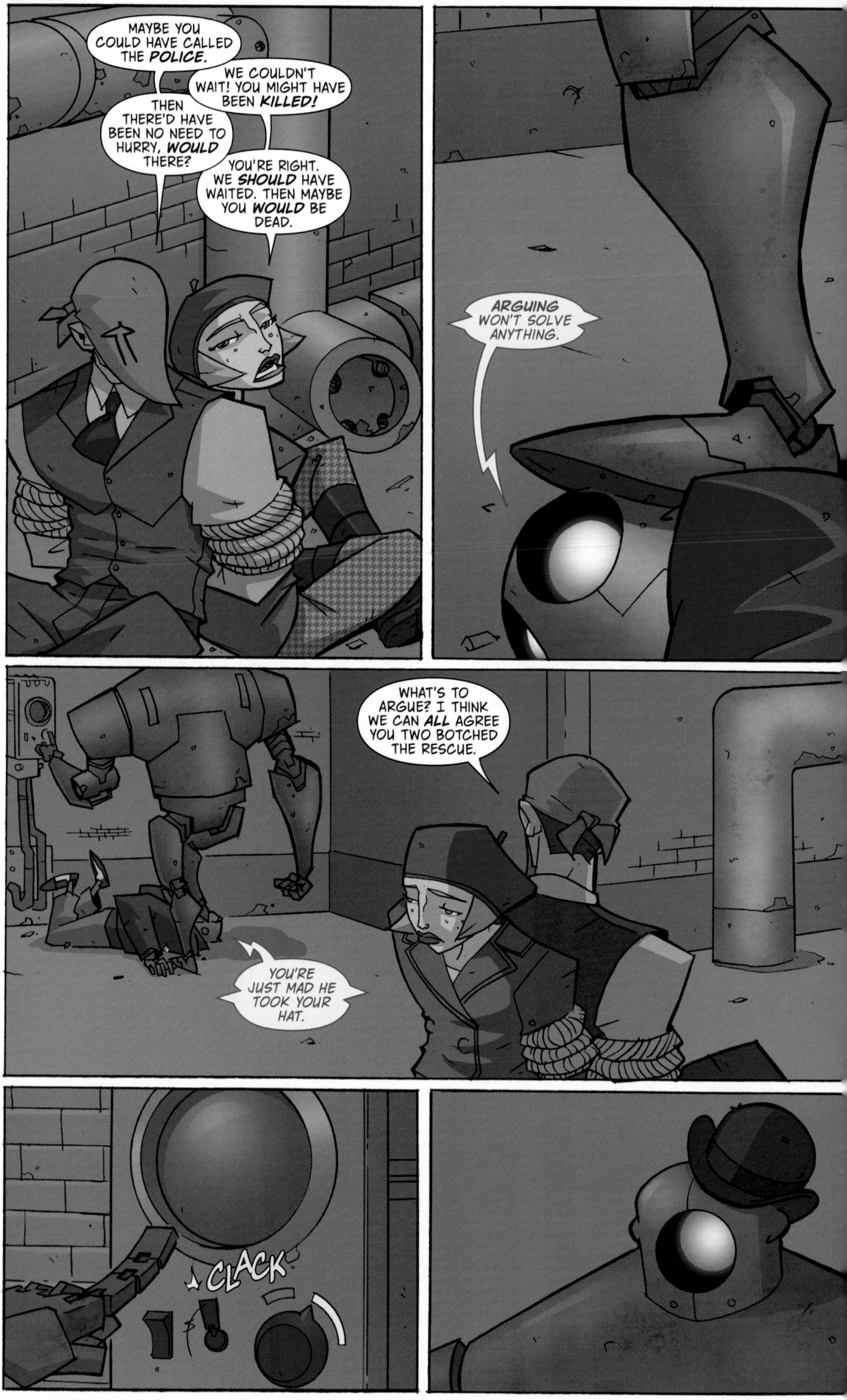
MAYBE YOU COULD HAVE CALLED THE ***POLICE.***
WE COULDN'T WAIT! YOU MIGHT HAVE BEEN ***KILLED!***
THEN THERE'D HAVE BEEN NO NEED TO HURRY, ***WOULD*** THERE?
YOU'RE RIGHT. WE ***SHOULD*** HAVE WAITED. THEN MAYBE YOU ***WOULD*** BE DEAD.
ARGUING *WON'T SOLVE ANYTHING.*
WHAT'S TO ARGUE? I THINK WE CAN ***ALL*** AGREE YOU TWO BOTCHED THE RESCUE.
YOU'RE JUST MAD HE TOOK YOUR HAT.
CLACK

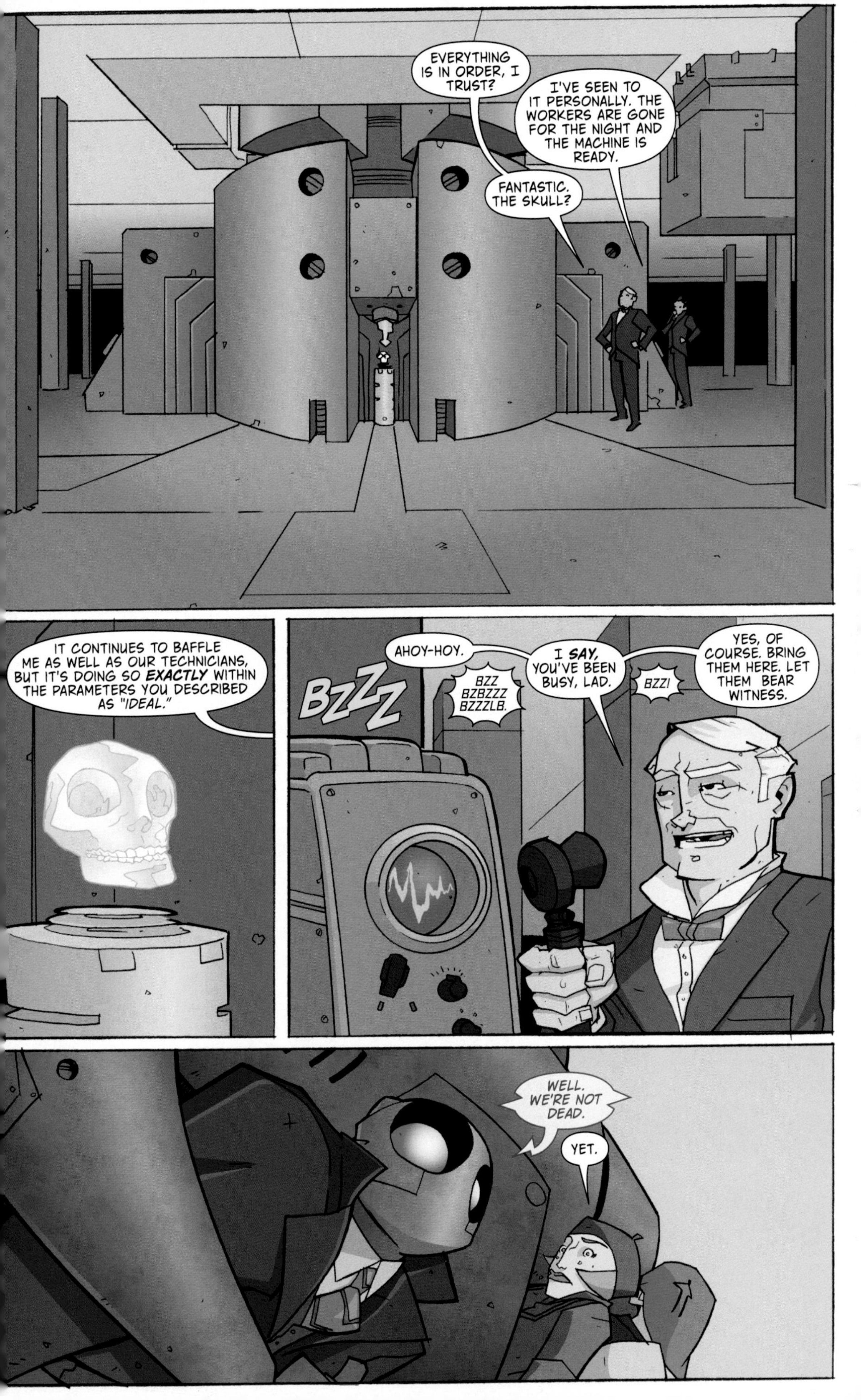
EVERYTHING IS IN ORDER, I TRUST?
I'VE SEEN TO IT PERSONALLY. THE WORKERS ARE GONE FOR THE NIGHT AND THE MACHINE IS READY.
FANTASTIC. THE SKULL?
IT CONTINUES TO BAFFLE ME AS WELL AS OUR TECHNICIANS, BUT IT'S DOING SO EXACTLY WITHIN THE PARAMETERS YOU DESCRIBED AS "IDEAL."
BZZZ
AHOY-HOY.
BZZ BZBZZZ BZZZLB.
I SAY, YOU'VE BEEN BUSY, LAD.
BZZ!
YES, OF COURSE. BRING THEM HERE. LET THEM BEAR WITNESS.
WELL. WE'RE NOT DEAD.
YET.

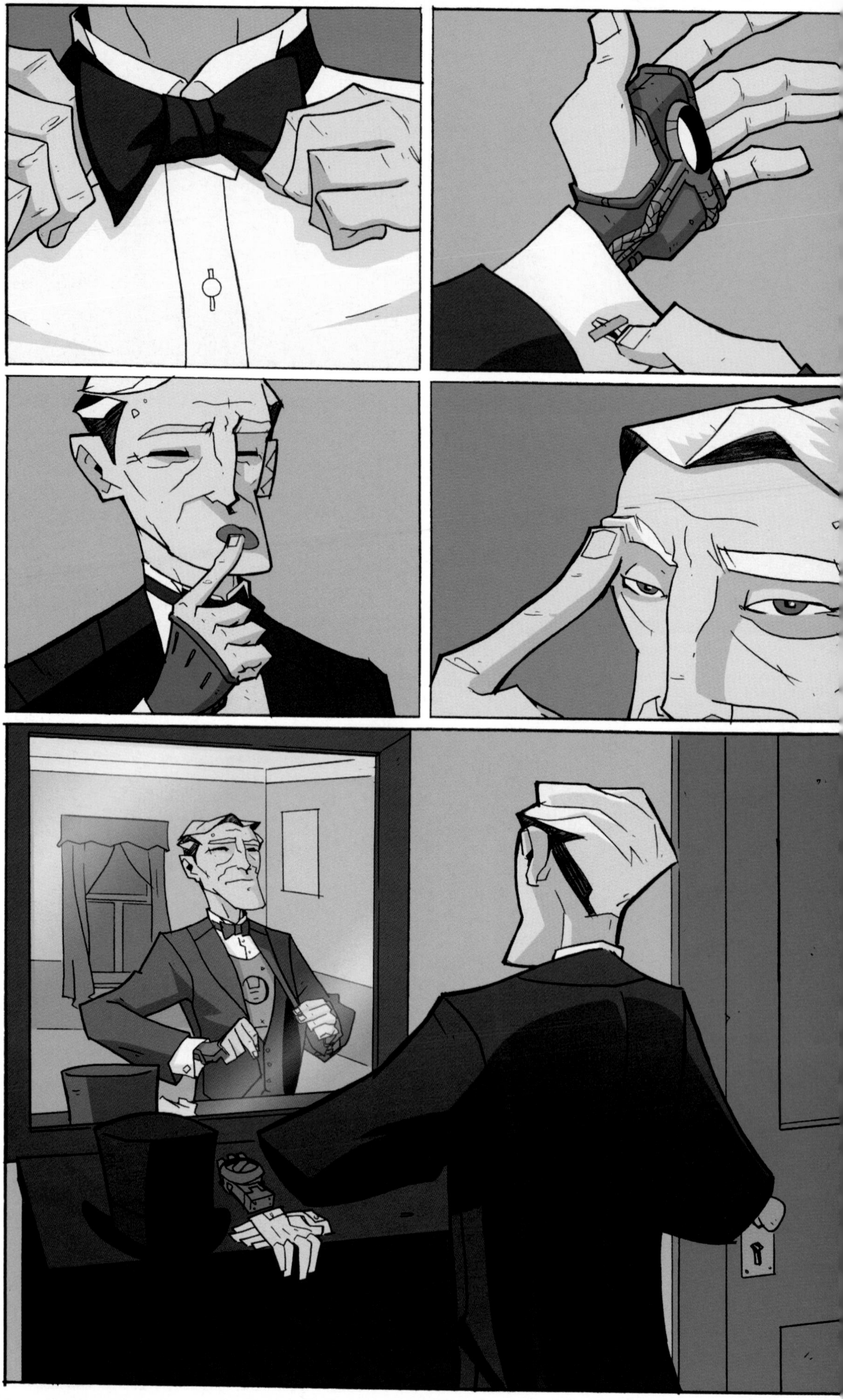

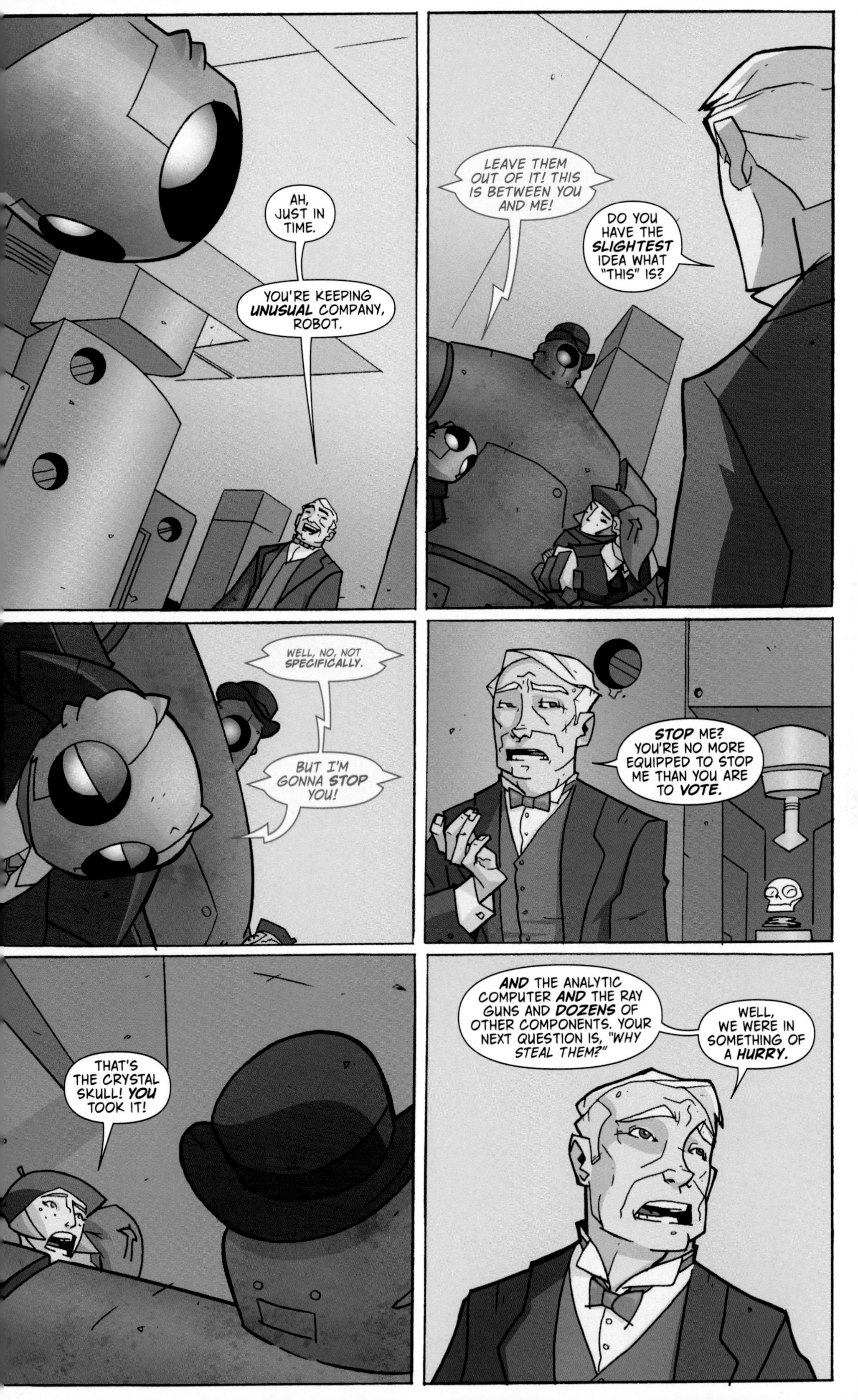
AH, JUST IN TIME.
YOU'RE KEEPING *UNUSUAL* COMPANY, ROBOT.
LEAVE THEM OUT OF IT! THIS IS BETWEEN YOU AND ME!
DO YOU HAVE THE *SLIGHTEST* IDEA WHAT "THIS" IS?
WELL, NO, NOT *SPECIFICALLY.*
BUT I'M GONNA *STOP* YOU!
STOP ME? YOU'RE NO MORE EQUIPPED TO STOP ME THAN YOU ARE TO *VOTE.*
THAT'S THE CRYSTAL SKULL! *YOU* TOOK IT!
AND THE ANALYTIC COMPUTER *AND* THE RAY GUNS AND *DOZENS* OF OTHER COMPONENTS. YOUR NEXT QUESTION IS, "WHY STEAL THEM?"
WELL, WE WERE IN SOMETHING OF A *HURRY.*

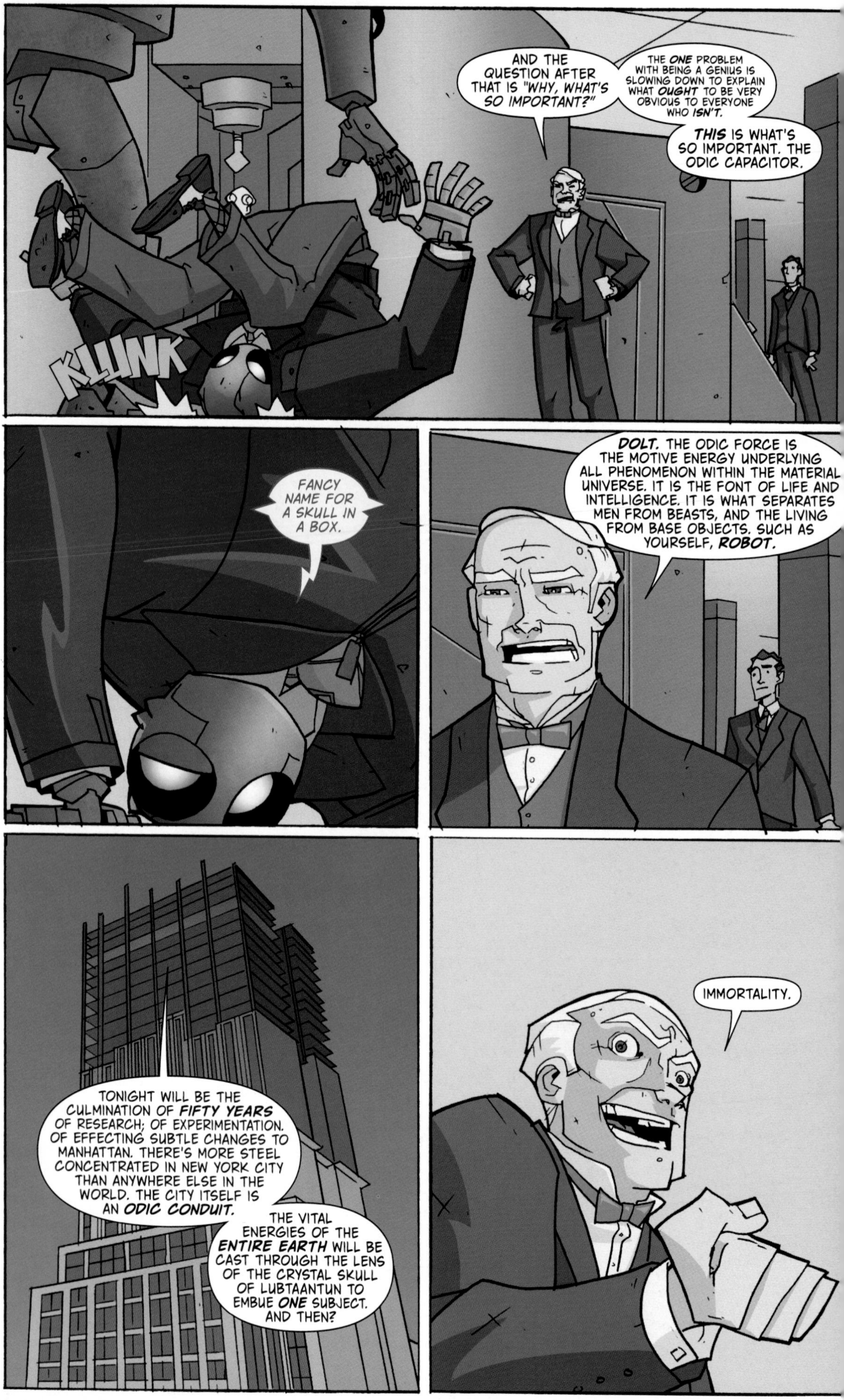
KLUNK
AND THE QUESTION AFTER THAT IS "WHY, WHAT'S SO IMPORTANT?"
THE ONE PROBLEM WITH BEING A GENIUS IS SLOWING DOWN TO EXPLAIN WHAT OUGHT TO BE VERY OBVIOUS TO EVERYONE WHO ISN'T.
THIS IS WHAT'S SO IMPORTANT. THE ODIC CAPACITOR.
FANCY NAME FOR A SKULL IN A BOX.
DOLT. THE ODIC FORCE IS THE MOTIVE ENERGY UNDERLYING ALL PHENOMENON WITHIN THE MATERIAL UNIVERSE. IT IS THE FONT OF LIFE AND INTELLIGENCE. IT IS WHAT SEPARATES MEN FROM BEASTS, AND THE LIVING FROM BASE OBJECTS. SUCH AS YOURSELF, ROBOT.
TONIGHT WILL BE THE CULMINATION OF FIFTY YEARS OF RESEARCH; OF EXPERIMENTATION. OF EFFECTING SUBTLE CHANGES TO MANHATTAN. THERE'S MORE STEEL CONCENTRATED IN NEW YORK CITY THAN ANYWHERE ELSE IN THE WORLD. THE CITY ITSELF IS AN ODIC CONDUIT.
THE VITAL ENERGIES OF THE ENTIRE EARTH WILL BE CAST THROUGH THE LENS OF THE CRYSTAL SKULL OF LUBTAANTUN TO EMBUE ONE SUBJECT. AND THEN?
IMMORTALITY.

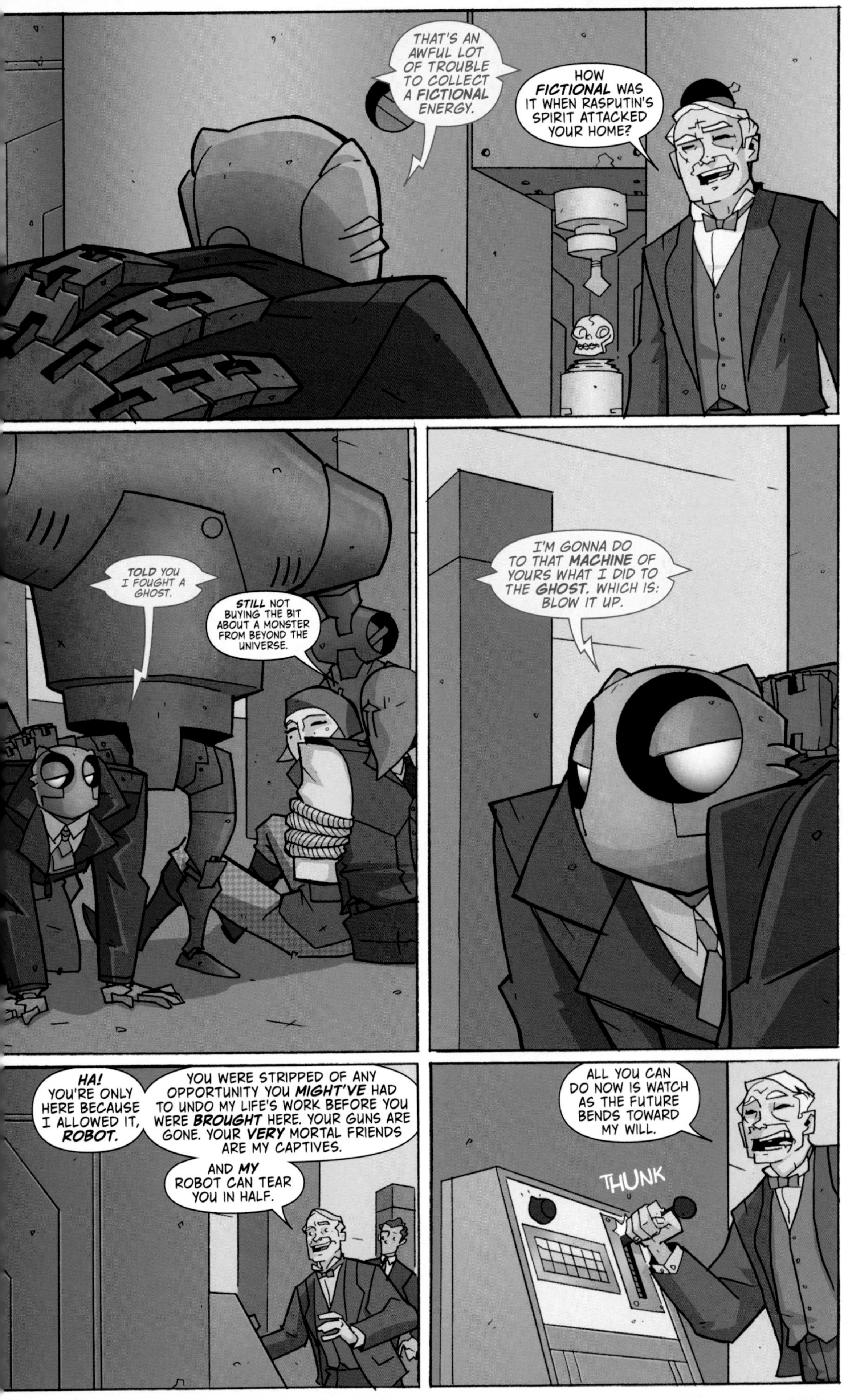
THAT'S AN AWFUL LOT OF TROUBLE TO COLLECT A FICTIONAL ENERGY.
HOW FICTIONAL WAS IT WHEN RASPUTIN'S SPIRIT ATTACKED YOUR HOME?
TOLD YOU I FOUGHT A GHOST.
STILL NOT BUYING THE BIT ABOUT A MONSTER FROM BEYOND THE UNIVERSE.
I'M GONNA DO TO THAT MACHINE OF YOURS WHAT I DID TO THE GHOST. WHICH IS: BLOW IT UP.
HA! YOU'RE ONLY HERE BECAUSE I ALLOWED IT, ROBOT.
YOU WERE STRIPPED OF ANY OPPORTUNITY YOU MIGHT'VE HAD TO UNDO MY LIFE'S WORK BEFORE YOU WERE BROUGHT HERE. YOUR GUNS ARE GONE. YOUR VERY MORTAL FRIENDS ARE MY CAPTIVES.
AND MY ROBOT CAN TEAR YOU IN HALF.
ALL YOU CAN DO NOW IS WATCH AS THE FUTURE BENDS TOWARD MY WILL.
THUNK

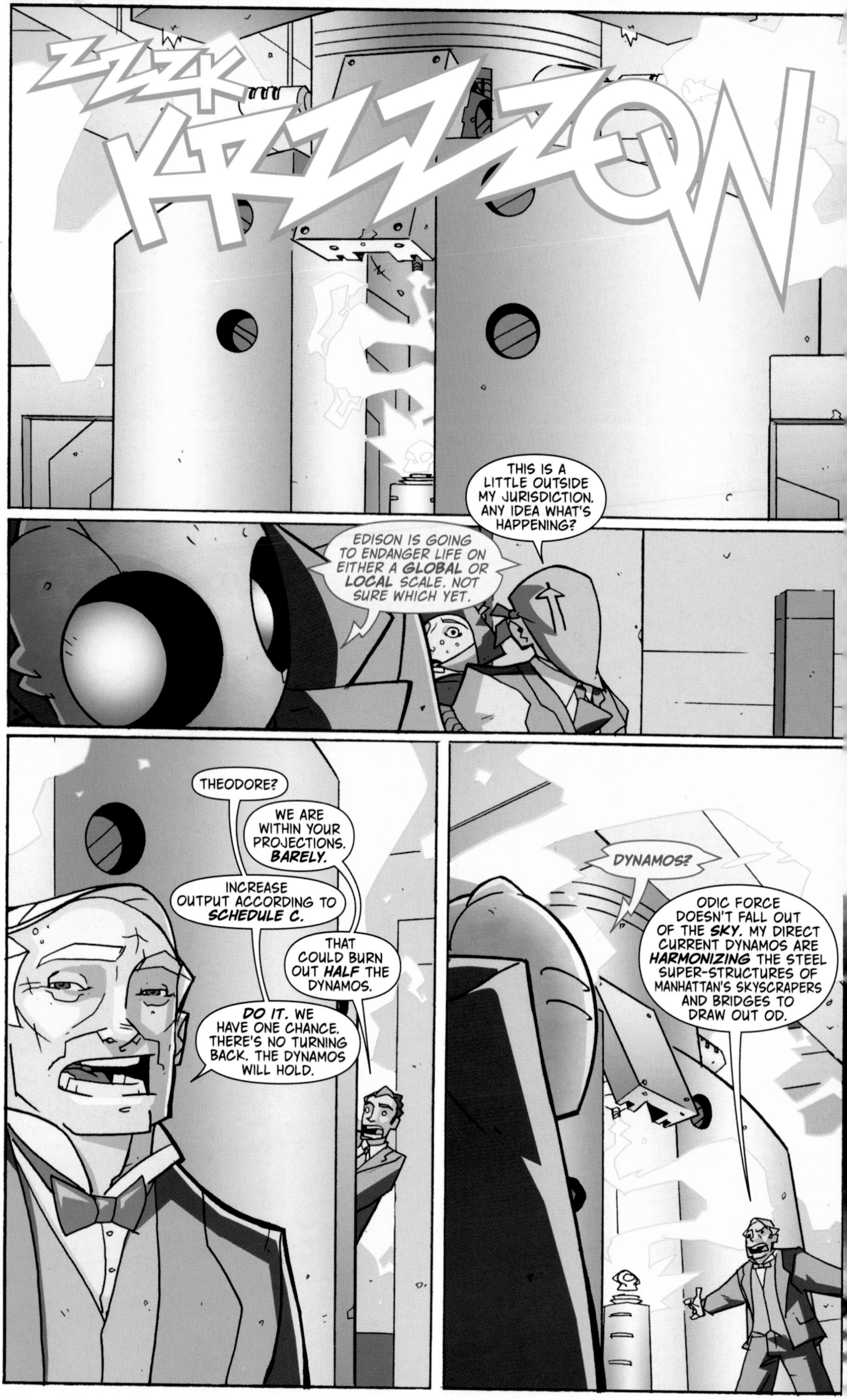
ZZZK
KRZZZZOW
THIS IS A LITTLE OUTSIDE MY JURISDICTION. ANY IDEA WHAT'S HAPPENING?
EDISON IS GOING TO ENDANGER LIFE ON EITHER A **GLOBAL** OR **LOCAL** SCALE. NOT SURE WHICH YET.
THEODORE?
WE ARE WITHIN YOUR PROJECTIONS. ***BARELY.***
INCREASE OUTPUT ACCORDING TO ***SCHEDULE C.***
THAT COULD BURN OUT ***HALF*** THE DYNAMOS.
DO IT. WE HAVE ONE CHANCE. THERE'S NO TURNING BACK. THE DYNAMOS WILL HOLD.
DYNAMOS?
ODIC FORCE DOESN'T FALL OUT OF THE ***SKY.*** MY DIRECT CURRENT DYNAMOS ARE ***HARMONIZING*** THE STEEL SUPER-STRUCTURES OF MANHATTAN'S SKYSCRAPERS AND BRIDGES TO DRAW OUT OD.

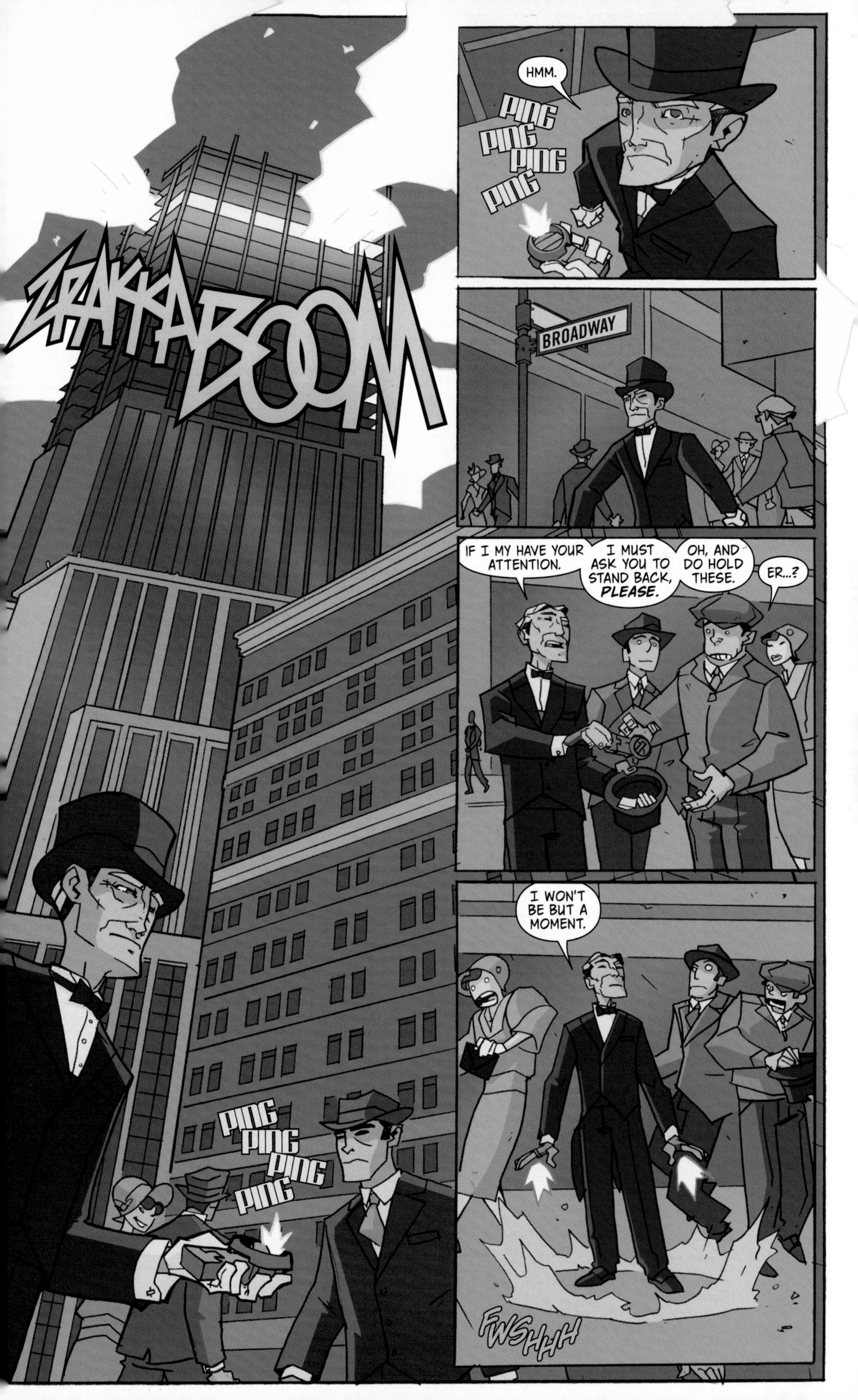
ZRAKKABOOM
PING PING PING PING
HMM.
PING PING PING PING
BROADWAY
IF I MY HAVE YOUR ATTENTION.
I MUST ASK YOU TO STAND BACK, PLEASE.
OH, AND DO HOLD THESE.
ER...?
I WON'T BE BUT A MOMENT.
FWSHHH

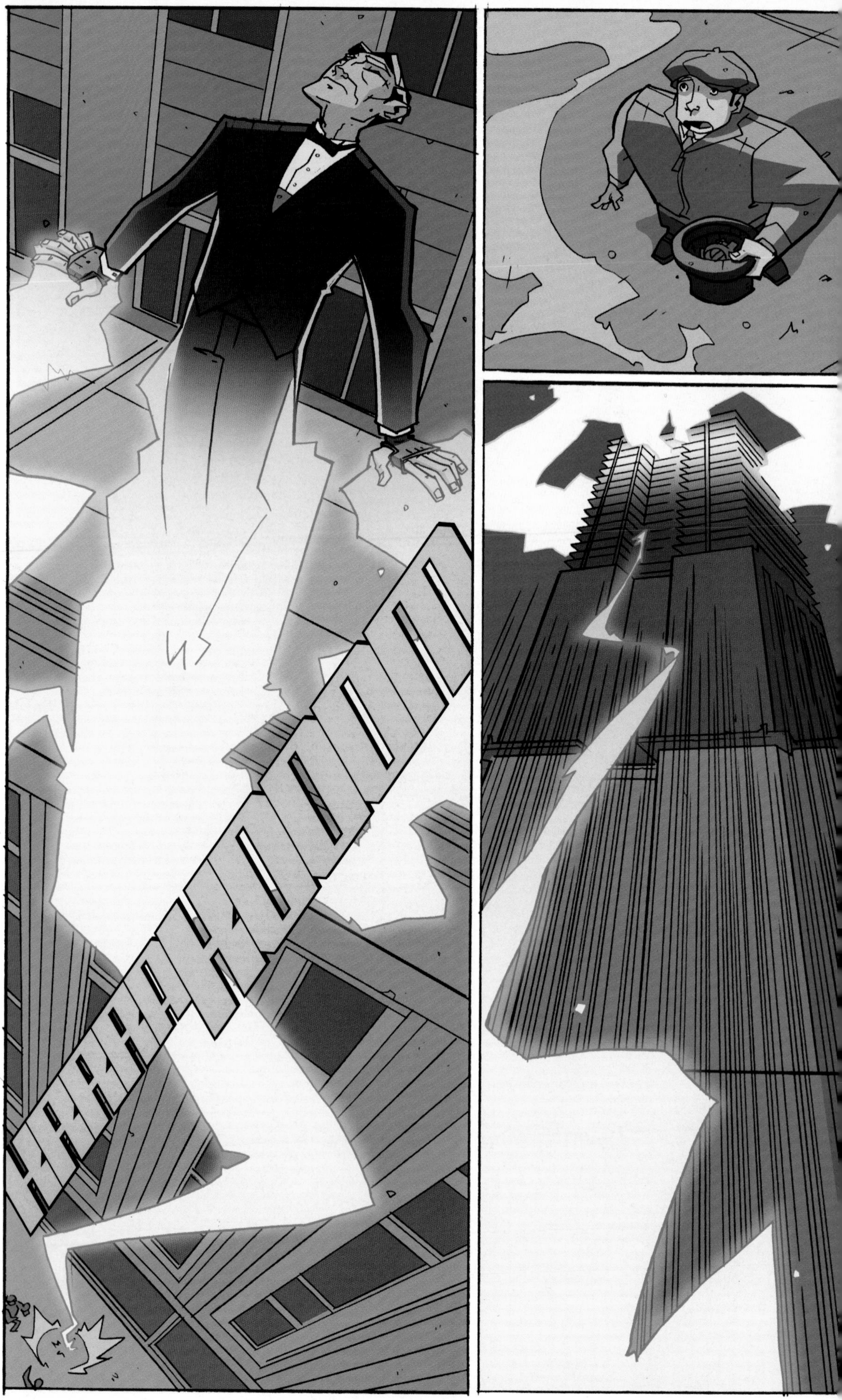

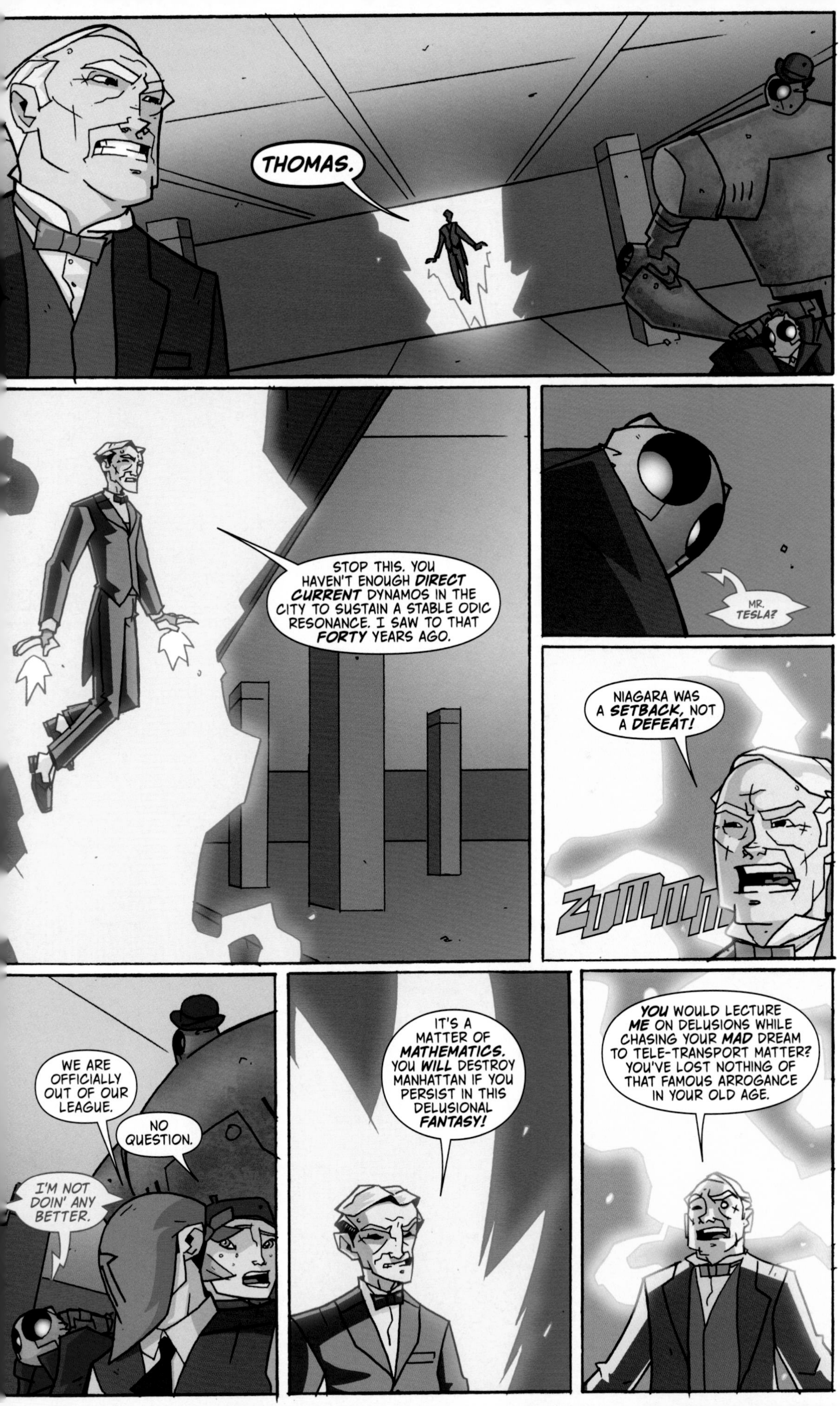
THOMAS.
STOP THIS. YOU HAVEN'T ENOUGH DIRECT CURRENT DYNAMOS IN THE CITY TO SUSTAIN A STABLE ODIC RESONANCE. I SAW TO THAT FORTY YEARS AGO.
MR. TESLA?
NIAGARA WAS A SETBACK, NOT A DEFEAT!
ZUMMM
WE ARE OFFICIALLY OUT OF OUR LEAGUE.
NO QUESTION.
I'M NOT DOIN' ANY BETTER.
IT'S A MATTER OF MATHEMATICS. YOU WILL DESTROY MANHATTAN IF YOU PERSIST IN THIS DELUSIONAL FANTASY!
YOU WOULD LECTURE ME ON DELUSIONS WHILE CHASING YOUR MAD DREAM TO TELE-TRANSPORT MATTER? YOU'VE LOST NOTHING OF THAT FAMOUS ARROGANCE IN YOUR OLD AGE.

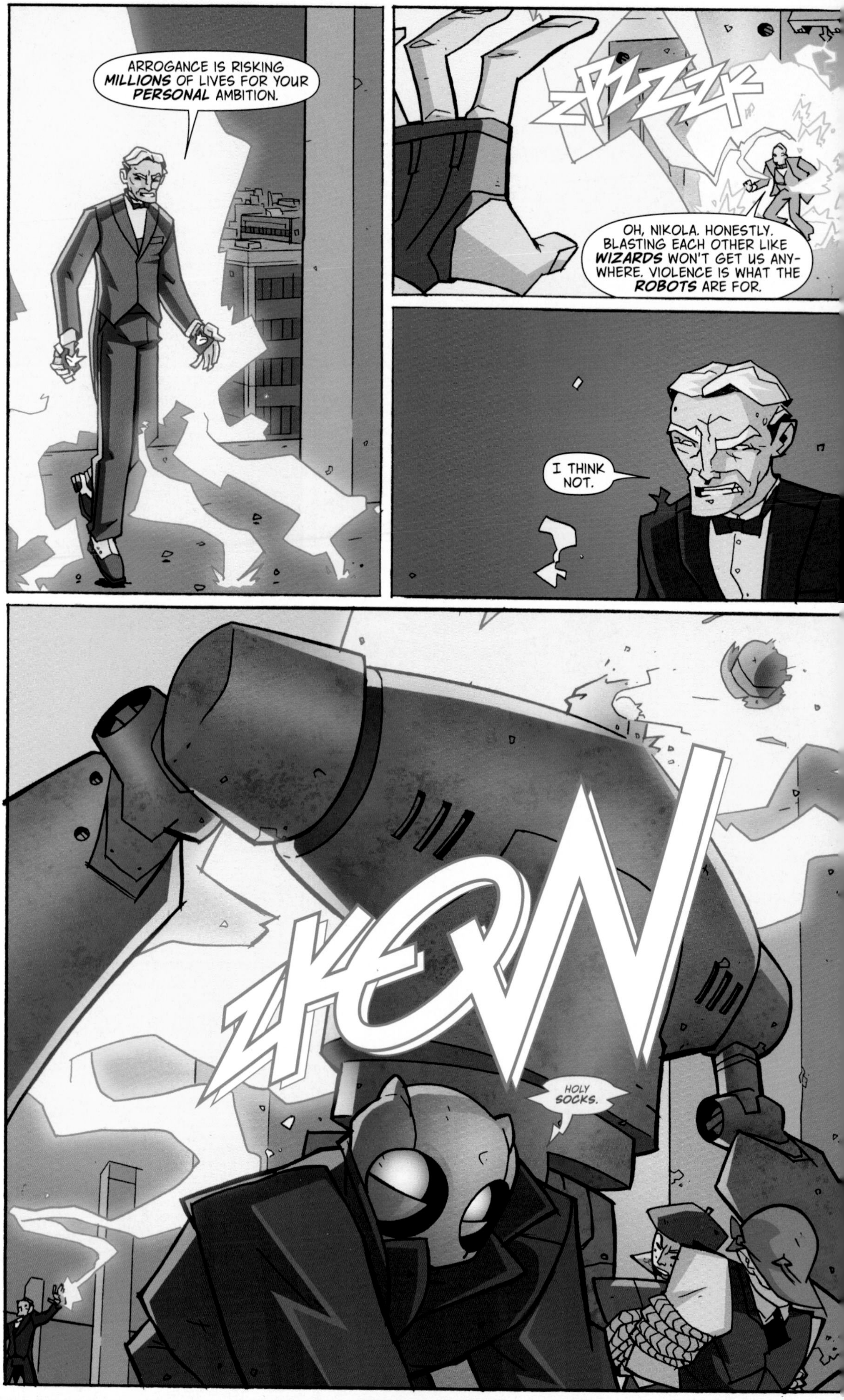
ARROGANCE IS RISKING MILLIONS OF LIVES FOR YOUR PERSONAL AMBITION.
ZRRZZZK
OH, NIKOLA. HONESTLY. BLASTING EACH OTHER LIKE WIZARDS WON'T GET US ANYWHERE. VIOLENCE IS WHAT THE ROBOTS ARE FOR.
I THINK NOT.
ZKEOW
HOLY SOCKS.

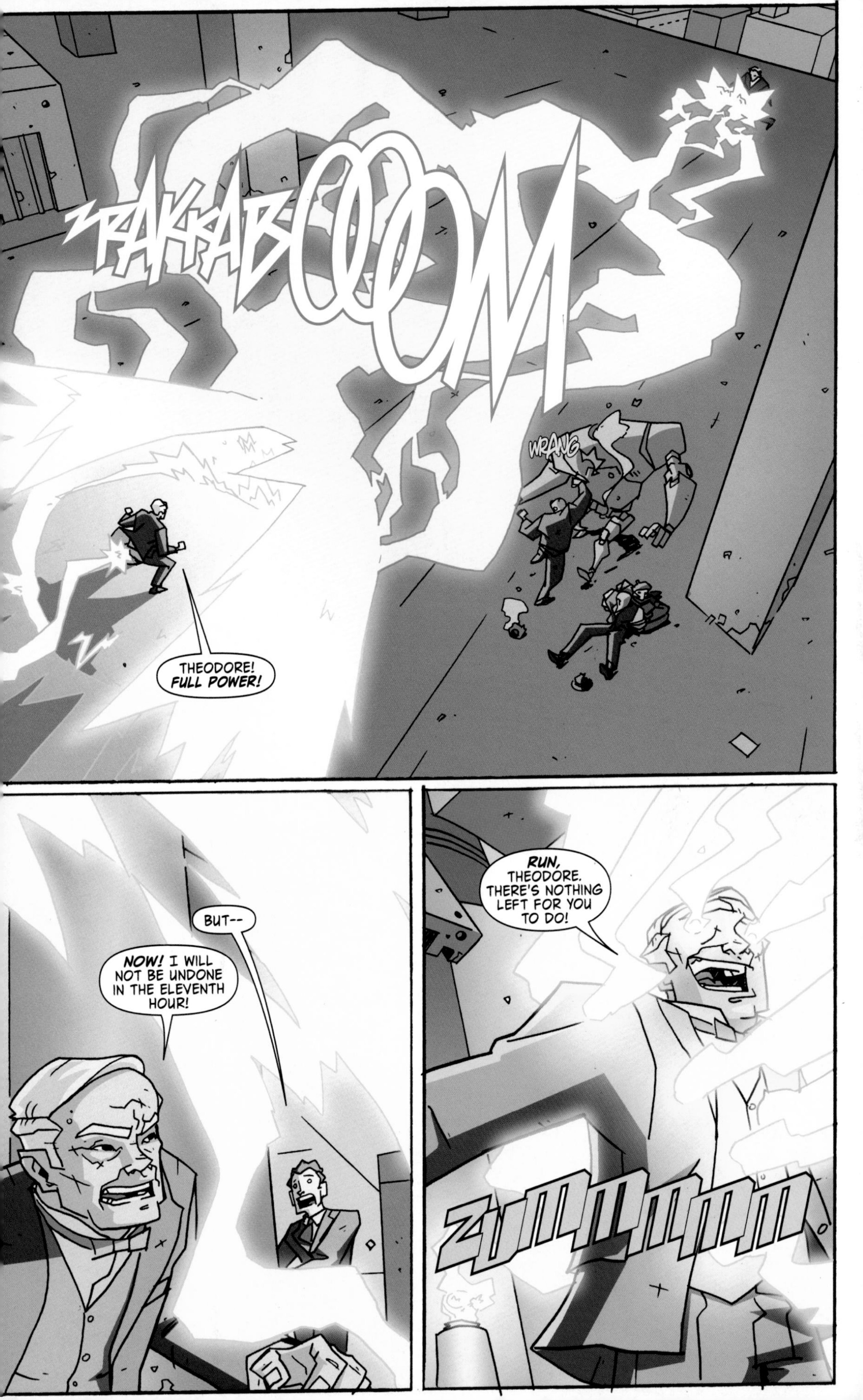
ZRAKKABOOOOM
WRANG
THEODORE! *FULL POWER!*
NOW! I WILL NOT BE UNDONE IN THE ELEVENTH HOUR!
BUT--
RUN, THEODORE. THERE'S NOTHING LEFT FOR YOU TO DO!
ZUMMMMMM

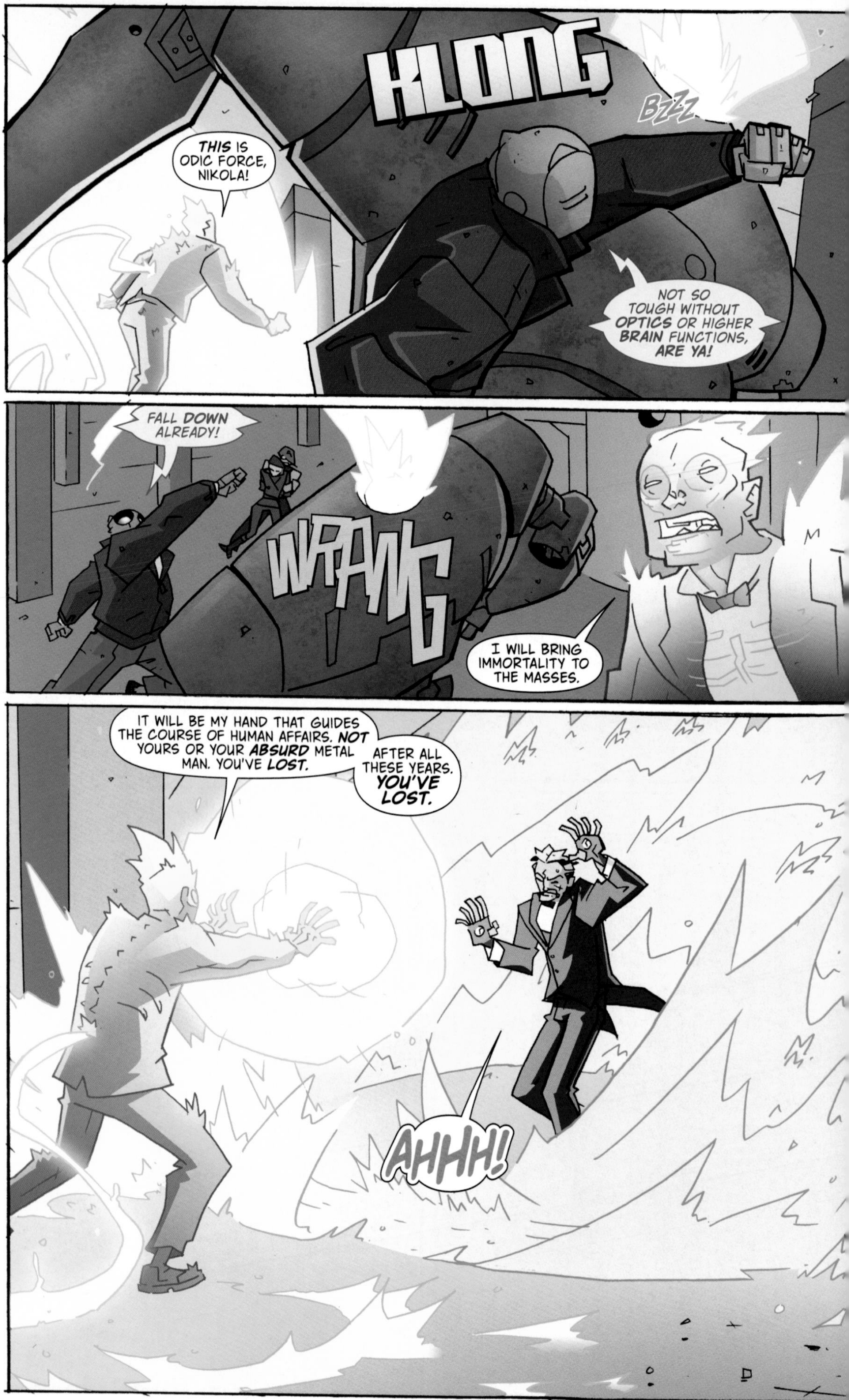
KLONG
BZZZ
THIS IS ODIC FORCE, NIKOLA!
NOT SO TOUGH WITHOUT OPTICS OR HIGHER BRAIN FUNCTIONS, ARE YA!
FALL DOWN ALREADY!
WRANG
I WILL BRING IMMORTALITY TO THE MASSES.
IT WILL BE MY HAND THAT GUIDES THE COURSE OF HUMAN AFFAIRS. NOT YOURS OR YOUR ABSURD METAL MAN. YOU'VE LOST.
AFTER ALL THESE YEARS. YOU'VE LOST.
AHHH!

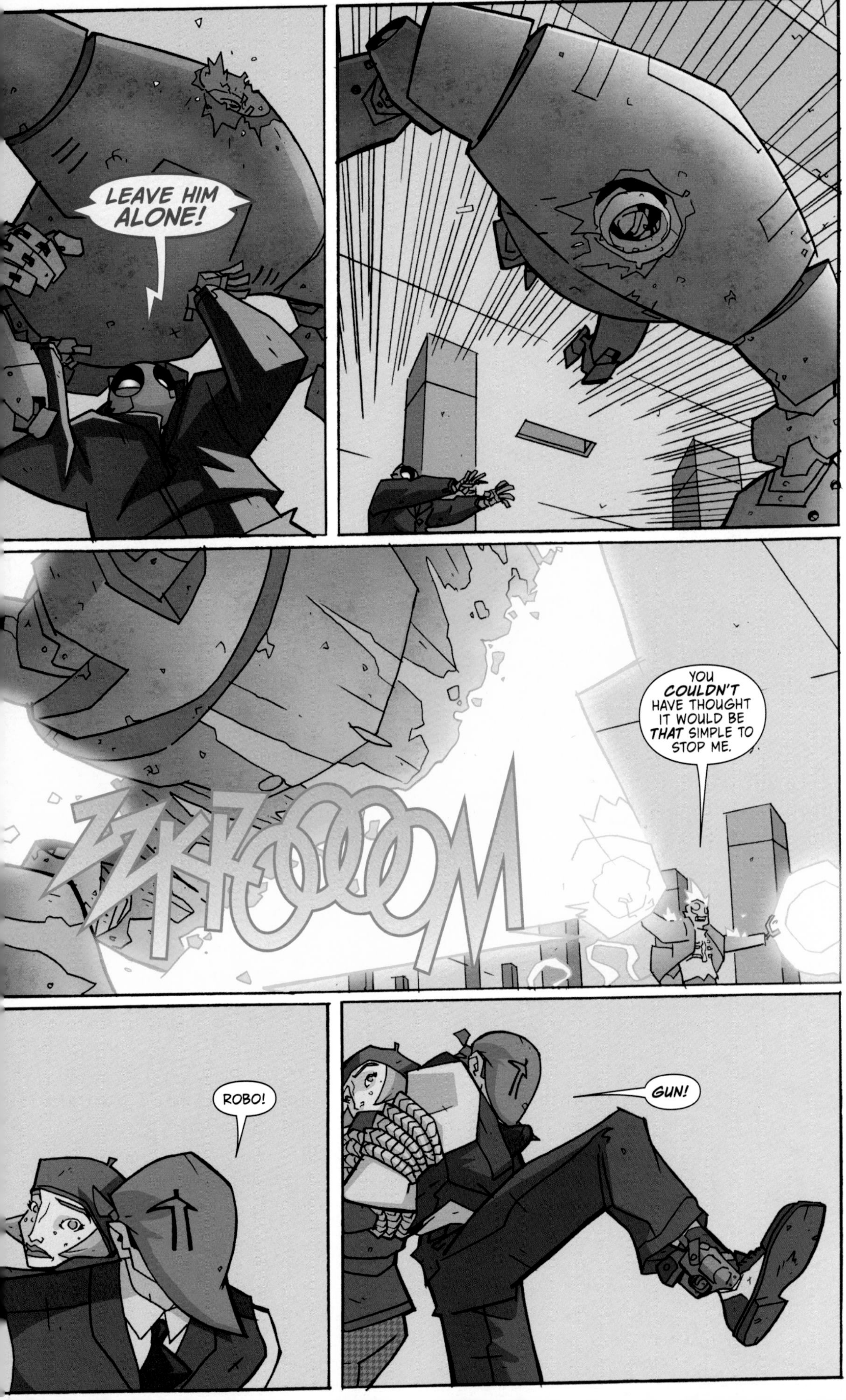
LEAVE HIM ALONE!
ZZKKOOOOOM
YOU COULDN'T HAVE THOUGHT IT WOULD BE THAT SIMPLE TO STOP ME.
ROBO!
GUN!

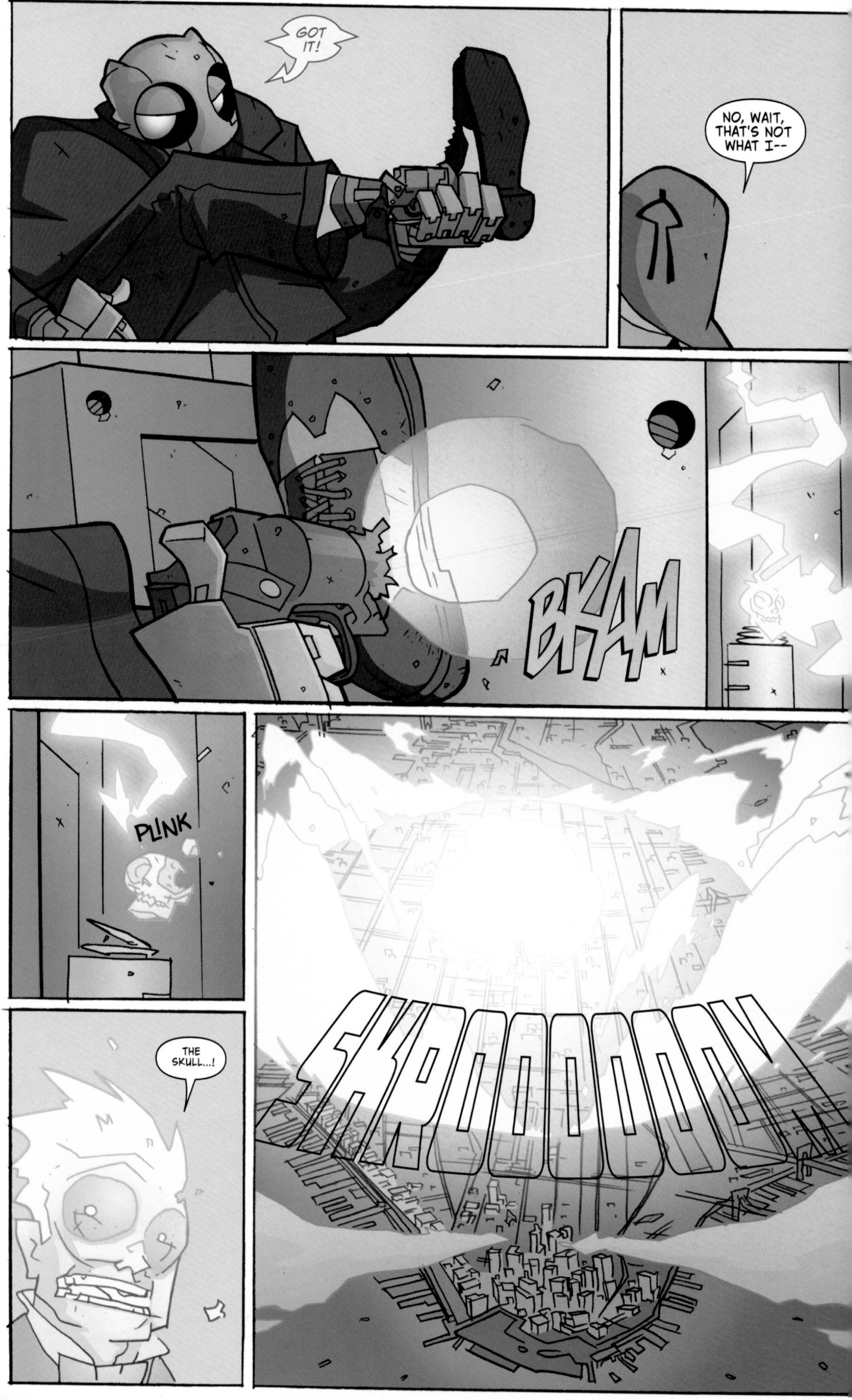
GOT IT!
NO, WAIT, THAT'S NOT WHAT I--
BKAM
PLINK
THE SKULL...!
SKPOOOOOOM

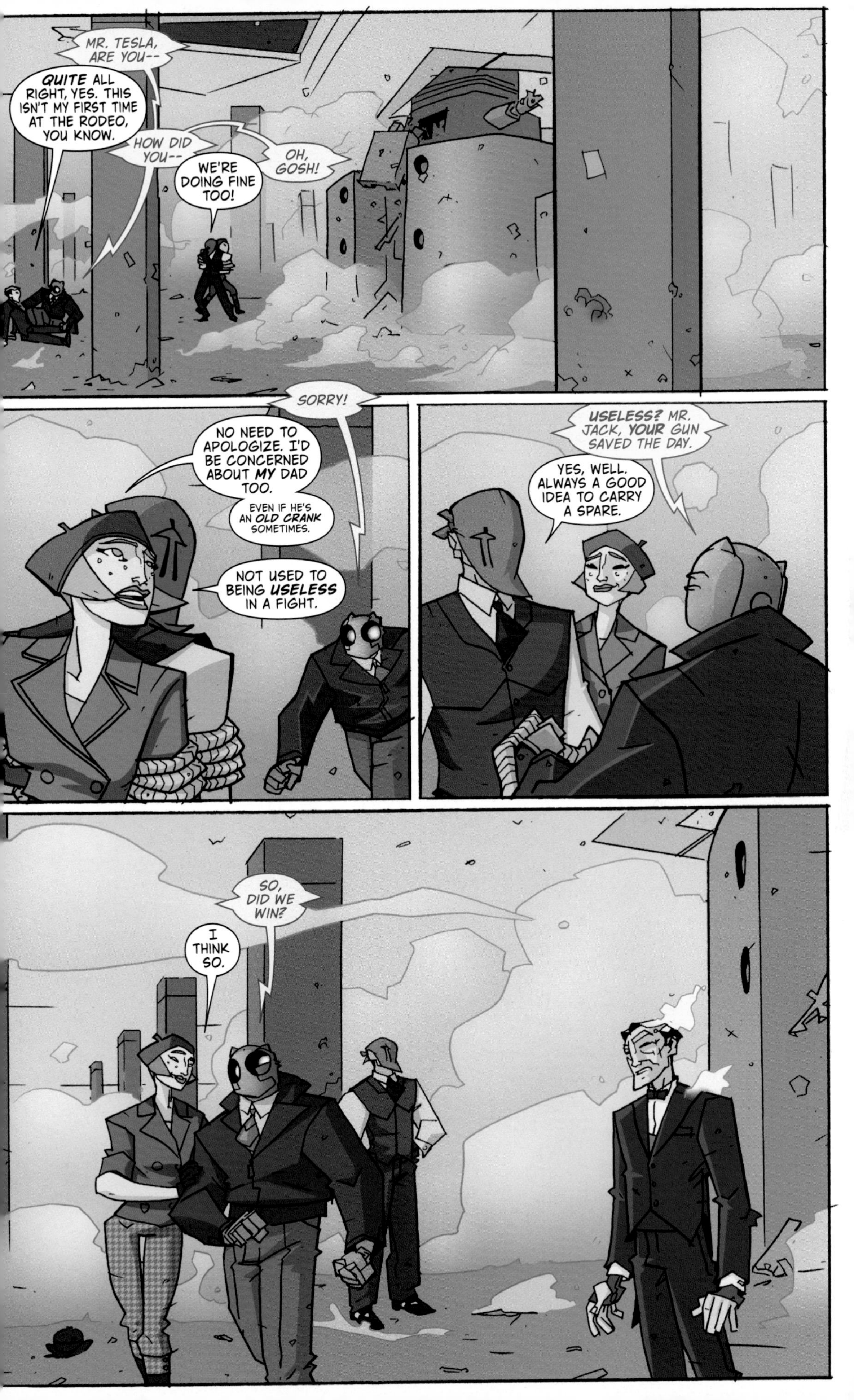
MR. TESLA, ARE YOU--
QUITE ALL RIGHT, YES. THIS ISN'T MY FIRST TIME AT THE RODEO, YOU KNOW.
HOW DID YOU--
OH, GOSH!
WE'RE DOING FINE TOO!
SORRY!
NO NEED TO APOLOGIZE. I'D BE CONCERNED ABOUT MY DAD TOO.
EVEN IF HE'S AN OLD CRANK SOMETIMES.
NOT USED TO BEING USELESS IN A FIGHT.
USELESS? MR. JACK, YOUR GUN SAVED THE DAY.
YES, WELL. ALWAYS A GOOD IDEA TO CARRY A SPARE.
SO, DID WE WIN?
I THINK SO.

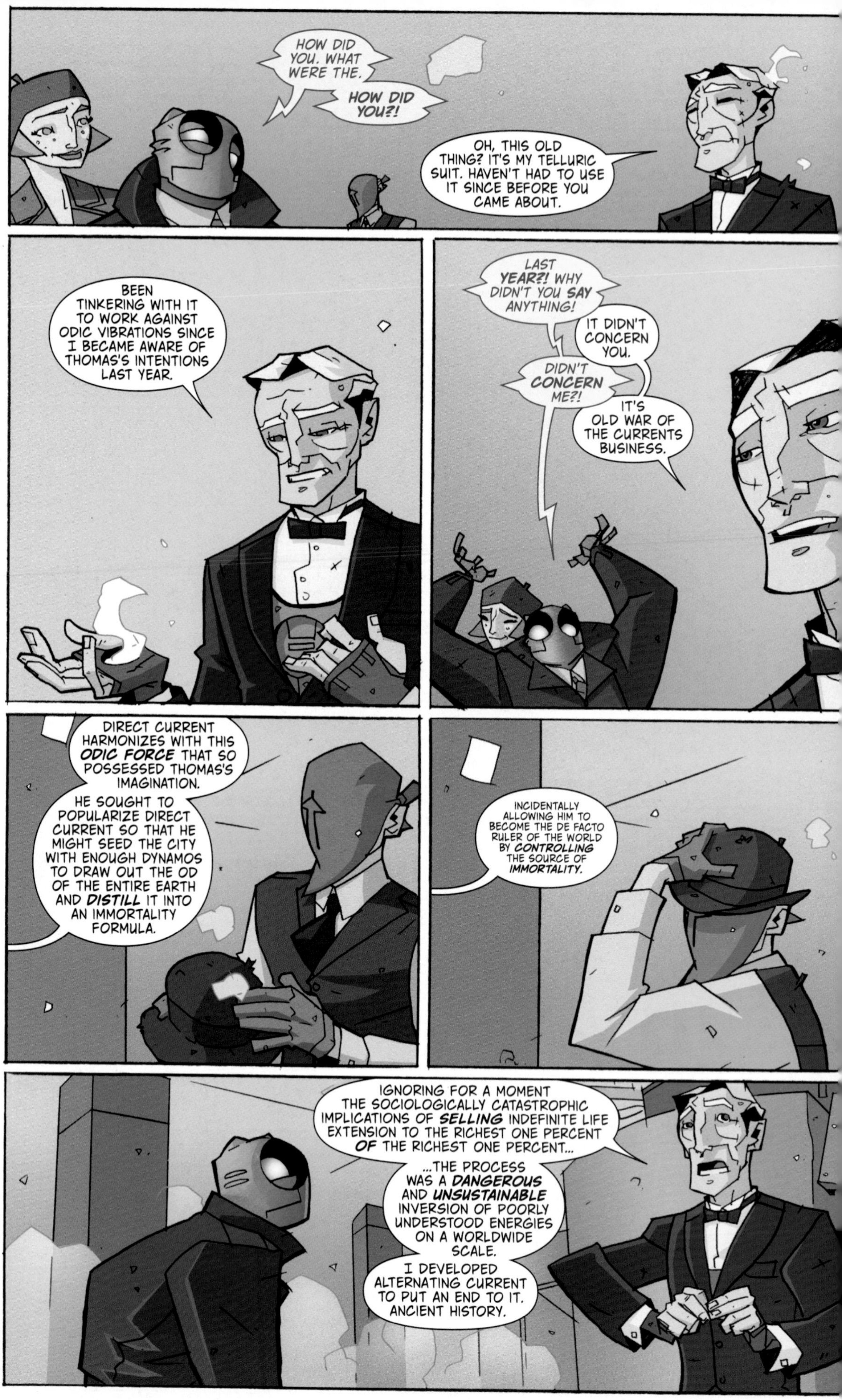
HOW DID YOU. WHAT WERE THE.
HOW DID YOU?!
OH, THIS OLD THING? IT'S MY TELLURIC SUIT. HAVEN'T HAD TO USE IT SINCE BEFORE YOU CAME ABOUT.
BEEN TINKERING WITH IT TO WORK AGAINST ODIC VIBRATIONS SINCE I BECAME AWARE OF THOMAS'S INTENTIONS LAST YEAR.
LAST **YEAR?!** WHY DIDN'T YOU **SAY** ANYTHING!
IT DIDN'T CONCERN YOU.
DIDN'T **CONCERN** ME?!
IT'S OLD WAR OF THE CURRENTS BUSINESS.
DIRECT CURRENT HARMONIZES WITH THIS **ODIC FORCE** THAT SO POSSESSED THOMAS'S IMAGINATION.
HE SOUGHT TO POPULARIZE DIRECT CURRENT SO THAT HE MIGHT SEED THE CITY WITH ENOUGH DYNAMOS TO DRAW OUT THE OD OF THE ENTIRE EARTH AND **DISTILL** IT INTO AN IMMORTALITY FORMULA.
INCIDENTALLY ALLOWING HIM TO BECOME THE DE FACTO RULER OF THE WORLD BY **CONTROLLING** THE SOURCE OF **IMMORTALITY.**
IGNORING FOR A MOMENT THE SOCIOLOGICALLY CATASTROPHIC IMPLICATIONS OF **SELLING** INDEFINITE LIFE EXTENSION TO THE RICHEST ONE PERCENT **OF** THE RICHEST ONE PERCENT...
...THE PROCESS WAS A **DANGEROUS** AND **UNSUSTAINABLE** INVERSION OF POORLY UNDERSTOOD ENERGIES ON A WORLDWIDE SCALE.
I DEVELOPED ALTERNATING CURRENT TO PUT AN END TO IT. ANCIENT HISTORY.

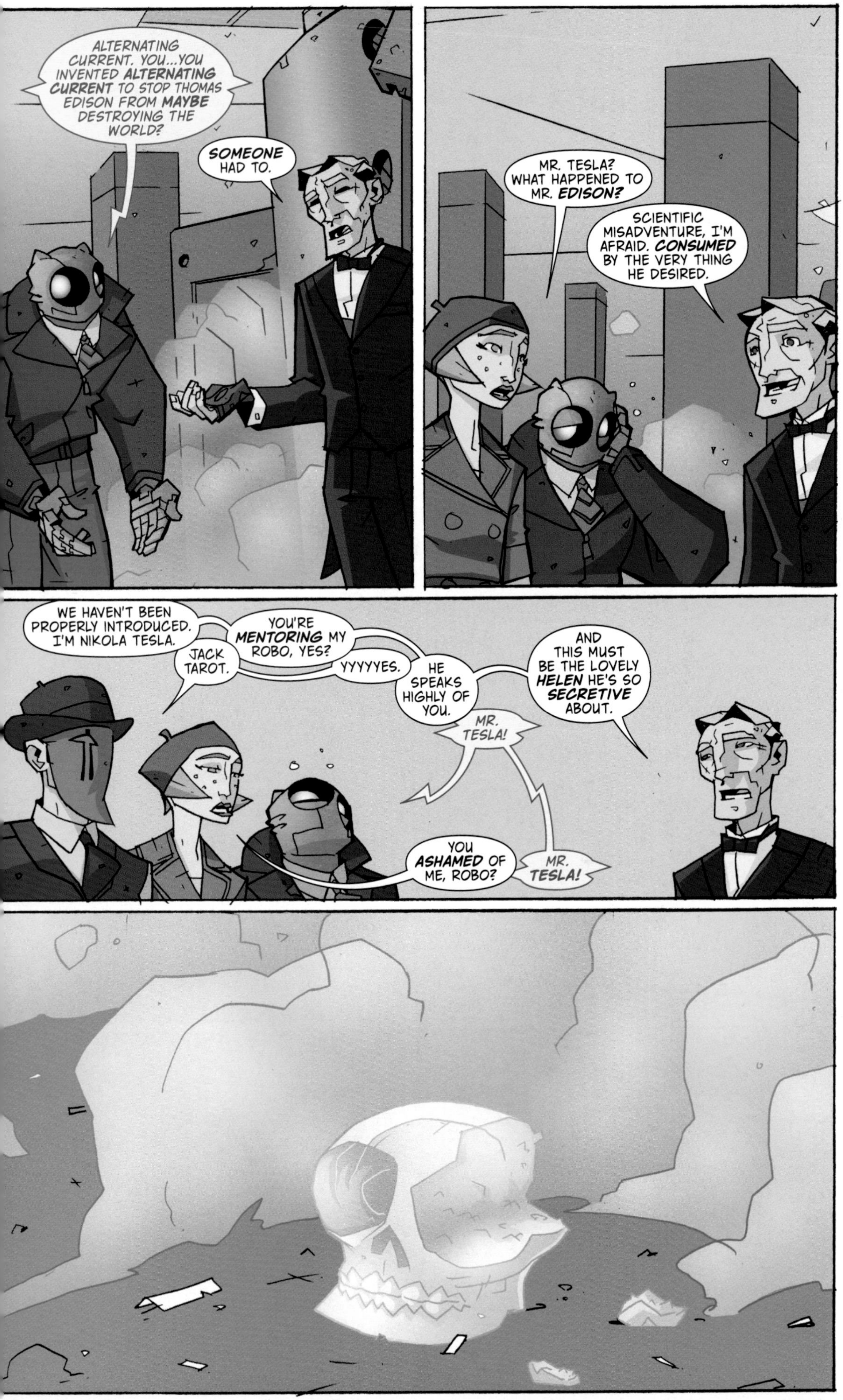
ALTERNATING CURRENT. YOU...YOU INVENTED ALTERNATING CURRENT TO STOP THOMAS EDISON FROM MAYBE DESTROYING THE WORLD?
SOMEONE HAD TO.
MR. TESLA? WHAT HAPPENED TO MR. EDISON?
SCIENTIFIC MISADVENTURE, I'M AFRAID. CONSUMED BY THE VERY THING HE DESIRED.
WE HAVEN'T BEEN PROPERLY INTRODUCED. I'M NIKOLA TESLA.
JACK TAROT.
YOU'RE MENTORING MY ROBO, YES?
YYYYYES.
HE SPEAKS HIGHLY OF YOU.
AND THIS MUST BE THE LOVELY HELEN HE'S SO SECRETIVE ABOUT.
MR. TESLA!
YOU ASHAMED OF ME, ROBO?
MR. TESLA!

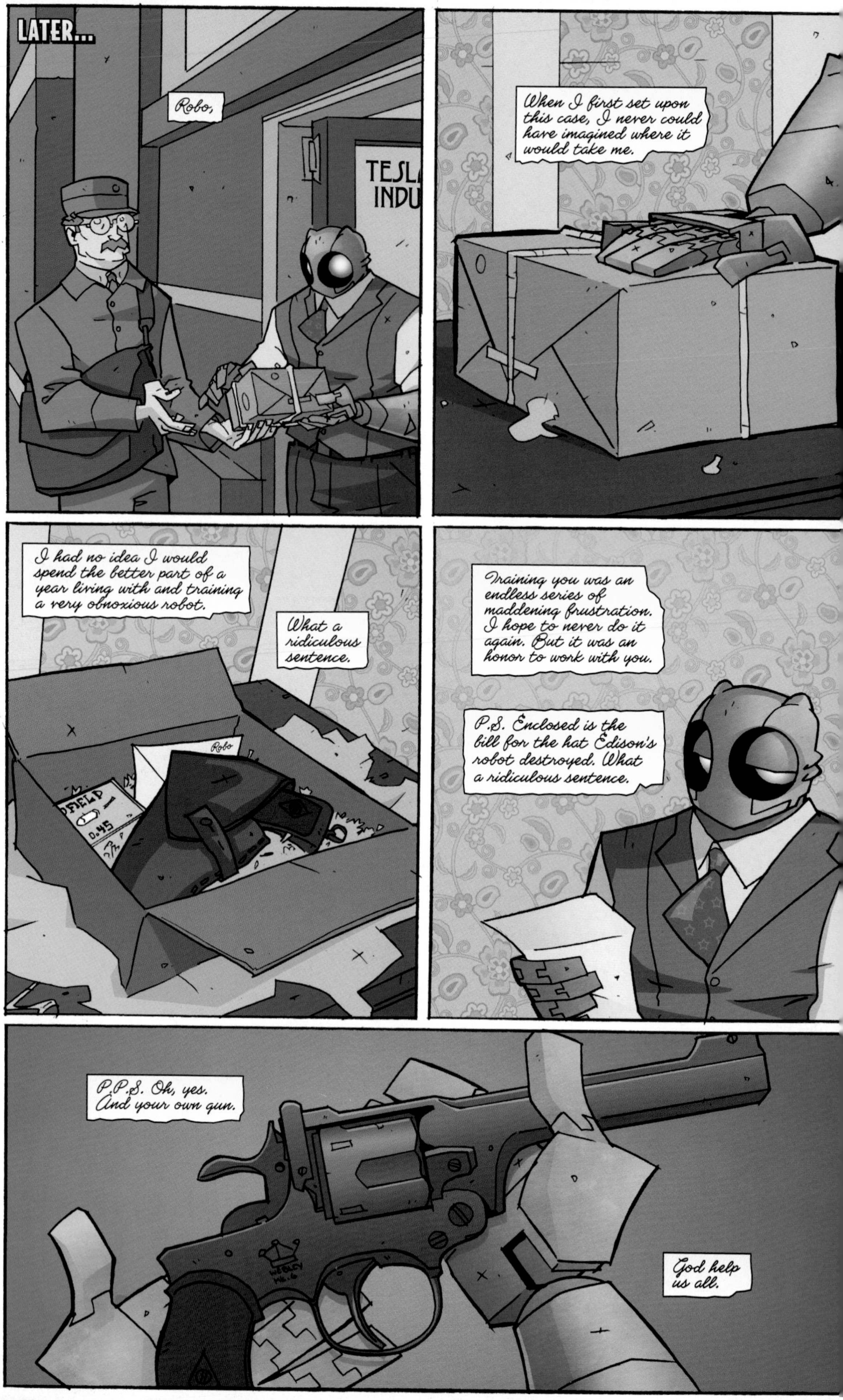
LATER...
Robo,
When I first set upon this case, I never could have imagined where it would take me.
I had no idea I would spend the better part of a year living with and training a very obnoxious robot.
What a ridiculous sentence.
Training you was an endless series of maddening frustration. I hope to never do it again. But it was an honor to work with you.
P.S. Enclosed is the bill for the hat Edison's robot destroyed. What a ridiculous sentence.
P.P.S. Oh, yes. And your own gun.
God help us all.

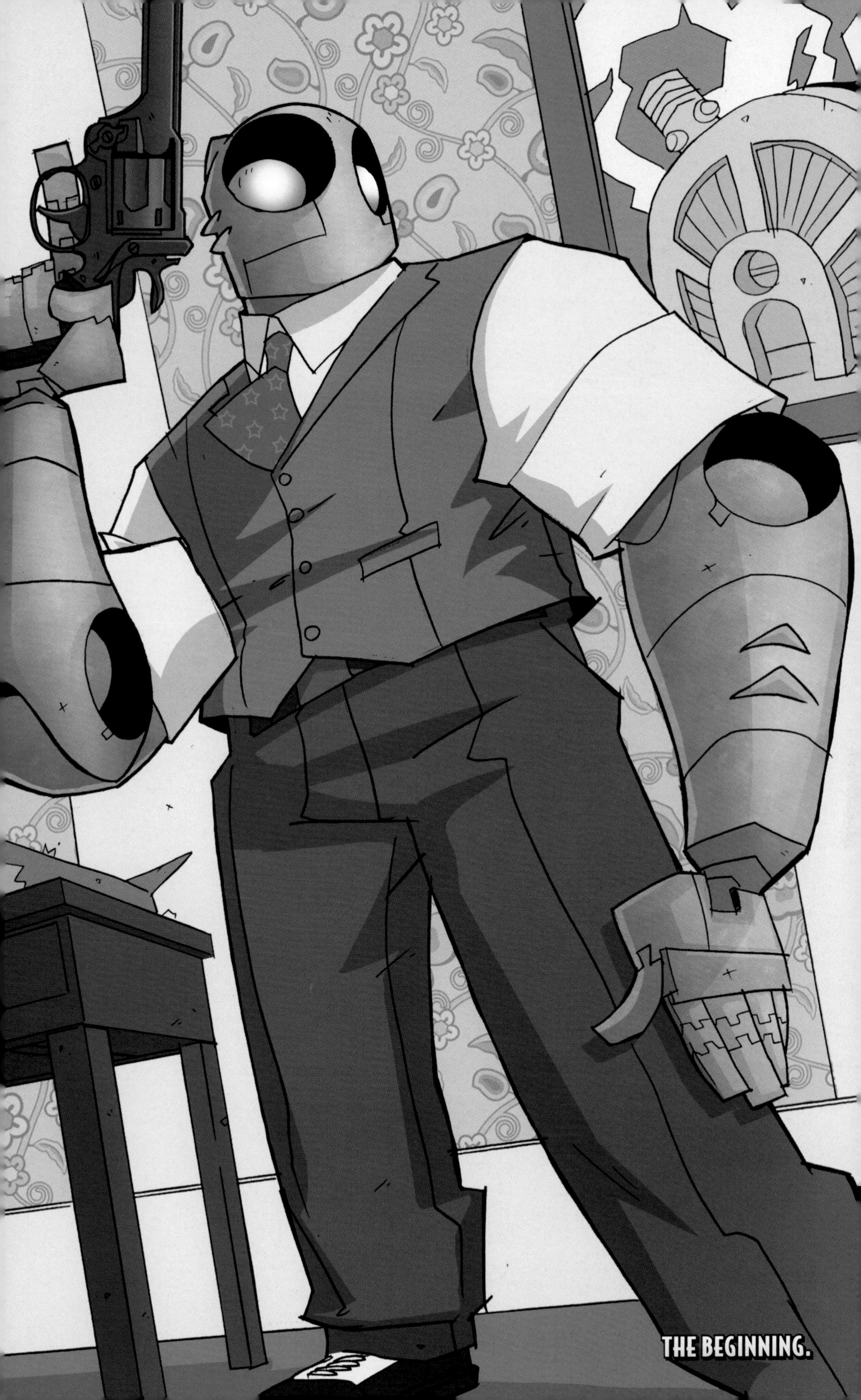
THE BEGINNING.

FREE COMIC BOOK DAY
2011

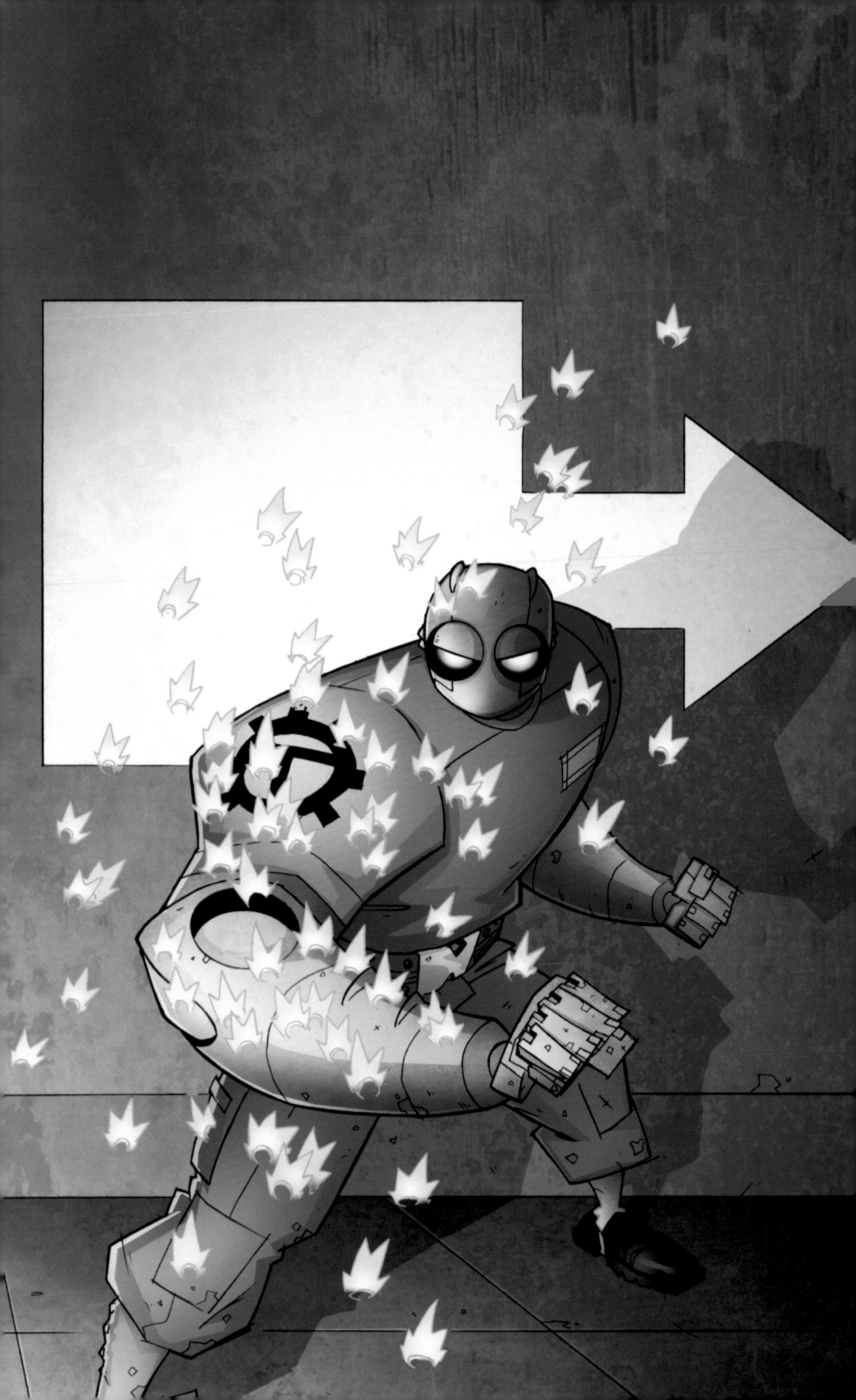

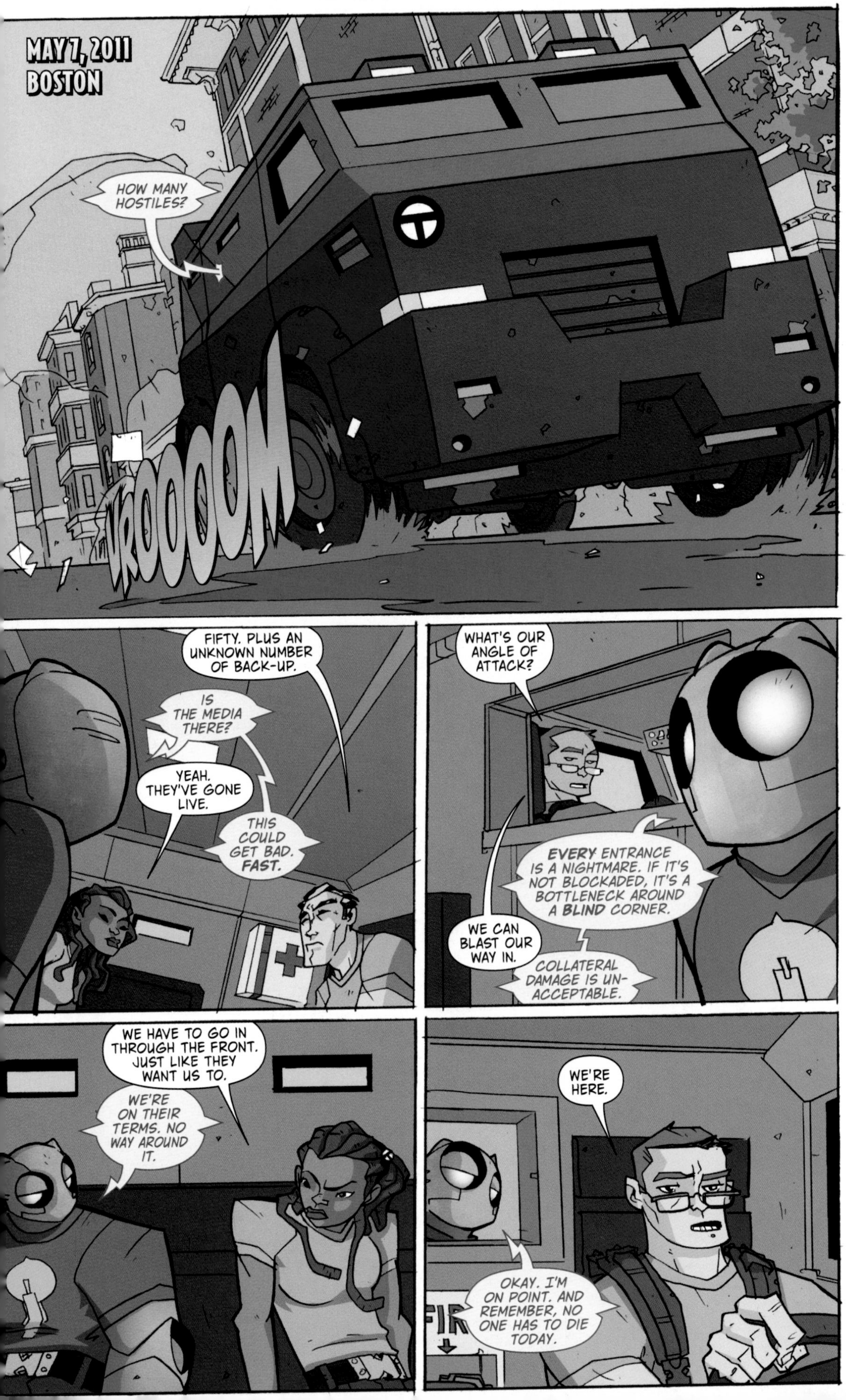
MAY 7, 2011
BOSTON
HOW MANY HOSTILES?
VROOOOM
FIFTY. PLUS AN UNKNOWN NUMBER OF BACK-UP.
IS THE MEDIA THERE?
YEAH. THEY'VE GONE LIVE.
THIS COULD GET BAD. FAST.
WHAT'S OUR ANGLE OF ATTACK?
EVERY ENTRANCE IS A NIGHTMARE. IF IT'S NOT BLOCKADED, IT'S A BOTTLENECK AROUND A BLIND CORNER.
WE CAN BLAST OUR WAY IN.
COLLATERAL DAMAGE IS UN-ACCEPTABLE.
WE HAVE TO GO IN THROUGH THE FRONT. JUST LIKE THEY WANT US TO.
WE'RE ON THEIR TERMS. NO WAY AROUND IT.
WE'RE HERE.
OKAY. I'M ON POINT. AND REMEMBER, NO ONE HAS TO DIE TODAY.
FIR

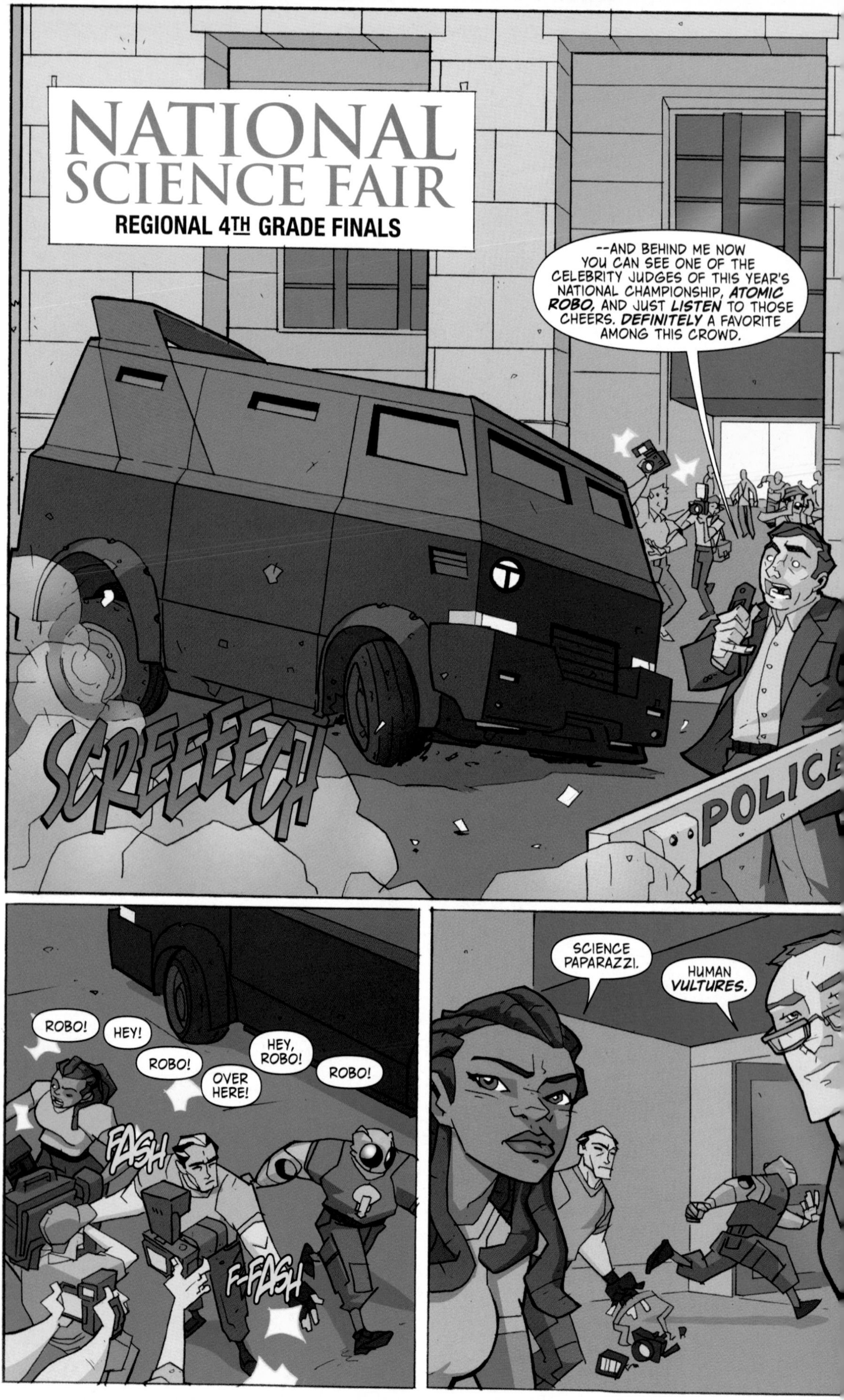
NATIONAL SCIENCE FAIR
REGIONAL 4TH GRADE FINALS
--AND BEHIND ME NOW YOU CAN SEE ONE OF THE CELEBRITY JUDGES OF THIS YEAR'S NATIONAL CHAMPIONSHIP, ATOMIC ROBO, AND JUST LISTEN TO THOSE CHEERS. DEFINITELY A FAVORITE AMONG THIS CROWD.
SCREEEECH
POLICE
ROBO!
HEY!
ROBO!
OVER HERE!
HEY, ROBO!
ROBO!
FASH
F-FASH
SCIENCE PAPARAZZI.
HUMAN VULTURES.

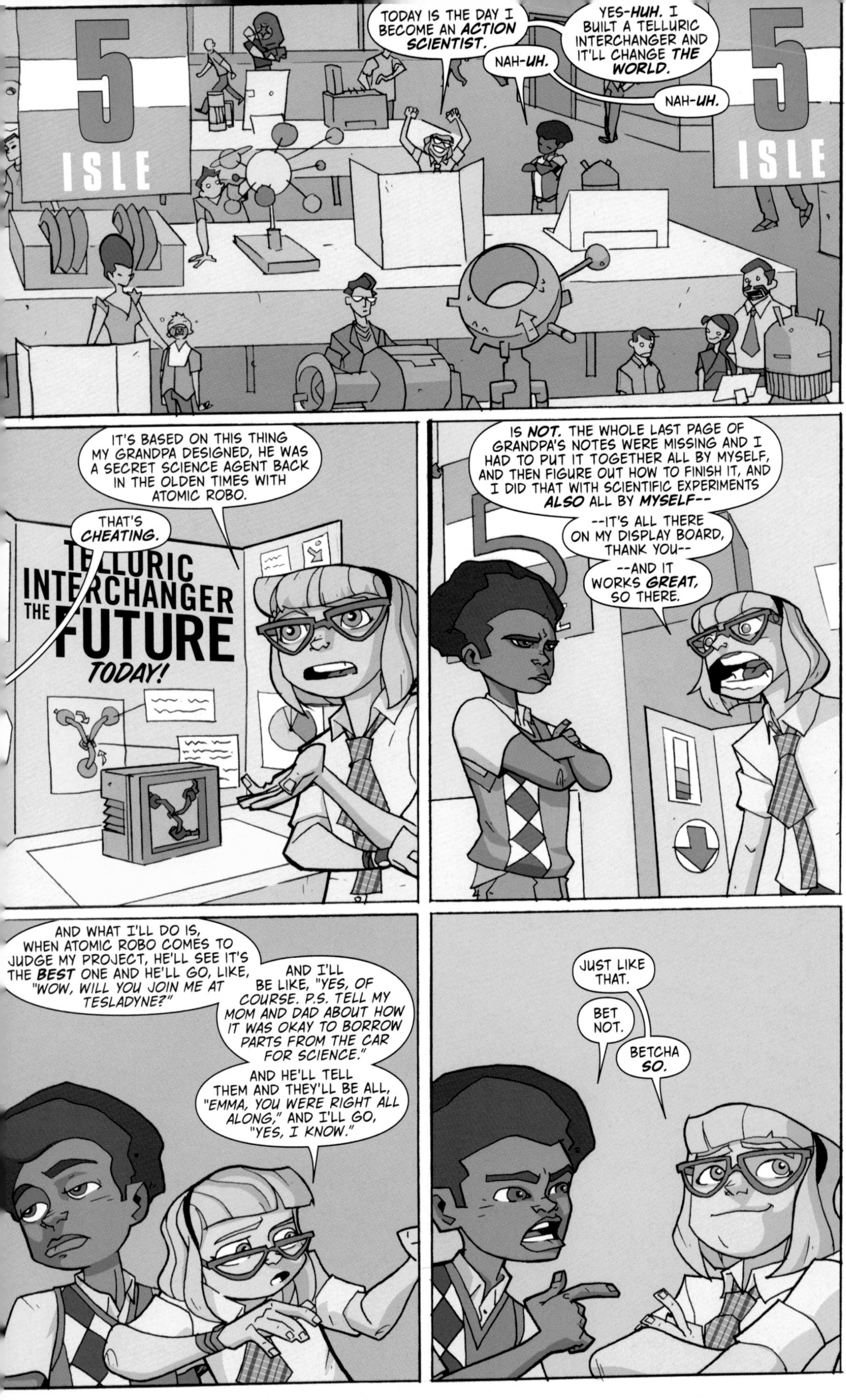
5 ISLE
TODAY IS THE DAY I BECOME AN *ACTION SCIENTIST.*
NAH-*UH.*
YES-*HUH.* I BUILT A TELLURIC INTERCHANGER AND IT'LL CHANGE *THE WORLD.*
NAH-*UH.*
5 ISLE
IT'S BASED ON THIS THING MY GRANDPA DESIGNED, HE WAS A SECRET SCIENCE AGENT BACK IN THE OLDEN TIMES WITH ATOMIC ROBO.
THAT'S *CHEATING.*
TELLURIC INTERCHANGER THE FUTURE TODAY!
IS *NOT.* THE WHOLE LAST PAGE OF GRANDPA'S NOTES WERE MISSING AND I HAD TO PUT IT TOGETHER ALL BY MYSELF, AND THEN FIGURE OUT HOW TO FINISH IT, AND I DID THAT WITH SCIENTIFIC EXPERIMENTS *ALSO* ALL BY *MYSELF--*
--IT'S ALL THERE ON MY DISPLAY BOARD, THANK YOU--
--AND IT WORKS *GREAT,* SO THERE.
AND WHAT I'LL DO IS, WHEN ATOMIC ROBO COMES TO JUDGE MY PROJECT, HE'LL SEE IT'S THE *BEST* ONE AND HE'LL GO, LIKE, *"WOW, WILL YOU JOIN ME AT TESLADYNE?"*
AND I'LL BE LIKE, *"YES, OF COURSE. P.S. TELL MY MOM AND DAD ABOUT HOW IT WAS OKAY TO BORROW PARTS FROM THE CAR FOR SCIENCE."*
AND HE'LL TELL THEM AND THEY'LL BE ALL, *"EMMA, YOU WERE RIGHT ALL ALONG,"* AND I'LL GO, *"YES, I KNOW."*
JUST LIKE THAT.
BET NOT.
BETCHA *SO.*

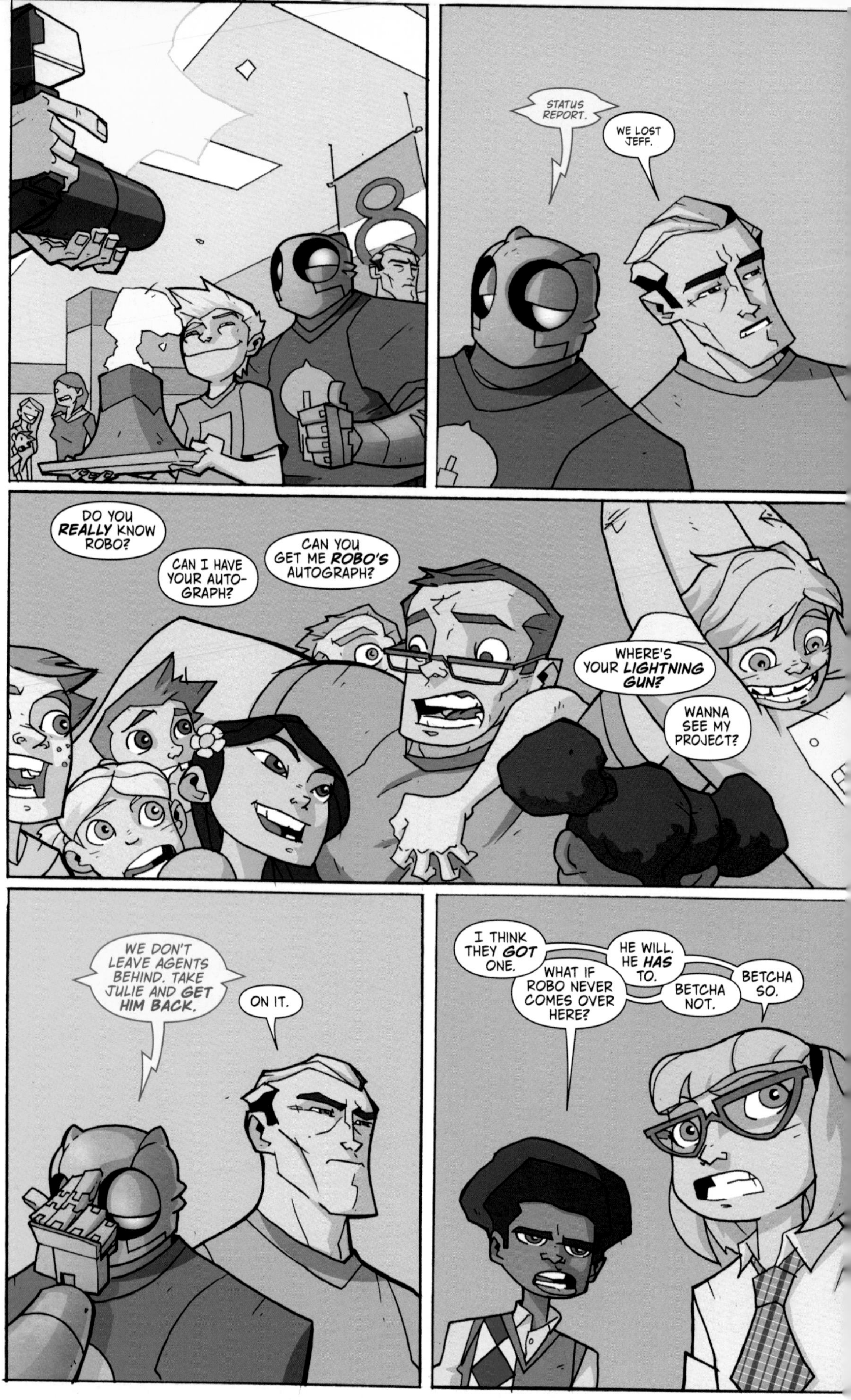
STATUS REPORT.
WE LOST JEFF.
DO YOU REALLY KNOW ROBO?
CAN I HAVE YOUR AUTO-GRAPH?
CAN YOU GET ME ROBO'S AUTOGRAPH?
WHERE'S YOUR LIGHTNING GUN?
WANNA SEE MY PROJECT?
WE DON'T LEAVE AGENTS BEHIND. TAKE JULIE AND GET HIM BACK.
ON IT.
I THINK THEY GOT ONE.
WHAT IF ROBO NEVER COMES OVER HERE?
HE WILL. HE HAS TO.
BETCHA NOT.
BETCHA SO.

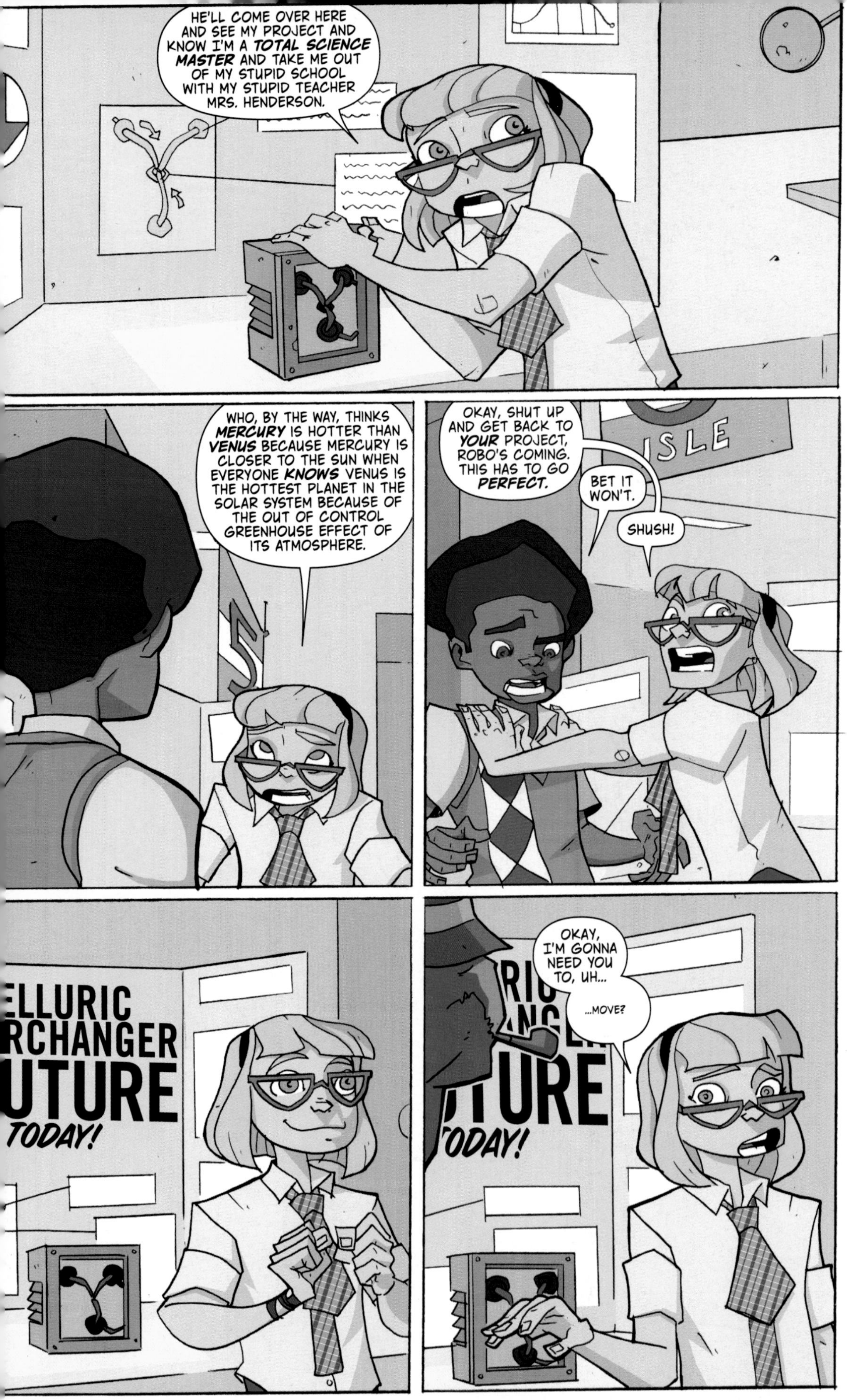
HE'LL COME OVER HERE AND SEE MY PROJECT AND KNOW I'M A ***TOTAL SCIENCE MASTER*** AND TAKE ME OUT OF MY STUPID SCHOOL WITH MY STUPID TEACHER MRS. HENDERSON.
WHO, BY THE WAY, THINKS ***MERCURY*** IS HOTTER THAN ***VENUS*** BECAUSE MERCURY IS CLOSER TO THE SUN WHEN EVERYONE ***KNOWS*** VENUS IS THE HOTTEST PLANET IN THE SOLAR SYSTEM BECAUSE OF THE OUT OF CONTROL GREENHOUSE EFFECT OF ITS ATMOSPHERE.
OKAY, SHUT UP AND GET BACK TO ***YOUR*** PROJECT, ROBO'S COMING. THIS HAS TO GO ***PERFECT.***
ISLE
BET IT WON'T.
SHUSH!
ELLURIC
RCHANGER
UTURE
TODAY!
OKAY, I'M GONNA NEED YOU TO, UH...
...MOVE?
TODAY!

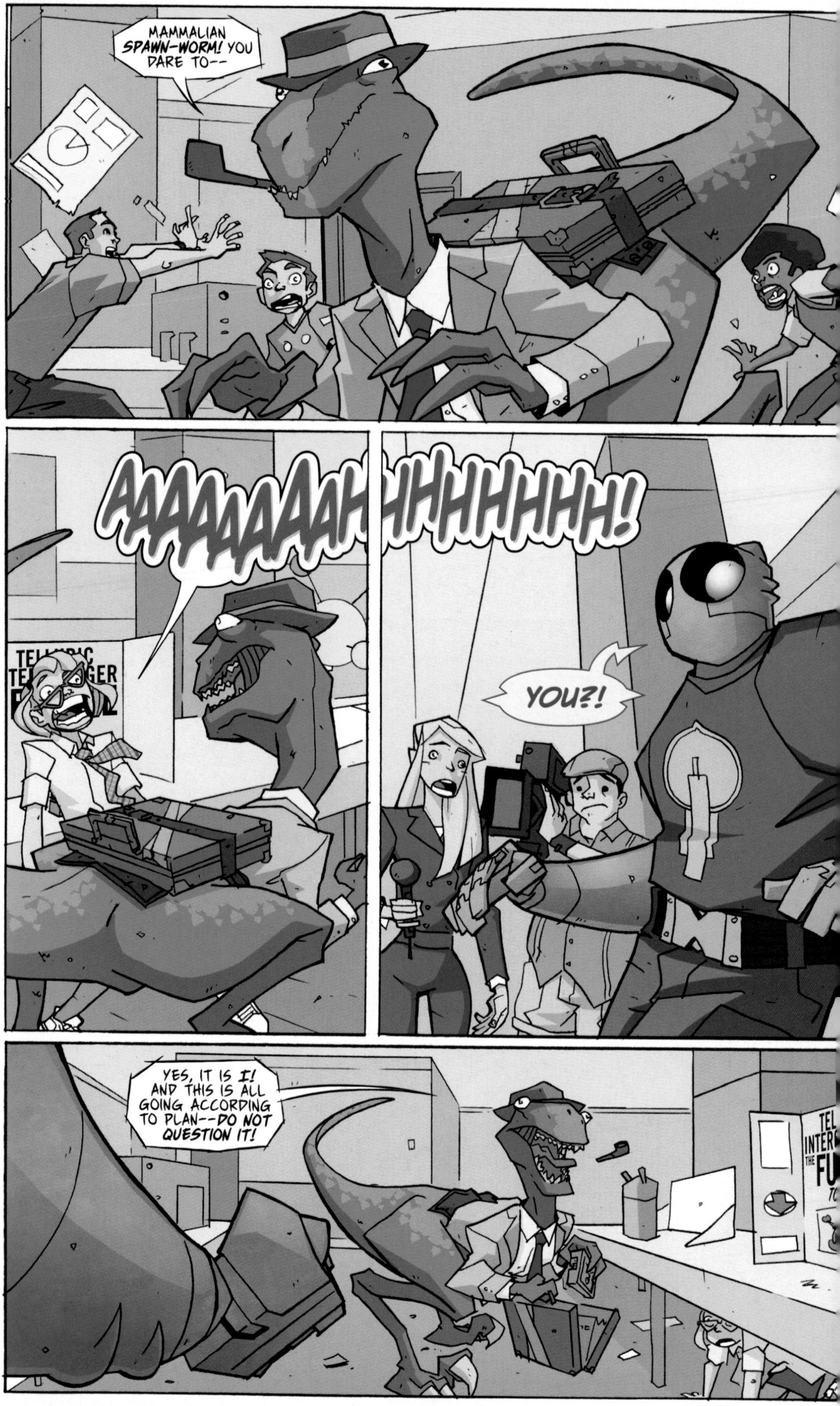
MAMMALIAN SPAWN-WORM! YOU DARE TO--
AAAAAAAAHHHHHHHHHH!
YOU?!
YES, IT IS I! AND THIS IS ALL GOING ACCORDING TO PLAN--DO NOT QUESTION IT!

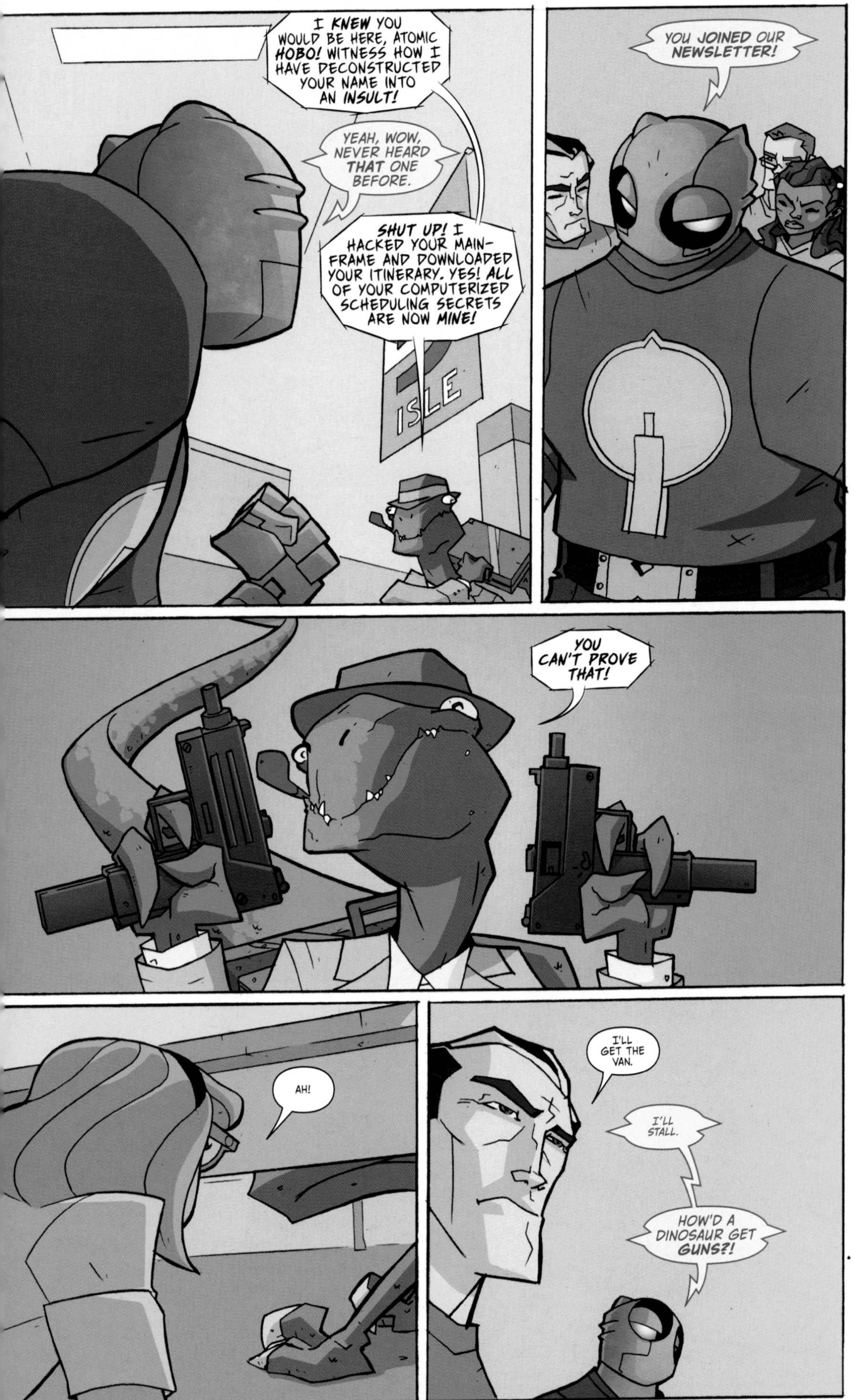
I KNEW YOU WOULD BE HERE, ATOMIC HOBO! WITNESS HOW I HAVE DECONSTRUCTED YOUR NAME INTO AN INSULT!
YEAH, WOW, NEVER HEARD THAT ONE BEFORE.
SHUT UP! I HACKED YOUR MAIN-FRAME AND DOWNLOADED YOUR ITINERARY. YES! ALL OF YOUR COMPUTERIZED SCHEDULING SECRETS ARE NOW MINE!
ISLE
YOU JOINED OUR NEWSLETTER!
YOU CAN'T PROVE THAT!
AH!
I'LL GET THE VAN.
I'LL STALL.
HOW'D A DINOSAUR GET GUNS?!

ONE WEEK AGO...

WE SELL GUNS
★★★★★
U.S.A. GUN SHOW!
NO BACKGROUND CHECKS
BUY ONE GET ONE FREE!

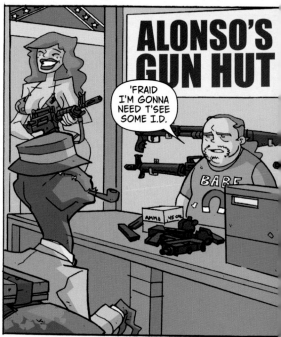

ALONSO'S GUN HUT

'FRAID I'M GONNA NEED T'SEE SOME I.D.

BIG BOOK OF DINOSAURS

DROMAEOSAURUS

AWRIGHT, LET'S RING Y'UP.

BABE

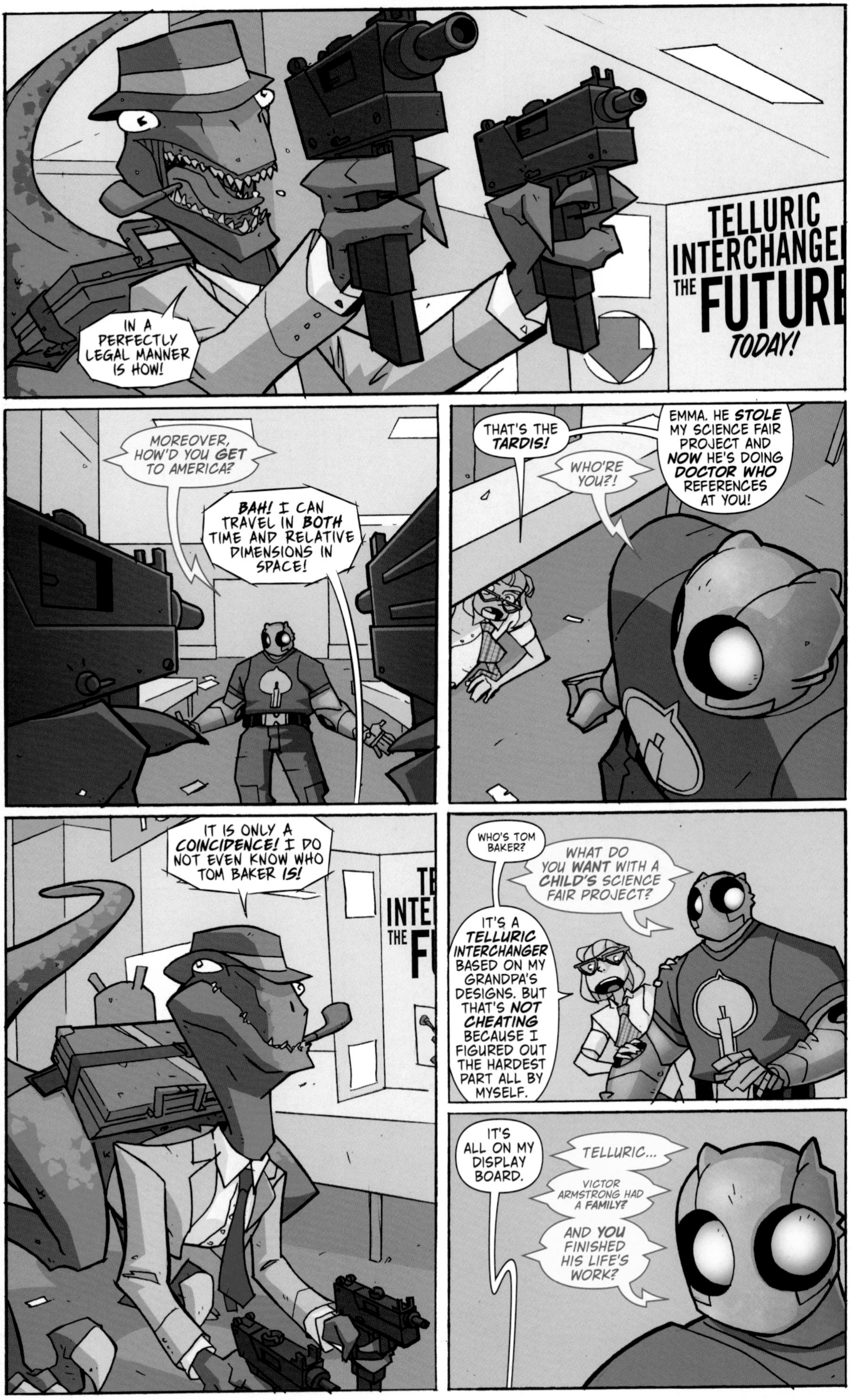
IN A PERFECTLY LEGAL MANNER IS HOW!
TELLURIC INTERCHANGER THE FUTURE TODAY!
MOREOVER, HOW'D YOU GET TO AMERICA?
BAH! I CAN TRAVEL IN BOTH TIME AND RELATIVE DIMENSIONS IN SPACE!
THAT'S THE TARDIS!
WHO'RE YOU?!
EMMA. HE STOLE MY SCIENCE FAIR PROJECT AND NOW HE'S DOING DOCTOR WHO REFERENCES AT YOU!
IT IS ONLY A COINCIDENCE! I DO NOT EVEN KNOW WHO TOM BAKER IS!
WHO'S TOM BAKER?
WHAT DO YOU WANT WITH A CHILD'S SCIENCE FAIR PROJECT?
IT'S A TELLURIC INTERCHANGER BASED ON MY GRANDPA'S DESIGNS. BUT THAT'S NOT CHEATING BECAUSE I FIGURED OUT THE HARDEST PART ALL BY MYSELF.
IT'S ALL ON MY DISPLAY BOARD.
TELLURIC...
VICTOR ARMSTRONG HAD A FAMILY?
AND YOU FINISHED HIS LIFE'S WORK?

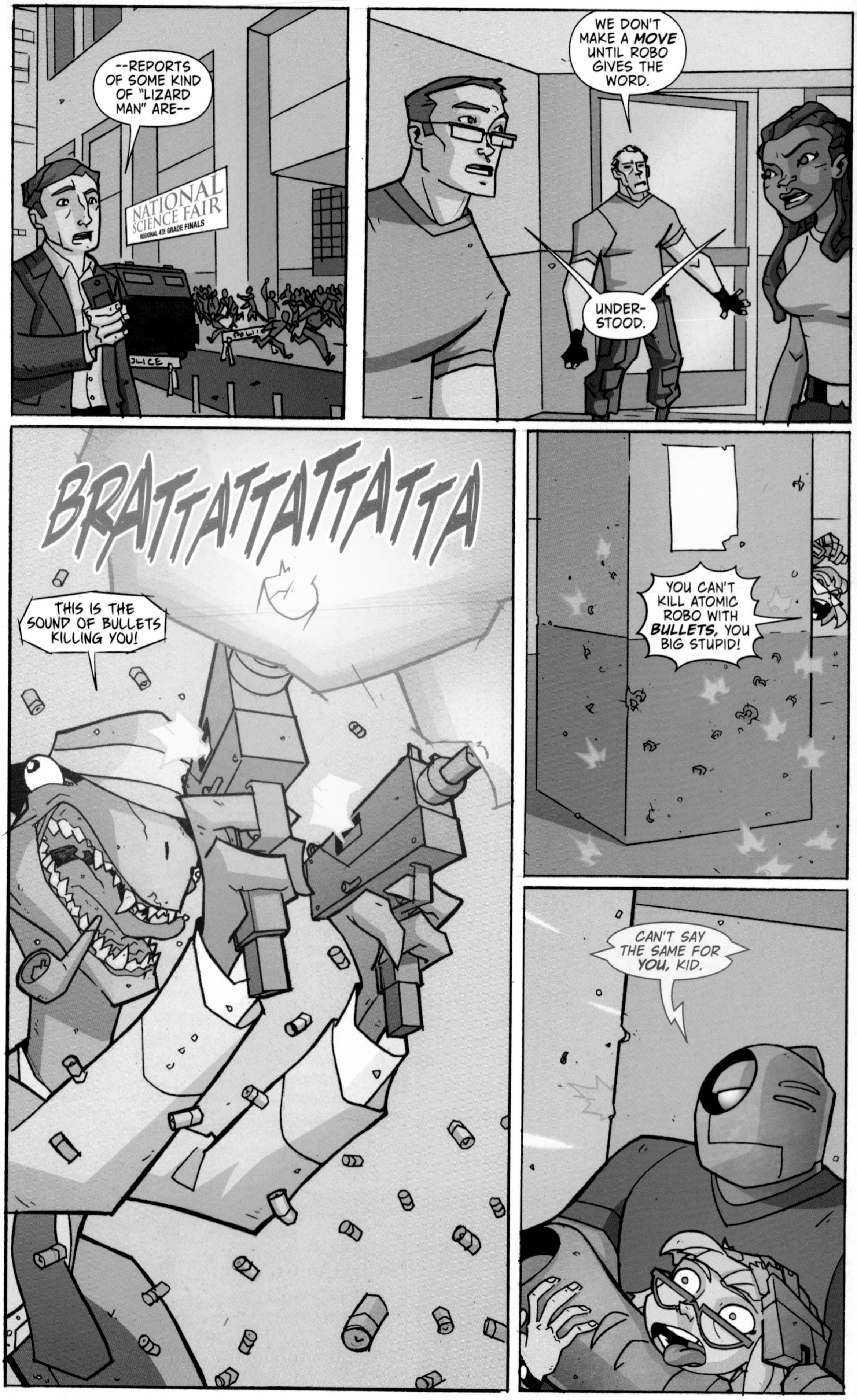
--REPORTS OF SOME KIND OF "LIZARD MAN" ARE--
NATIONAL SCIENCE FAIR
REGIONAL 4TH GRADE FINALS
POLICE
WE DON'T MAKE A MOVE UNTIL ROBO GIVES THE WORD.
UNDER-STOOD.
BRATTATTATTATTA
THIS IS THE SOUND OF BULLETS KILLING YOU!
YOU CAN'T KILL ATOMIC ROBO WITH BULLETS, YOU BIG STUPID!
CAN'T SAY THE SAME FOR YOU, KID.

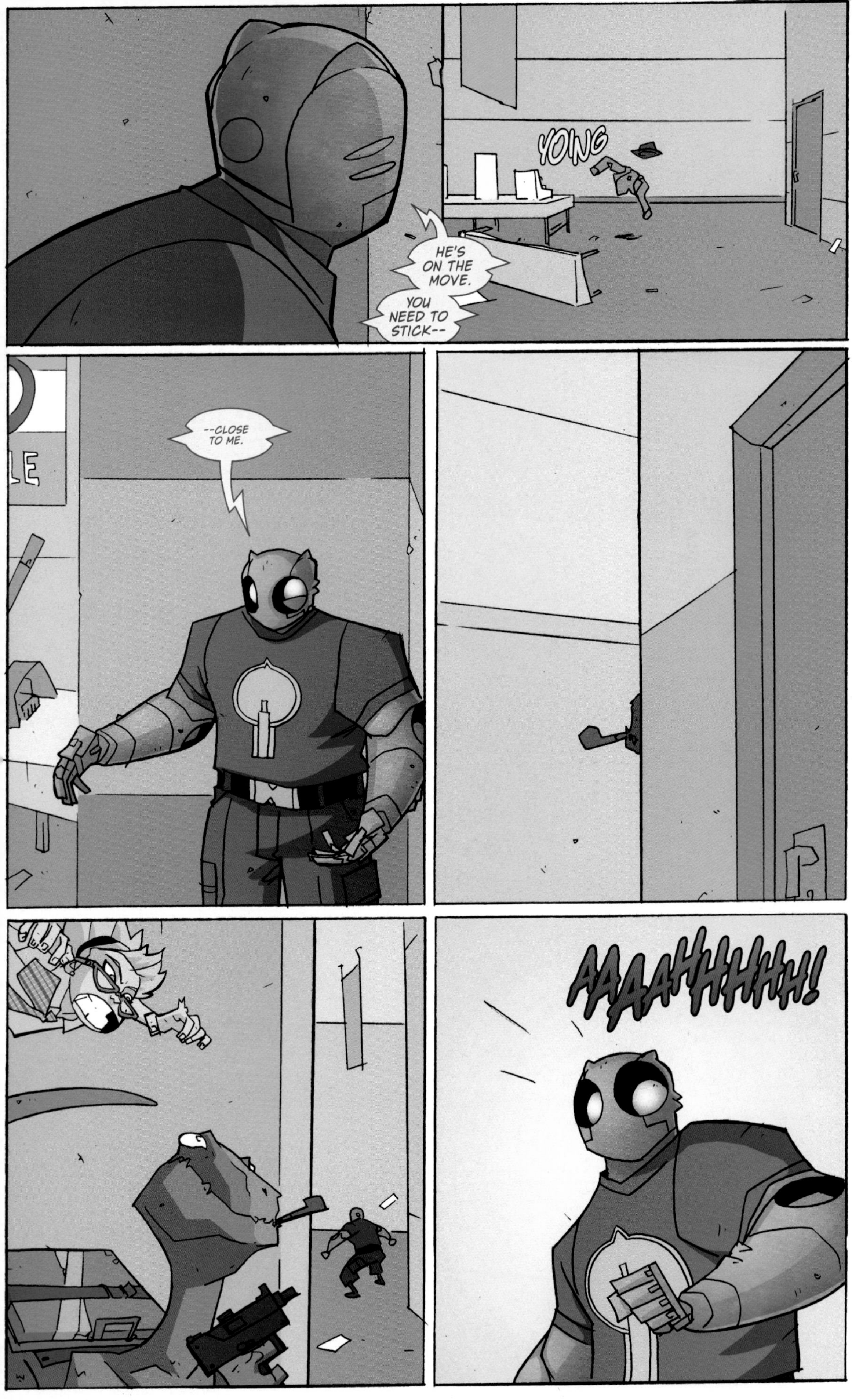
YOING
HE'S ON THE MOVE.
YOU NEED TO STICK--
--CLOSE TO ME.
AAAAHHHHH!

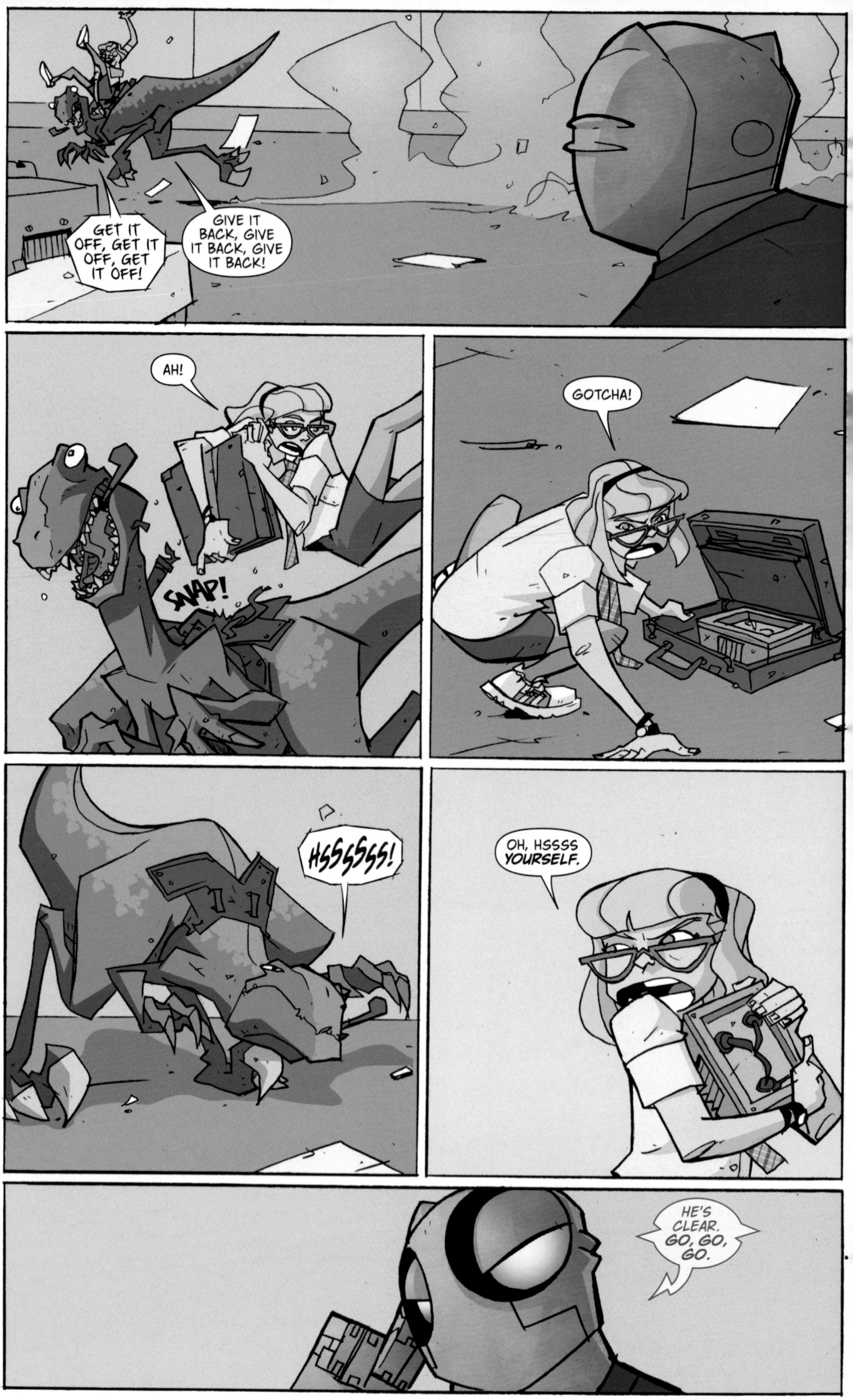
GET IT OFF, GET IT OFF, GET IT OFF!
GIVE IT BACK, GIVE IT BACK, GIVE IT BACK!
AH!
SNAP!
GOTCHA!
HSSSSSS!
OH, HSSSS *YOURSELF*.
HE'S CLEAR. **GO, GO, GO.**

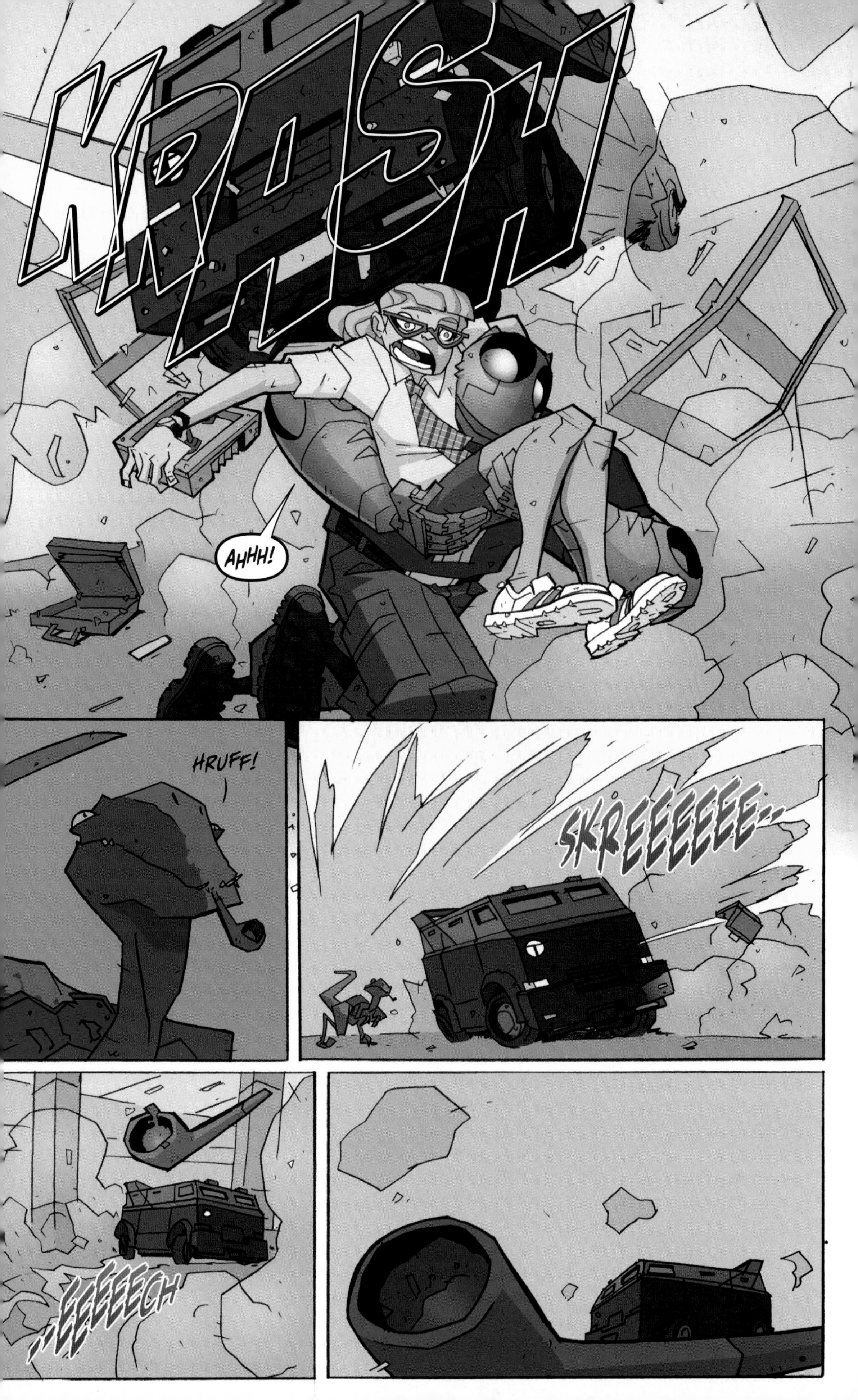
KRASH
AHHH!
HRUFF!
SKREEEEEEE...
...EEEEECH

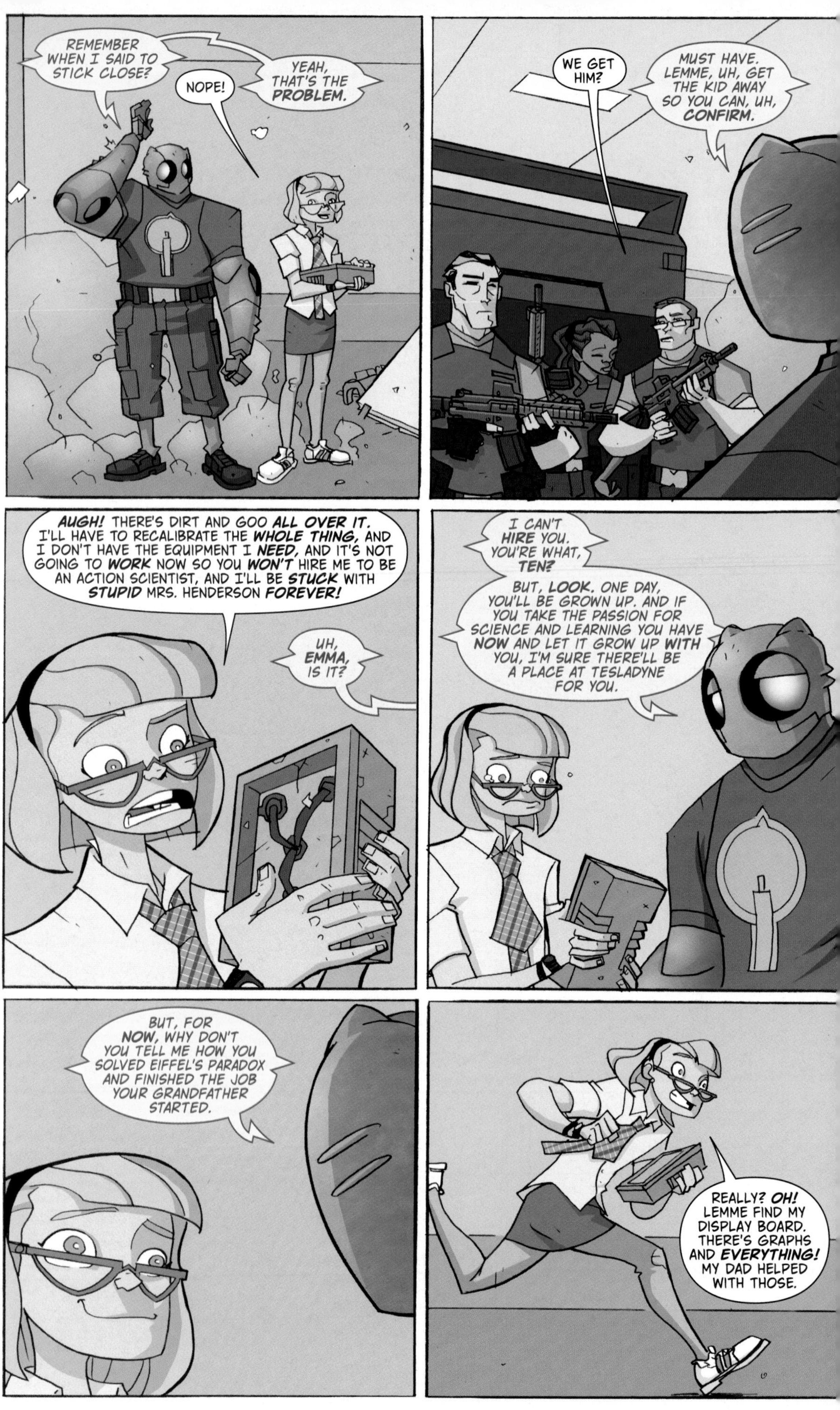
REMEMBER WHEN I SAID TO STICK CLOSE?
NOPE!
YEAH, THAT'S THE **PROBLEM.**
WE GET HIM?
MUST HAVE. LEMME, UH, GET THE KID AWAY SO YOU CAN, UH, **CONFIRM.**
AUGH! THERE'S DIRT AND GOO **ALL OVER IT.** I'LL HAVE TO RECALIBRATE THE **WHOLE THING,** AND I DON'T HAVE THE EQUIPMENT I **NEED,** AND IT'S NOT GOING TO **WORK** NOW SO YOU **WON'T** HIRE ME TO BE AN ACTION SCIENTIST, AND I'LL BE **STUCK** WITH **STUPID** MRS. HENDERSON **FOREVER!**
UH, **EMMA,** IS IT?
I CAN'T **HIRE** YOU. YOU'RE WHAT, **TEN?**
BUT, **LOOK.** ONE DAY, YOU'LL BE GROWN UP. AND IF YOU TAKE THE PASSION FOR SCIENCE AND LEARNING YOU HAVE **NOW** AND LET IT GROW UP **WITH** YOU, I'M SURE THERE'LL BE A PLACE AT TESLADYNE FOR YOU.
BUT, FOR **NOW,** WHY DON'T YOU TELL ME HOW YOU SOLVED EIFFEL'S PARADOX AND FINISHED THE JOB YOUR GRANDFATHER STARTED.
REALLY? **OH!** LEMME FIND MY DISPLAY BOARD. THERE'S GRAPHS AND **EVERYTHING!** MY DAD HELPED WITH THOSE.

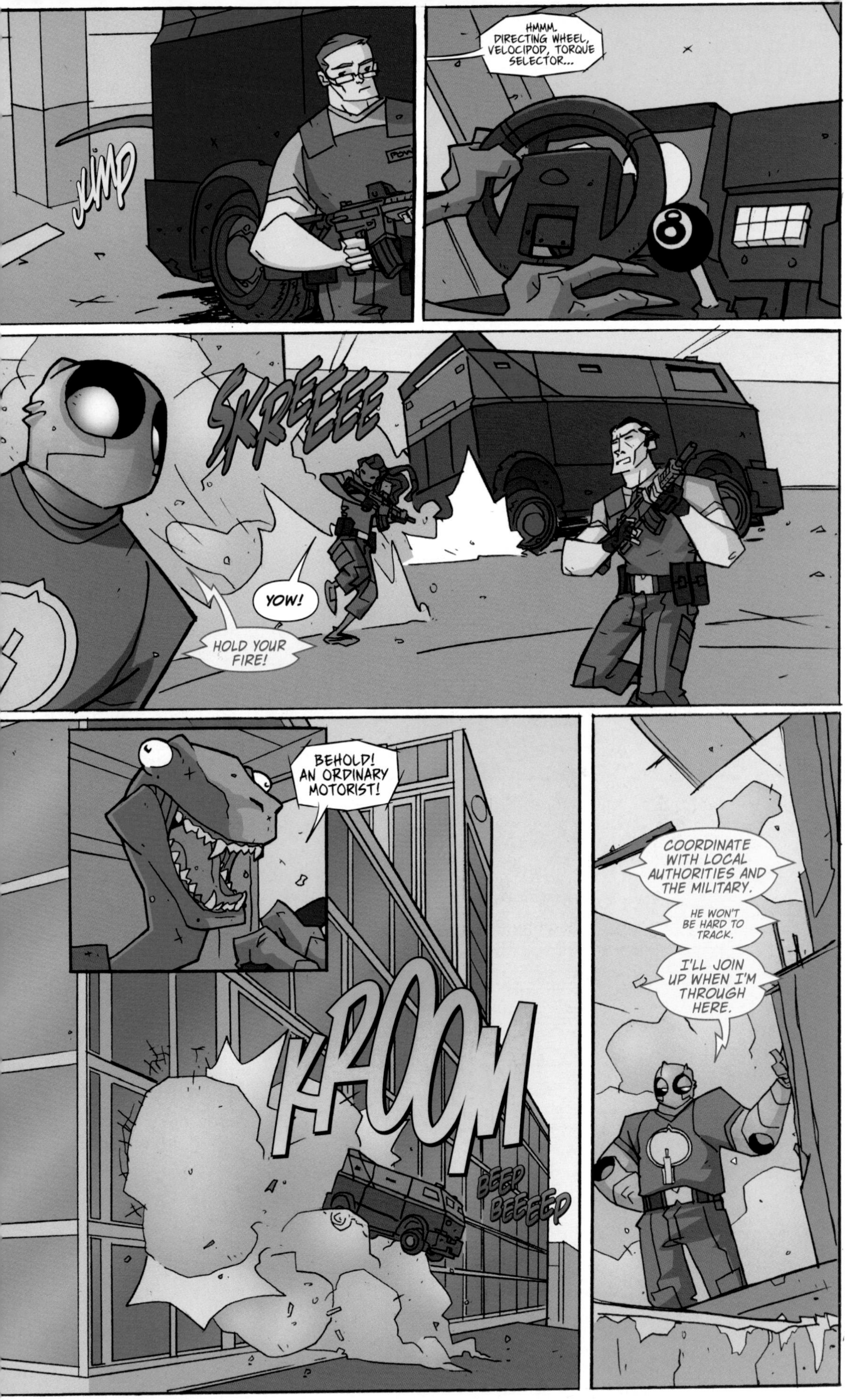
JUMP
HMMM. DIRECTING WHEEL, VELOCIPOD, TORQUE SELECTOR...
SKREEEE
YOW!
HOLD YOUR FIRE!
BEHOLD! AN ORDINARY MOTORIST!
KROOM
BEEP BEEEEP
COORDINATE WITH LOCAL AUTHORITIES AND THE MILITARY.
HE WON'T BE HARD TO TRACK.
I'LL JOIN UP WHEN I'M THROUGH HERE.

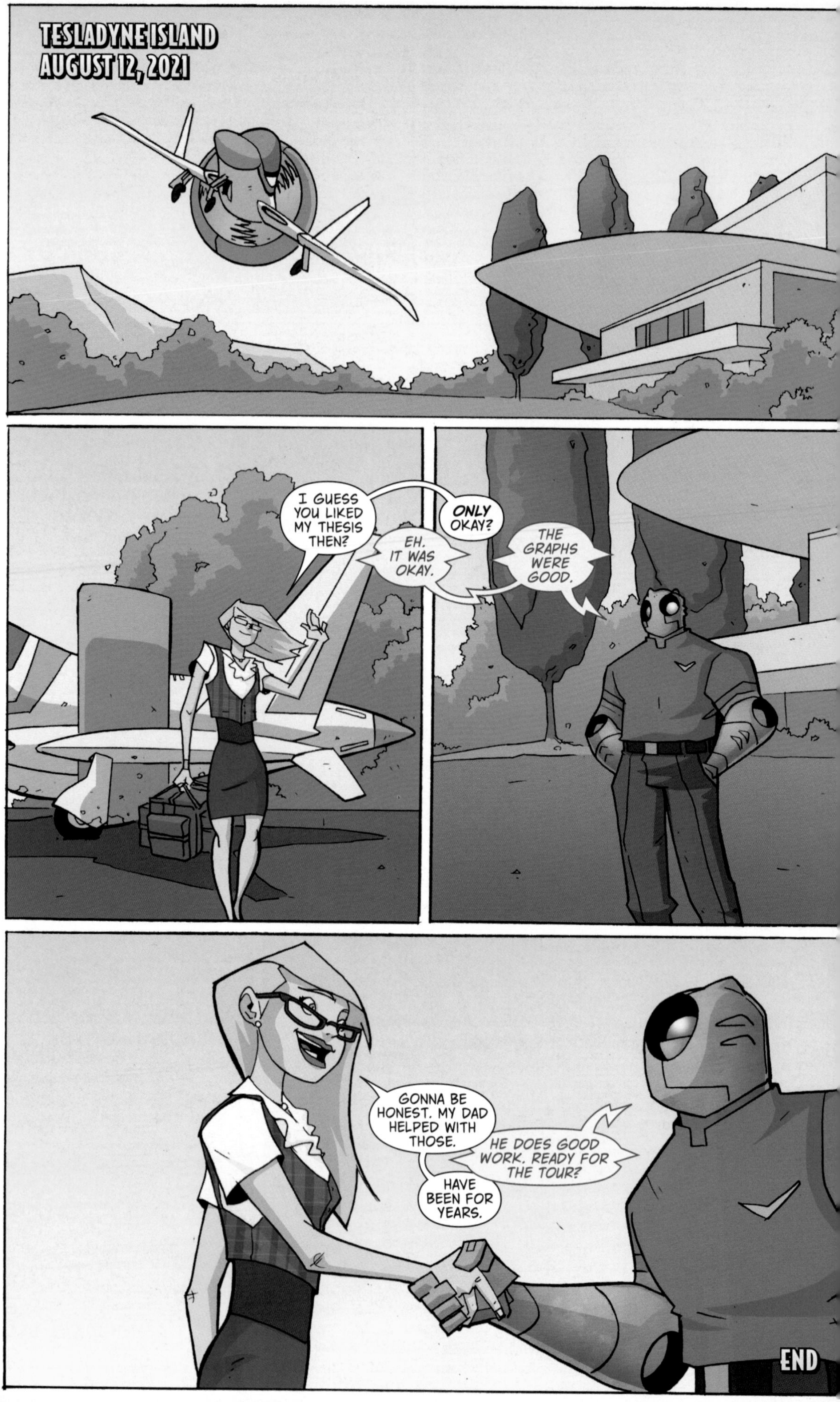
TESLADYNE ISLAND
AUGUST 12, 2021
I GUESS YOU LIKED MY THESIS THEN?
EH. IT WAS OKAY.
ONLY OKAY?
THE GRAPHS WERE GOOD.
GONNA BE HONEST. MY DAD HELPED WITH THOSE.
HE DOES GOOD WORK. READY FOR THE TOUR?
HAVE BEEN FOR YEARS.
END

SKETCHBOOK

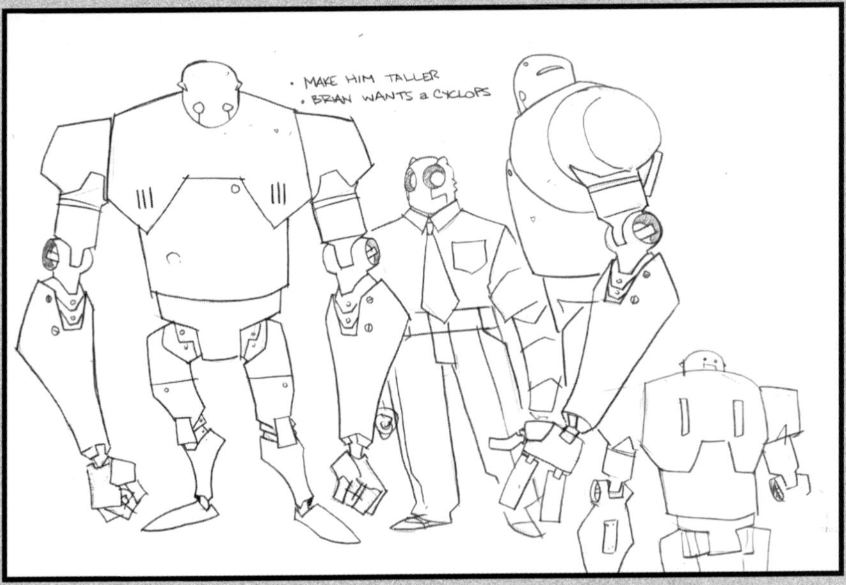
• MAKE HIM TALLER
• BRIAN WANTS a CYCLOPS

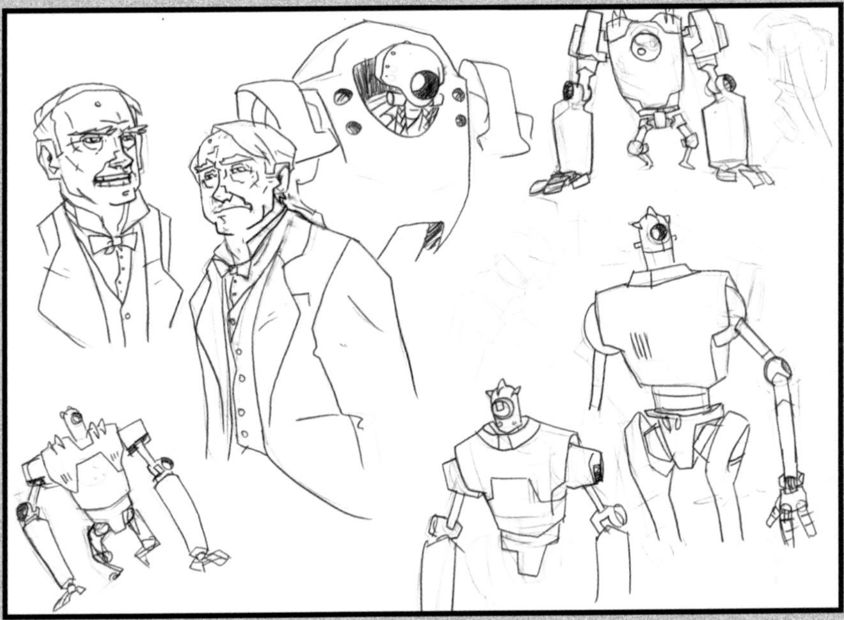

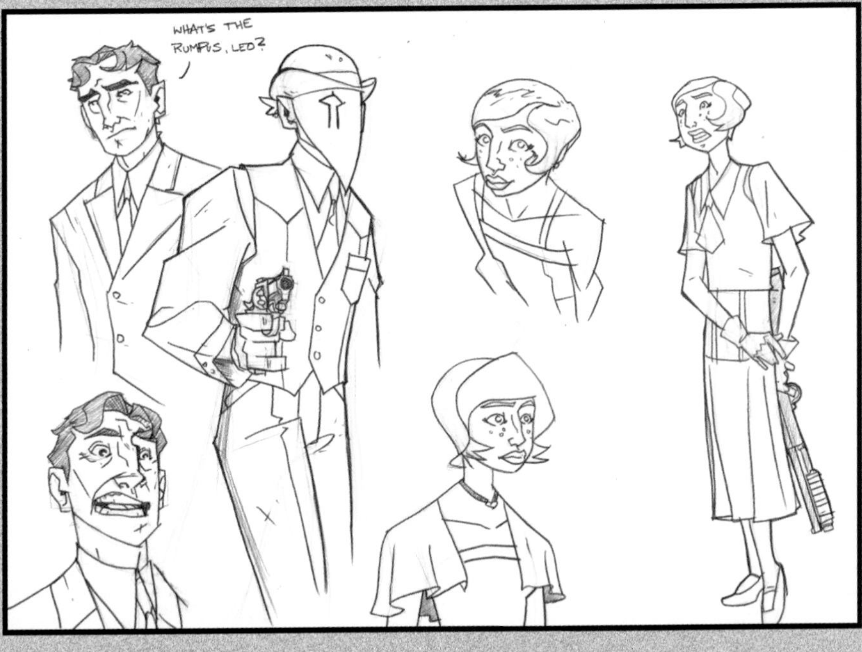
WHAT'S THE RUMPUS, LEO?

SKETCHBOOK

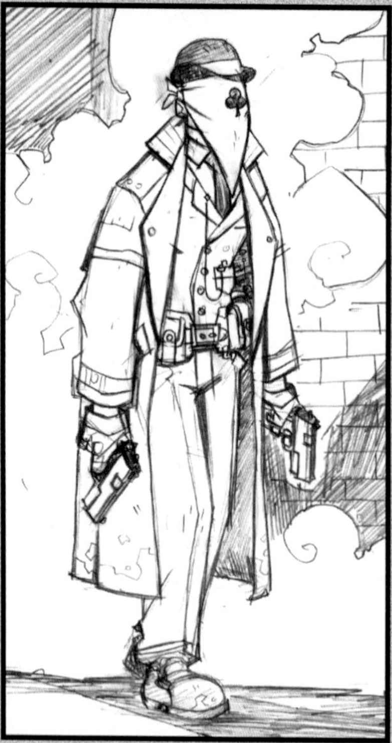

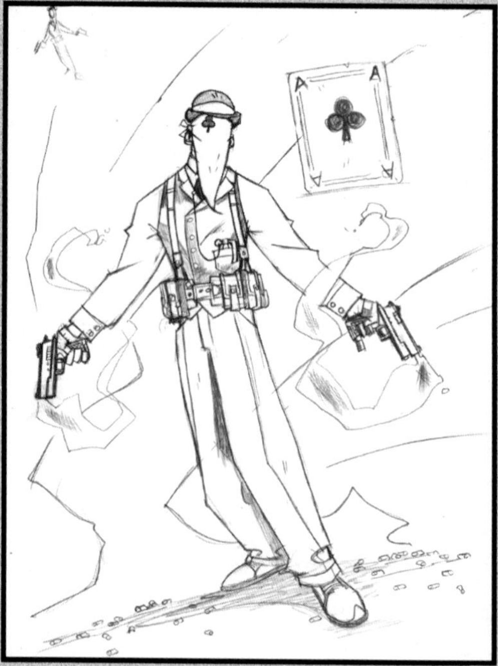

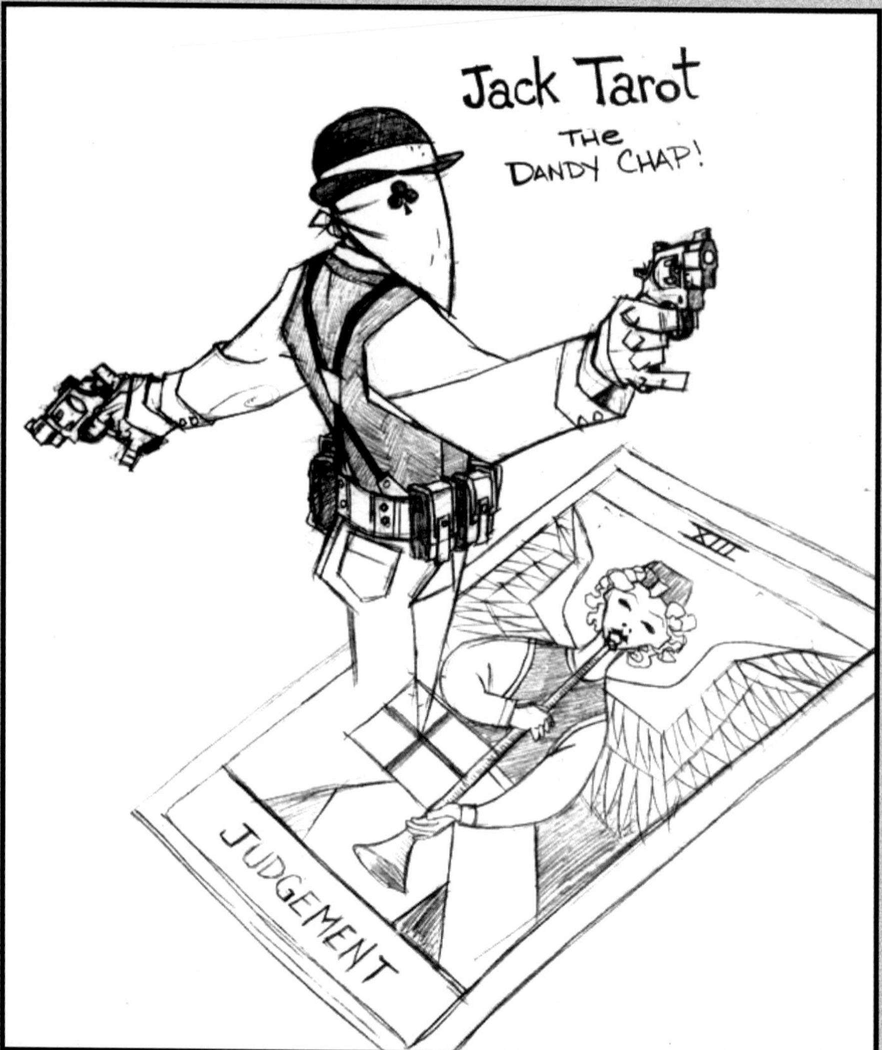
Jack Tarot
THE DANDY CHAP!
XIII
JUDGEMENT

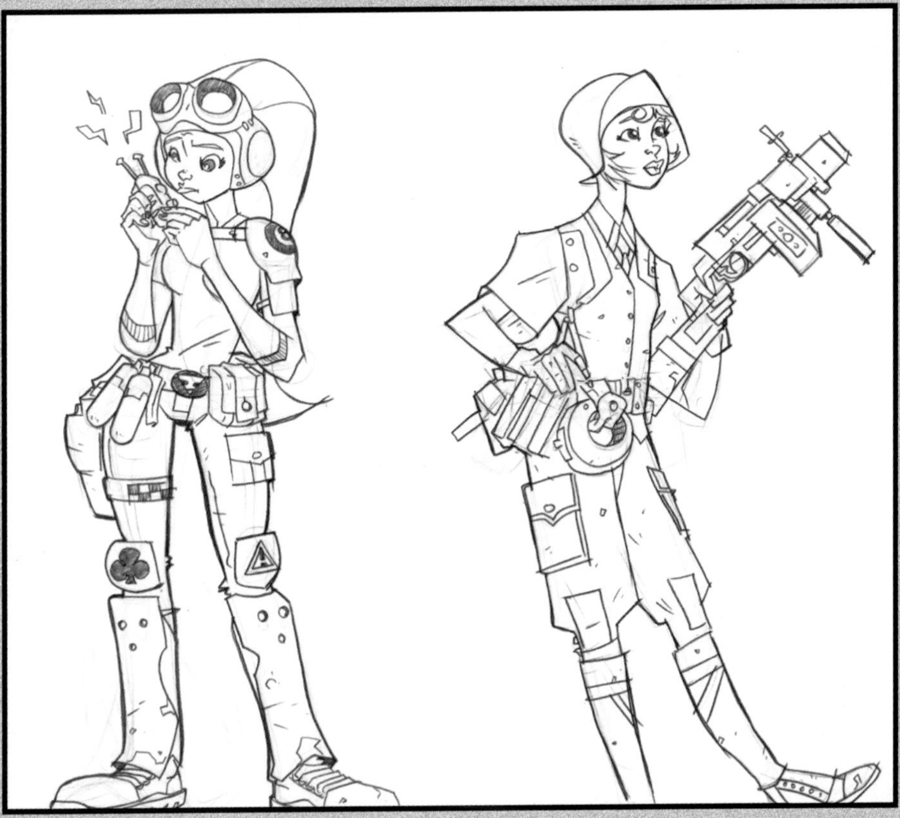

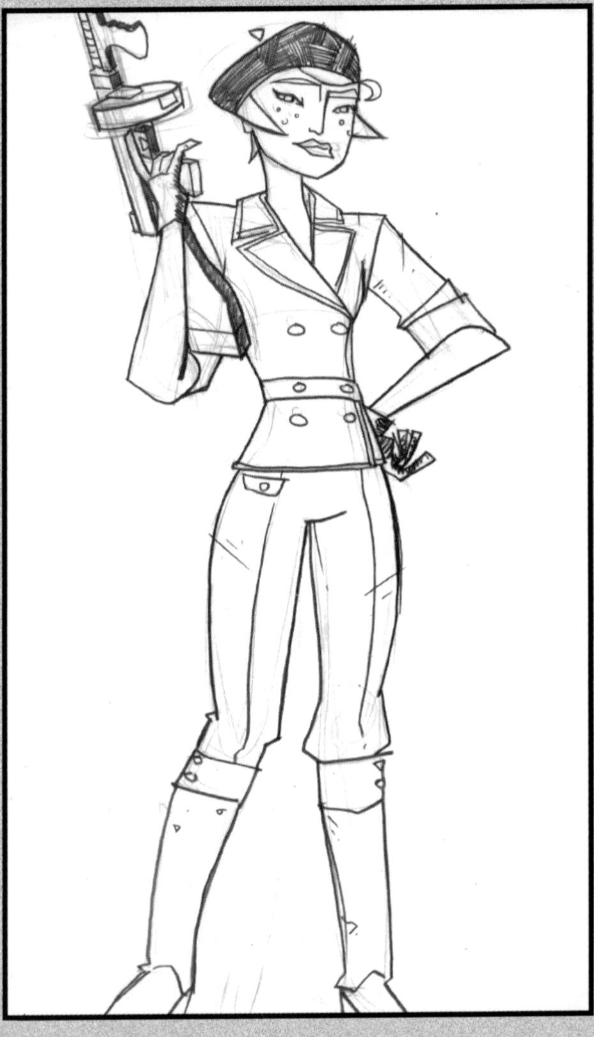

SKETCHBOOK

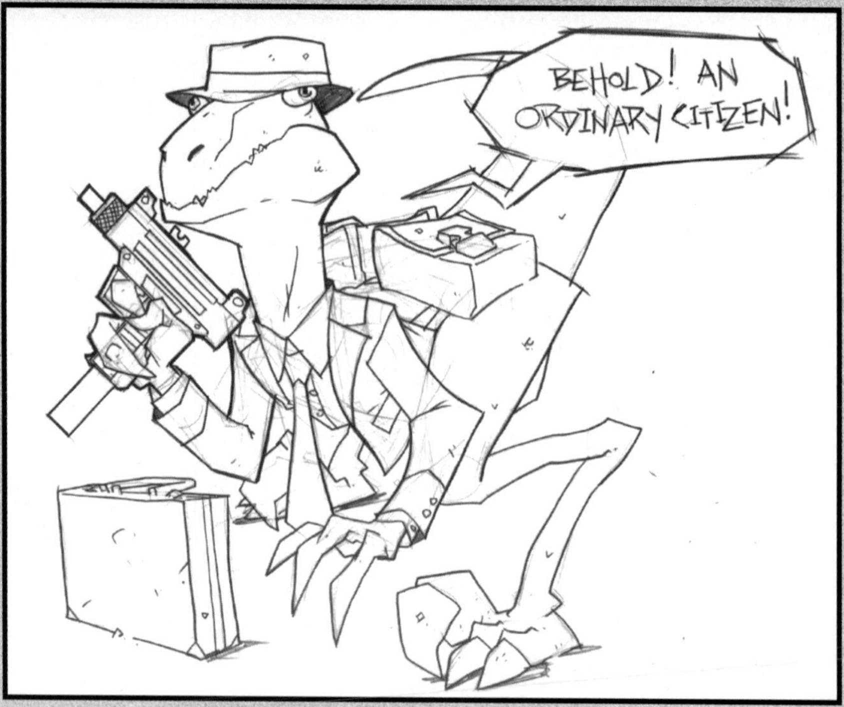
BEHOLD! AN ORDINARY CITIZEN!

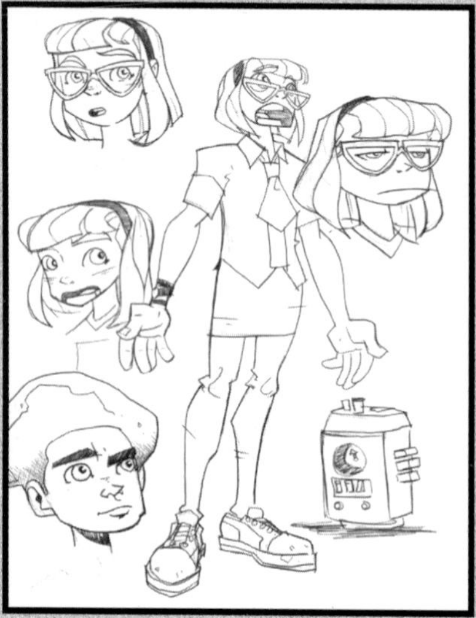

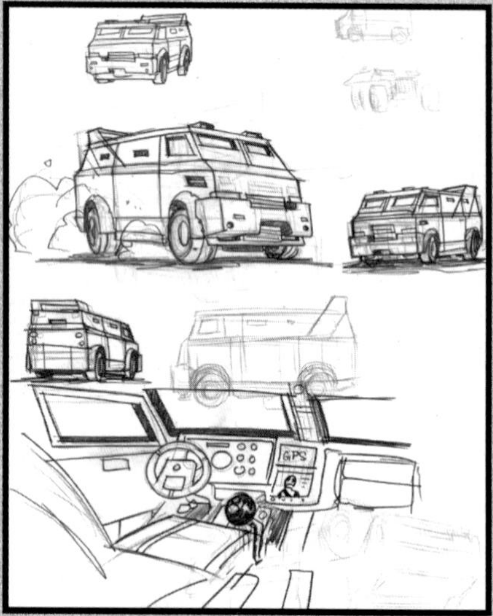
GPS

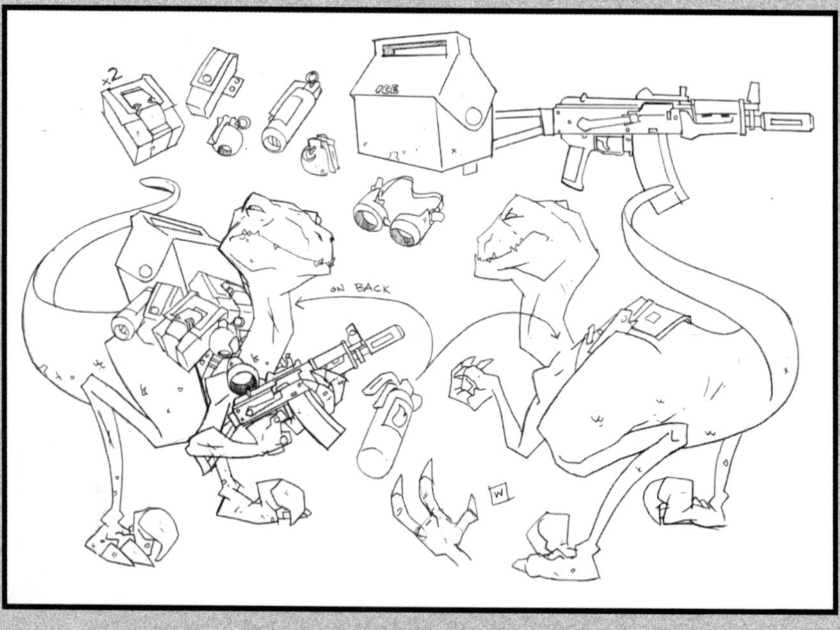
x2
ICE
ON BACK
W